Power and Conflict
in a Mexican Community

Power and Conflict in a Mexican Community

A STUDY OF POLITICAL INTEGRATION

BY ANTONIO UGALDE

Albuquerque
UNIVERSITY OF NEW MEXICO PRESS

© 1970 by the University of New Mexico Press. All rights reserved. Manufactured in the
United States of America by the University of New Mexico Printing Plant, Albuquerque.
Library of Congress Catalog Card No. 78-107100.
First Edition

To the memory of Camilo Torres
who gave his life for
a noble cause

Acknowledgments

Field Research is never the work of a single individual; its success depends to a large extent on the cooperation of the people in the community. I was very fortunate in that the people of Ensenada were understanding, patient, and cooperative. They did not mind the intrusion of a foreigner into their community, their organizations, and at times their homes. So many people cooperated with me during the nine months of field residence that it is not possible to name each of them here, but I am grateful for their valuable help.

I am particularly indebted to the Treviño family, through whom I was introduced to many other people in Ensenada and who, at the same time, provided meaningful insights into the community. I also would especially like to thank Luis de Basabe and his family; Ing. Basabe, Chief of the State Office of Public Works in Ensenada, was of great assistance from the day I arrived in the city. I am very grateful to Lic. Alfredo González Corral, President of the PRI Municipal Committee, with whom conversation was a most pleasurable learning experience. Through him and his secretary, Rebeca García, I had full access to the PRI archives.

For allowing me to research the archives of their organizations and offices, I wish to thank Lic. Armando Ramírez de la Garza, manager of the Centro Patronal, Pío Ventura Benavides, Secretary General of the CROC Labor Federation, Angel Díaz Prado, Secretary General of the CTM Labor Federation, Jesús Valencia León, Secretary General of the CRT Labor Federation, and Lic. Adolfo Castellanos de la Torre, President of the Municipal Labor Board.

Through the friendship of the Barajas family, to whom I am much indebted, I became well acquainted with some slum dwellers of the city, and ultimately learned a great deal about aspirations and political organization among them.

Municipal Treasurer Cliserio Bambrila Gil was very helpful in explaining the municipal budget and other problems of the municipality. Jose León

Toscano, former president of the PAN Municipal Committee, made many useful comments on the political life of the community.

I am deeply indebted to Professor Richard R. Fagen of Stanford University, who closely supervised the research project and made innumerable valuable comments and criticisms. Professor Martin C. Needler of the University of New Mexico and Professor William S. Tuohy of the University of California at Davis also made useful comments and suggestions. I would like to thank Henry Torres-Trueba, a doctoral candidate in anthropology at the University of Pittsburgh, for his assistance in conducting a survey of the city. I am very thankful to the Kent Foundation, which generously financed my field work and the writing of the manuscript. Finally, I wish to express my appreciation to Professor Francis X. Allard of the University of Washington, who put the manuscript in readable form.

Contents

Figures

Tables

Introduction

Approach

This study attempts to identify the main kinds of group conflict in a Mexican city and to investigate the ways in which the social system solves these conflicts. The theory behind the research was that conflict exists in all social systems, and that the survival of the system requires the creation of conflict-solving mechanisms.[1]

The assumption underlying this approach was that by studying the conflict, its participants, and their conflict-solving processes one might gain some knowledge of the nature of social power and of the components of the political system.

Most studies dealing with the Mexican political system have been done at the national level, that is, looking down on the system from above. The present study attempts to look into the system from below. Although the study does not provide a comprehensive view of the system, it may furnish new details and insights for a better understanding of the total system.

The city to be studied had to be large enough to present conflict between nationally organized groups but small enough so that one researcher could obtain a fairly good understanding of the community during a stay of nine months. Regional variations in Mexico precluded finding a "typical" Mexican city. However, I assumed that the study of conflicts among nationally organized groups would reveal the essential components of conflict and the essential processes for resolving these conflicts in the Mexican system, and that I would then be able to make some useful generalizations. Consequently the search was not for a typical Mexican community but rather for one in which the major national groups are present—labor and managerial organizations, bureaucratic groups, political parties, service and church organizations, and civic associations. Ensenada was one of several cities that seemed to meet these requirements.

Ensenada is not a university center and, therefore, student organizations were not present.[2] This was a limiting factor, since student organizations are politically active in Mexico. However, very few provincial cities in Mexico have universities.

Baja California is probably the most highly developed state in Mexico, and Ensenada has the most modern occupational structure of all the cities in the state. I believed that this factor would allow me to make some projections about the directions political development may take in Mexico as the other states become more modern.

The "conflict" approach used in this study differs from the "power" approach used in most political studies of communities. The power approach is primarily concerned with the power structure, decision-making processes, and identification of the power holders in the community. The power approach came into vogue in the fifties, when the findings of Floyd Hunter confirmed the earlier findings of the Lynds.[3] These studies challenged the assumption that power was diffused in the United States and questioned democratic behavior at the local level.[4] Then during the early sixties Robert Dahl's study reaffirmed the thesis that power was diffused.[5] The opposite findings of Hunter and Dahl spirited a lively controversy among students of communities and raised many methodological questions.[6]

A few weeks in the field at the outset of this research showed that the power approach was inappropriate for studying social power and the local political system in a Mexican city. The methodological questions raised by the students of American communities seemed to multiply in this study. It became obvious that most decisions affecting Ensenada were made by outside holders of political and economic power, and that the little power left in the community was diffused among political and economic groups.[7] Under these circumstances, the study of conflicting situations and the mechanisms used to resolve them seemed more likely to be productive in understanding the local power structure and decision-making processes.

Method

The data for the study were gathered during nine months of residence in Ensenada, from May 1967 to January 1968, from (1) research in the files and archives of local organizations, (2) informal interviewing of incumbents and of knowledgeable former officers of organizations, (3) attendance at official sessions and meetings, (4) study of official acts, and (5) formal interviewing.

The files and documents of three of the five labor federations, the two political parties, two business organizations, and one government office were extensively researched. I was allowed to copy any documents. Unfortunately, the files were in poor condition. The organizations usually throw away records and documents after two or three years. It was difficult and time consuming to locate complete data on electoral results, membership of some of the organizations, and financial matters. Several interesting case studies had to be discarded for lack of complete information. The files nonetheless provided invaluable information. Of greatest interest were the minutes of organization meetings, particularly those of the labor organizations. I evaluated the overall accuracy of the minutes by attending meetings and then later reading their minutes. They were accurate. The minutes provided reliable and interesting information about the labor organizations and the local political system.

Approximately eighty knowledgeable persons were interviewed, including two former municipal presidents, fifteen city officials, twelve labor leaders, fourteen leading businessmen, eighteen officers of political parties, and a few clergymen. Some of the respondents were interviewed several times. The names of the interviewees have been changed in the text. Most interviews took place at the informant's place of business, a few in the researcher's or informant's home. Some of the interviews were taped, but the majority were not. The untaped conversations were transcribed immediately afterward. The interviews were not structured, and the technique was that of an anthropologist conversing with respondents after first establishing a workable rapport.

The schedule of the interviews was different in each case because the purpose of the conversations was to elicit information about which the respondent was particularly knowledgeable. Thus, in the interviews with municipal officers the questions were designed to bring responses explaining the *de facto* municipal government; rapport was necessary in order to avoid ready-made answers and responses giving the *de jure* descriptions of the government.

This technique did not permit quantification of interview schedules. However, it is very doubtful that the questions asked in the informal interviews would have been answered in formal interviews, and the respondents frequently gave information for which I thought it improper to ask directly. It should be remembered that the Mexican political system does not allow for complete freedom of expression. For example, many members of an opposition political party do not want to be identified as such by strangers. Critical comments about the government are made with a certain amount of caution and discretion in front of strangers.

I was given permission to attend several sessions of organizations in the community, and observed about twenty-five meetings of political parties, labor unions, professional associations, civic groups, and business associations. Particularly interesting were the daily routines of many government offices. While searching the archives of the Municipal Labor Board of Conciliation, for instance, I was able to observe some of the hearings and to talk with the members of the Board. During several weeks of work at one of the party's headquarters, I had opportunities to see the party in operation and to talk at length with many members and officials. I also participated in the activities of some of the organizations, sometimes helping with secretarial chores or drawing up documents, sometimes working on organization projects.

A survey of 125 households in three *colonias* (neighborhoods) was carried out with the assistance of an anthropology graduate student. The survey consisted of a formal questionnaire with several categories of questions aimed at eliciting not behavioral but factual data, including information on living conditions, place of origin, size of family, income, education, and membership in organizations. The results of this survey have not been used in the present study, as it was not possible to randomize the sample for lack of adequate city maps. Nevertheless, the survey of the 125 households provided much information about the living conditions of the people and increased significantly my knowledge of the city. The limitations of this research technique in Ensenada became apparent rather quickly. The survey was made in the first weeks of residence in the field.

NOTES

1. See George Simmel, *Conflict and the Web of Group Affiliations* (Glencoe: The Free Press, 1955) and Lewis Coser, *The Functions of Social Conflict* (Glencoe: The Free Press, 1956).

2. In Ensenada there are two university preparatory schools *(preuniversitarias)*, one under the administration of the University of Baja California. The University also has in Ensenada a Department of Marine Sciences with approximately 80 students.

3. Floyd Hunter, *Community Power Structure: A Study of Decision Makers* (Chapel Hill: University of North Carolina Press, 1953); Robert S. Lynd and Helen M. Lynd, *Middletown in Transition, A Study in Cultural Conflicts* (New York: Harcourt, Brace and Company, 1937).

4. C. Wright Mills, *The Power Elite* (New York: Oxford University Press, Inc., 1959), also challenged the thesis that power was diffused at the national level.

5. Robert A. Dahl, *Who Governs? Democracy and Power in an American City* (New Haven: Yale University Press, 1961).

6. The profusion of literature on the issue led to the following comment: "As the literature on community power grows, none but the most diligent readers of journals can hope to keep pace with the reports of findings, criticisms, and critiques of criticisms that wash over us with every tide. If the present trend continues long in the future, the field will be better suited to a sociologist of knowledge who can disentangle who said what, than to the scholar who wants to know about political decision in American communities." Nelson W. Polsby, "Community Power: Some Reflections on the Recent Literature," *American Sociological Review,* Vol. 27 (1962), pp. 838-41. See among many other recent articles: Linton C. Freeman, Thomas J. Fararo, Warner Bloomberg, Jr., and Morris H. Sunshine, "Locating Leaders in Local Communities: A Comparison of Some Alternative Approaches," *American Sociological Review,* Vol. 28 (1963), pp.

791-98; Donald A. Clelland and William H. Form, "Economic Dominants and Community Power: A Comparative Analysis," *American Journal of Sociology,* Vol. 69 (1964), pp. 511-21; Jerry B. Michel, "The Measurement of Social Power on the Community Level: An Exploratory Study," *The American Journal of Economics and Sociology* (April 1964), pp. 189-93.

7. Students of another border town have made similar remarks. See Orrin E. Klapp and L. Vincent Padgett, "Power Structure and Decision-Making in a Mexican Border Town," *American Journal of Sociology,* Vol. 65 (January 1960), pp. 400-406.

1
Setting

Ensenada, one of Mexico's more prosperous Pacific harbors, lies approximately 65 miles south of the United States-Mexican border, in the vicinity of San Diego, California. It can be reached by a new turnpike that follows the coast southward from Tijuana. The city of Ensenada is the seat of the municipality of the same name, which is geographically the largest municipality in Mexico (20,600 square miles). It is one of four municipalities of the state of Baja California.[1] See Figure 1.

The city of Ensenada, with an estimated population in 1967 of 65,000, is a provincial town ranking nineteenth in size among other provincial Mexican towns, closely following Salamanca (state of Guanajuato) and Orizaba (state of Veracruz). If state capitals are included in the ranking, Ensenada occupies the forty-first position, according to the 1960 Mexican national census.

The natural beauty of its surroundings, its proximity to San Diego and Los Angeles, the excellent conditions for sport fishing, and a pleasant climate have made Ensenada a tourist town.[2] Fishing and related industry are the most important economic activities of its inhabitants.

Ensenada is a quiet town and the absence of a center of higher education probably contributes to its air of provincialism and the sense of a cultural vacuum. On the other hand, the many tourists and foreign residents in the community and the ships from all over the world that dock at the port give the city a certain cosmopolitan flavor.[3]

History

In 1931 the Peninsula of Baja California was divided politically into two districts, the Northern Territory and the Southern Territory, both directly dependent on the Federal Executive in Mexico City.[4] The economic bases of

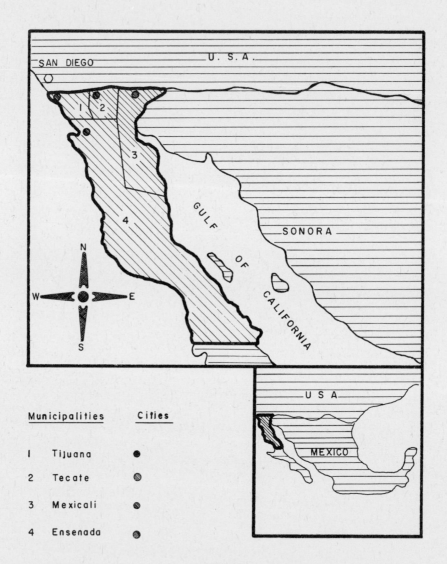

FIGURE 1.
STATE OF BAJA CALIFORNIA AND ITS FOUR MUNICIPALITIES

development of the Northern Territory had been established in the 1920s with the successful introduction of cotton in the fertile valley of Mexicali.

The 1920s in the United States saw prohibition and the outlawing of gambling in the state of California. These two events promoted the beginnings of a tourist industry in Baja California. Thousands of Californians crossed the border to drink and gamble. Casinos and bars mushroomed in the border towns of Baja and prostitution became a well-organized business.

The international price of cotton collapsed during the Depression of the 1930s, producing a serious economic crisis in the rapidly growing Northern Territory. In 1933, the United States repealed prohibition; a few years later Mexican President Lázaro Cárdenas outlawed gambling in Mexico. These events and the Depression brought the economy of the region almost to a standstill.

In an attempt to help the territory, the federal government granted free custom duty privileges to the cities of Tijuana and Ensenada, an exemption that was extended to the rest of the Peninsula in 1939. Basically, the custom exemptions allowed for the duty-free import of foreign products that were to be used, consumed, or transformed in the zone. Local producers were also exempted from export taxes for locally manufactured merchandise. National industries were attracted to the region by local and federal tax reductions, and national manufacturers supplying the Free Zone received subsidies from the federal government for transportation costs. The Free Zone privileges, due to expire in 1956, were instead extended for ten years. Then in 1966, local organizations pressed the government for a new extension which was granted reluctantly for an additional five years. With every renewal, limitations were imposed on the Free Zone privileges with the clear understanding that the local economy would have to be integrated into that of the rest of the country.[5]

The custom privileges of the Free Zone accelerated the economic growth of Baja California during the 1940s, and the economy was favored during World War II by the expansion of naval installations at San Diego and Los Angeles. The United States *bracero* program of the 1950s also affected Baja California, because it attracted to the border towns thousands of farm workers expecting jobs in the California fields.

The government of President Miguel Alemán (1946–52) supported heavy spending on works in the infrastructure, such as the building of the state's basic transportation system. The roads from Tijuana to Mexicali and from Mexicali to San Felipe were built, and the Sonora-Baja California railroad, which links Baja to the rest of the country, was completed. During the same period the important Morelos Dam was built and work on the port of Ensenada was planned.

In December 1951, the Federal Executive gave statehood to the Northern

Territory of the Peninsula of Baja California. The first gubernatorial elections were held in August 1953, and the municipal councils were elected in February of the following year. Four municipalities were organized in the new state: Mexicali, which became the state capital; Tijuana, which had become a large commercial center; Ensenada, which had a fast-growing fishing industry, and the small municipality of Tecate.

Population

Table 1 shows the population growth of the state of Baja California and of the municipality of Ensenada after 1930. The population growth rates of the state and municipality are phenomenal. In the 1950s the state had a co-efficient rate of growth of 129.5, the highest in the nation. Quintana Roo followed Baja with a coefficient of 93.9, and the Federal District was third with a coefficient of 58.3.

Immigration was the main source of population growth. According to the 1960 census, only 50.8 percent of the population of Ensenada had been born in Baja California. The immigrants came from every state of the federation.[6]

Economy

The regional economic study of Mexico by British economist Paul Yates Lamartine shows the privileged economic position of Baja California.[7] Lamartine used such standard indicators as G.N.P. per capita, economic development, minimum wages, health services, literacy, protein intake, capital investments, and agricultural and industrial productivity to construct a welfare index for ranking the states of the federation. Baja California ranks first in the general welfare index with 204 (the national average is 100), followed by the Federal District with 188.

The favorable economic position of Baja California can also be seen in a comparison of the labor force's occupational structure in the state to that in the rest of the nation. As shown in Table 2, Baja California has a more modern structure. The percentage of persons working in the primary sector is considerably lower than the national average, the percentage of persons working in the secondary sector is slightly higher, and the percentage of persons in the tertiary sector is significantly higher. Table 2 also shows that modernization of the occupational structure between 1950 and 1960 took place faster in Baja California than in the rest of the country. The occupational structure in the municipality of Ensenada is more modern than in the rest of the state of Baja California, and modernization of the structure took place faster during the same years in the municipality than in the state.

TABLE 1
POPULATION GROWTH OF STATE OF BAJA CALIFORNIA AND MUNICIPALITY OF ENSENADA (1930–70)

Year	State			Ensenada		
	Total	Urban	Rural	Total	Urban[a]	Rural
1930	48,327	26,268	22,059	7,072	3,043	4,029
1940	79,007	39,977	39,030	12,531	4,616	7,915
1950	226,965	146,391	80,574	31,077	18,149	12,928
1960	520,165	404,063	116,102	64,934	45,099	19,835
1970[b]	1,192,114	979,237	212,877	105,000	75,000	30,000

[a]The city of Ensenada had in 1960 a population of 42,561 inhabitants. The difference between this figure and the urban figure represents the town of El Sauzal, which became urban in 1960. The Mexican census considers centers above 2,500 persons as urban. The urban figures prior to 1960 represent the population of the city of Ensenada.

[b]Estimates for the state are by Román Hirales Corrales, *Estudio Demográfico de Baja California*. Unpublished manuscript, Instituto de Investigaciones Sociales y Económicas, Universidad de Baja California, 1964, pp. 15 ff. The estimates for the municipality of Ensenada are my own based on figures from the office of the Civil Register and on estimated migration.

From Estados Unidos Mexicanos, Secretaría de Industria y Comercio, Dirección General de Estadística, *VIII Censo General de Población* (Mexico, D.F.: 1960).

TABLE 2
COMPOSITION OF LABOR FORCE IN MEXICO, STATE OF BAJA CALIFORNIA, AND MUNICIPALITY OF ENSENADA, 1950 AND 1960 (PERCENT)

Occupation	1950a			1960b		
	Mexico	Baja	Ensenada	Mexico	Baja	Ensenada
Agriculture, livestock, fishing, and forestry	58.3	45.6	44.0	54.2	39.5	34.0
Extractive industries	1.2	0.5	1.4	1.2	0.4	0.4
Manufacturing industries	11.7	11.1	14.8	13.7	12.9	15.0
Construction industries	2.7	4.1	3.5	3.6	5.0	5.6
Public utilities	0.3	0.5	0.6	0.4	0.7	0.9
Commerce	8.3	11.7	10.1	9.5	13.1	10.6
Transportation	2.6	3.0	3.2	3.3	4.0	5.2
Services	10.6	17.2	22.4	13.4	19.2	20.2
Unspecified and others	4.3	6.2		0.7	5.2	8.0

aTotal labor force in 1950: Mexico, 8,272,093; Baja California, 75,876; Ensenada, 10,782.

bTotal labor force in 1960: Mexico, 11,322,016; Baja California, 167,436; Ensenada, 21,999.

From Estados Unidos Mexicanos, Secretaría de Industria y Comercio, Dirección General de Estadística, *VII Censo General de Población* and *VIII Censo General de Población* (México, D.F.: 1950 and 1960, respectively).

Baja's wealth is due in large part to its proximity to one of the most prosperous regions in the United States. The greater San Diego area provides thousands of jobs for Tijuana residents, a factor that stimulates the economy of the entire state. Citizens of Tijuana and of Northern Baja can import easily and cheaply such second-hand articles as clothing, furniture, home and industrial appliances, cars and trucks. The poorest homes in Ensenada have refrigerators and gas ranges, even if at times the refrigerators have to be used as iceboxes for lack of electricity. In 1966 there was one motor vehicle per five persons in the municipality of Ensenada, and television sets are becoming a common item in most households.[8]

Local industry has also benefited from the prosperity of the San Diego and Los Angeles areas by buying second-hand tools and equipment that would otherwise be unavailable. For example, when canneries in Monterey, California closed down they frequently sold their machinery and fishing boats to Ensenada canneries. Even the dry dock in the port of Ensenada was bought second-hand in Oakland. In 1960 the municipality of Ensenada imported 307.5 million pesos worth of goods from foreign markets but goods from other Mexican markets worth only 112.5 million pesos.[9]

The proximity of Baja to the United States has promoted particularly the tourist industry. Baja California has an estimated average daily floating population of 32,000 North American visitors and 44,000 Mexicans who are residents of the United States. In 1960, eighteen million persons visited the city of Tijuana, and the total yearly income from tourism in the state was estimated to be one billion pesos.[10] Although no estimates of the number of visitors to Ensenada are available, Table 3 presents industrial sales during 1960 and shows that in that year tourism was the second most important industry in the municipality. Total sales of the municipality in 1960 amounted to 465 million pesos (Table 3). Because purchases amounted to only 420 million pesos, Ensenada enjoyed a favorable balance of trade of 45 million pesos during 1960, a figure that suggests a healthy local economy.

Fishing, fish processing, and tourism are the economic backbone of the municipality. In 1960 there were fourteen fish canneries with an estimated total capital investment of 200 million pesos, and two large factories manufacturing tin cans for the canneries. The tourism industry had forty-seven hotels and motels with accommodations for more than 1,000 guests, nineteen trailer camps with a total capacity of 1,175 trailers, and thirty restaurants with a total capacity to serve 2,035 persons at one time.[11] Sport fishing is one of the main attractions for tourists, and in 1967 a fleet of forty-six vessels with an average capacity of 25 passengers provided this service.

Agriculture and food processing are fast-growing industries. Three major wineries and two olive oil factories serve the national markets, and in the late 1960s three important vegetable canneries were established. These vegetable

TABLE 3
TOTAL SALES IN MUNICIPALITY OF ENSENADA BY INDUSTRY, 1960
(in millions of pesos)

Industry[a]	Foreign Sales	Domestic Sales	Total	Percent of Total Sales
Fishing and fish processing	127.5	122.5	250.0	53.8
Tourism	110.0	12.5	122.5	26.3
Agriculture	—	23.7	23.7	5.1
Cement	—	22.5	22.5	4.8
Wines and liquors	—	20.0	20.0	4.3
Others	—	26.3	26.3	5.6
Total	237.5	227.5	465.0	

[a]There are two large salt mines in the municipality; the one in Gurerrero Negro is one of the largest in the world. These industries are owned by North American concerns and most of the salt is exported. Apparently these businesses to not provide any income for the municipality except for employees' salaries.

Calculated from Programa Nacional Fronterizo, *Ensenada, B.C.*, Part 1, Report No. 7, (Mexico City: n.d.), pp. 15 ff.

canneries receive their produce from the prosperous valley of Maneadero, a few miles to the south, and from San Quintín, 105 miles south of Ensenada. Tomatoes, artichokes, peppers, and olives are among important products canned by the new factories.[12] During the summer of 1967, considerable quantities of fresh tomatoes and canned vegetables were exported to the United States. The future potential of this industry appears very large; a shortage of irrigation water for the growers is the main limiting factor at the moment. Several other firms produce foods for local consumption.

A large cement factory on the outskirts of the city employs more than 200 persons and supplies the state of Baja California with cement. It is the single largest factory in the municipality. Other small businesses include a tannery, two packing houses, a paint factory, a fertilizer factory, an ice plant, and a soap factory.

One other important source of economic wealth in Ensenada is the port. The new deep-water port was completed only in 1967, although deep-water ships have been able to dock there since 1958. During 1962, 282 deep-water ships called at the port of Ensenada. Total overseas and coastal shipments in that year amounted to 285,063 tons, and the industry employed 665 persons with an annual payroll of 8.5 million pesos.[13] The port includes a dry dock and two small shipyards that construct small pleasure boats and offer a variety of repair services.

The municipality of Ensenada is one of the most economically privileged areas of Mexico. Although it does not have heavy industry, it does have a modern occupational structure and a healthy economy. In 1960 the average income per person was 634 dollars, the national average 280 dollars.

Political System

Baja California is one of the few states of the federation that has a competitive two-party system. The two parties, the Partido Revolucionario Institucional (PRI) and the Partido de Acción Nacional (PAN), have been fighting at the polls—and occasionally in the streets—since the territory became a state in 1951. The 1959 state elections (for governor and deputies) and municipal elections were heavily contested in the four municipalities. The PAN claimed that it had won the elections and accused the State Electoral Commission, under the control of the PRI, of fraud and of tampering with the election results.[14] Although the PAN frequently makes such allegations in elections in other parts of the nation, the evidence supporting its claim in this case was overwhelming. Almost ten years later, in the municipal elections of 1968, history repeated itself in Mexicali and Tijuana, the two most important municipalities of the state. This time the fraudulent behavior of the State Electoral Commission was so obvious that the Federal Electoral Commission took unprecedented action and annulled the elections.[15] The 1968 election showed the political strength of the PAN in the state; the PRI had made every effort in preparing for the elections, using all its power and electoral experience to guarantee a victory, yet the election was annulled. Table 4 shows election results from selected years for the PRI and PAN in Baja California and in the nation.

Baja California is second only to the Federal District as a political stronghold of the PAN. Students of Mexico have somewhat limitingly identified the PAN with the Church, but if church attendance and the reception of sacraments are used as indicators of religiosity, then Baja California must be one of the most secular states in Mexico.[16] There is not hostility but indifference toward the Church. According to the 1960 census, 94.3 percent of the population considered itself Catholic, 2.4 percent Protestant, and 1 percent as having no religious affiliation. The rest of the population indicated membership in other churches or gave "don't know" answers. In spite of the high percentage of Catholics, Baja California ranks only twenty-seventh in Catholic affiliation among the states, followed by Chihuahua and four southern states (Campeche, Chiapas, Quintana Roo, and Tabasco) where Protestantism is particularly strong. During several weeks of observation at the three Catholic churches in the city, only 10 to 15 percent of the city's population attended mass on Sunday, and as few as 150 persons, most of them women and children, received communion.[17]

TABLE 4

VOTES FOR PRI AND PAN IN STATE OF BAJA CALIFORNIA AND IN NATION

(selected elections)

Year	Election	State			Nation		
		PRI Votes	PAN Votes	Percent PAN Votes[a]	PRI Votes	PAN Votes	Percent PAN Votes[a]
1958	President	82,405	53,399	39.3	6,767,754	705,303	9.4
1961	Federal deputies	91,413	35,817	28.2	6,178,434	518,652	8.4
1962	State deputies	94,041	27,204	22.4	—	—	—
1964	Federal deputies	115,230	41,039	26.3	7,807,912	1,042,396	11.8
1964	President	143,074	38,946	21.4	8,368,446	1,034,337	i1.0
1965	Governor	102,508	37,069	26.6	—	—	—
1967	Federal deputies	141,748	42,333	23.0	8,312,143	1,227,512	12.9

[a]This percentage is of the PRI and PAN total votes. The combined votes of the three other parties—PPS (Partido Popular Socialista), PARM (Partido Auténtico de la Revolución Mexicana), and PNM (Partido Nacional Mexicano)—in the State of Baja California do not generally amount to 3% of the total vote.

State data from the State Electoral Commision in Mexicali. National data from Pablo González Casanova, *La Democracia en México* (México, D.F.: Ed. Era, S.A., 1965). The 1967 figures are from *El Universal* (Mexico City), July 11, 1967.

The tiny Protestant minority does not have problems of integration with the rest of the population, although there is a certain degree of latent suspicion. Children and youths have thrown stones at windows in the Protestant churches on a few occasions, with the knowledge and perhaps the blessing of some of the Catholic priests. (There are five Protestant churches in Ensenada.)

Social Organization

Ensenada has a high organizational density. Organizations in the city include approximately 150 sport groups, more than 100 labor unions, 30 cultural and social associations, 20 professional and business groups, and several religious and political associations. Each school has a parent-teacher association. Several of the *colonias* have Boards of Moral, Civic, and Material Improvements, and others have Associations of Neighbors organized to improve the physical conditions of the neighborhoods. In the rural areas of the municipality farmers are organized into 27 *ejidos* and 27 New Centers of Agriculture. *Ad hoc* committees and associations usually can be organized without difficulty when the need for common action arises.

By using the 1960 census, population growth estimates, membership lists of unions, and party affiliation figures, one can estimate roughly the occupational structure of the municipality (Table 5).

TABLE 5
OCCUPATIONAL STRUCTURE OF LABOR FORCE
IN MUNICIPALITY OF ENSENADA
(estimates in 1967)

Occupation	Number	Percent
Professional and managerial	1,500	5.0
White collar private	5,500	18.3
White collar public	2,000	6.7
Organized workers	7,000	23.3
Organized farmers *(ejidatarios)*	2,000	6.7
Nonorganized workers	4,000	13.3
Nonorganized farmers	8,000	26.7
Total Labor Force	30,000	

The number of professionals holding university degrees is very small—about 200—and breaks down as follows: 35 percent medical doctors, 30 percent engineers and architects, 22 percent lawyers, and 13 percent other professions. Most of the businesses are managed by nonprofessional personnel. On the other hand, literacy rates are high. According to the 1960 census, 84 percent of the population over six years of age was literate. With some exceptions, most children attend school, and two private normal schools, one nursing school, and several secretarial schools provide training in semiprofessional skills. With the exception of one very small and poorly financed vocational school, the city has no institutions that provide training in technical skills. Workers have to learn their trades on the job.

The social structure of the community is flexible, with a high degree of social mobility that migration may have helped to bring about. People frequently refer to Baja California as a frontier with opportunities and possibilities for many. Geographically, Ensenada reflects this freedom; there are many well-built homes in the slum *colonias,* and in the downtown area poor and wealthy homes are mingled.

The inhabitants of Ensenada agree on one issue: The community's most important need is water. The rapid growth of the city has aggravated this problem, which becomes acute during the summer months when natural water resources are low and the demands from tourism and industry are highest. The city has artesian wells only, and its water system is obsolete and insufficient. The water pipes are contaminated and drinking water has to be bought from private artesian wells.

The high rates of migration have produced some serious problems in housing, city services, and employment, because the resources of the community cannot cope fast enough with the demands put upon them. However, the city is reasonably attractive and its slums are not as dismal as those in Tijuana and in some other fast-growing Mexican cities.

As has been previously mentioned, the municipality of Ensenada is geographically the largest in Mexico. The most distant population center from the city of Ensenada, yet still a part of the municipality, is Isla de Cedros, an important fishing center about 215 miles away. Communications between the city and the rest of the municipality are very poor. There are practically no paved roads, and the dirt roads are in bad condition and may even disappear during the rainy season. Most communication within the municipality is by air, and there is a local airline that has irregular service to most important points. Most of the rural population, however, is concentrated in the immediate vicinity of the city of Ensenada and in the valley of San Quintín; most of the rest of the municipality is desert or high sierra with limited water resources. The city of Ensenada has little interest in the rest of the municipality, yet there are twenty-two political delegations that are dependent upon the Municipal Council, which is located in the city.

To summarize, Ensenada is a young and progressive Mexican community with a mixed atmosphere of provincialism and cosmopolitanism. In spite of its peculiarities it is very much culturally integrated into the rest of the nation. The proximity and economic influence of the United States have affected only minimally the social and cultural institutions of its inhabitants.

NOTES

1. The municipality is the smallest autonomous politico-administrative unit in Mexico. The municipality of Ensenada covers 74% of the area of Baja California and is larger than 13 of the states of the federation.

2. The lowest average temperature is 55.6° F in February, the highest average temperature 70.3° F in August.

3. There are several foreign groups in Ensenada: North Americans, Chinese, Russians, and smaller groups of Spaniards, Italians, French, Arabs, and Indians. It is difficult to assess precisely the number of these foreign groups since many of them are nationalized citizens and the census only gives the figures of foreign residents in Ensenada. In 1960 the total number of foreign residents was 1,374. Of these, 985 were North Americans, most of whom are retired couples who live on the outskirts of the city in their own *colonias* and trailer camps. The North Americans very seldom attempt any integration with the local people. The second large foreign group is the Chinese. For the government's racial prejudice in Baja California against the Chinese see Baja California, Territorio Norte, *Memoria Administrativa del Gobierno del Territorio Norte de la Baja California, 1924–1927.* The author of the report was the late governor of the Territory, General Abelardo Rodríguez.

4. Before 1920 the Peninsula of Baja California was little more than an uninhabited desert. According to the national census of 1910, what is today the state of Baja California then had a total population of 9,760 persons. For the early history of the Peninsula and the several attempts at colonization by European and North American companies, see Pablo Martínez, *Historia de Baja California* (México, D.F.: Editorial Libros Mexicanos, 1965), the most complete history of Baja California; Alfonso Salazar Ruvirosa, *Cronología de Baja California: del Territorio y del Estado 1500 a 1956* (México, D.F.: 1957). For contemporary history see Lowell L. Blaisdell, *The Desert Revolution. Baja California 1911* (Madison: University of Wisconsin Press, 1962); Ulises Irigoyen, *Carretera Transpeninsular de la Baja California* (México, D.F.: Editorial América, 1943). For a complete bibliographical report of Baja California see Ellen C. Barret, *Baja California 1535–1964; a Bibliography of Historical, Geographical and Scientific Literature Relating to the Peninsula of Baja California and to the Adjacent Islands in the Gulf of California and the Pacific Ocean* (Los Angeles: Westernlore Press, 2 vol., Vol. 1 published by Bennet and Marshall, 1957-67).

5. Not all the Mexican economists have viewed favorably the Free Zone status of Baja California. For various views, see Lázaro Cárdenas, *El Problema de los Territorios Federales . . . Mensaje Dirigido a la Nación, el 28 de Septiembre de 1936* (México, D.F.: Talleres Gráficos de la Nación, 1936); Ulises Irigoyen, *El Problema Económico de las Fronteras Mexicanas, Tres Monografías: Zona Libre, Puertos Libres y Perímetros Libres* (México, D.F.: 1935).

6. The principal states of origin of immigrants were Baja California Southern Territory (10.7%), Jalisco (8.6%), Sinaloa (4.9%), Michoacan (3.8%), Sonora (3.1%). Colima, the Federal District, Guanajuato, and Zacatecas were represented each with approximately 2%.

7. Paul Yates Lamartine, *El Desarrollo Regional de México* (México, D.F.: Banco de México, Departamento de Investigaciones Industriales, 1962). For a similar analysis see Miguel Huerta Maldonado, "El Nivel de Vida en México," *Revista Mexicana de Sociología,* Vol. 22, No. 2 (May–September 1960), pp. 463-527.

8. Gobierno del Estado, *Baja California en Cifras* (Mexicali, Baja California: Talleres Tipográficos del Gobierno del Estado de Baja California, 1967). p. 62.

9. Programa Nacional Fronterizo, *Ensenada, B.C.,* Part 1, Report No. 7 (Mexico City: n.d.), p. 14. Since 1954 the monetary rate of exchange has been 12.49 pesos per U.S. dollar.

10. René Treviño Arredondo, *La Industrialización y el Desarrollo Económico del Estado de Baja California.* (Unpublished *licenciatura* thesis, Universidad Nacional Autónoma de México, Escuela Nacional de Economía, 1962, p. 144. This work is perhaps one of the most complete and accurate sources of economic data for the region.

11. Dirección General de Turismo del Estado de Baja California, Oficina de Ensenada, "Boletin" (1967), p. 3. The figures correspond to 1967, and include only those first- and second-class services that catered to the tourists.

12. In 1955 Baja California had approximately half a million olive trees, which had been planted without previous agricultural surveys. According to U.S. studies of the area, it does not have the proper climate for the olive industry. Olivares Mexicanos, S.A., which owns a large number of the trees and is partially financed by Nacional Financiera, a government financing agency, is going through a serious economic crisis. For a study of the olive industry in Baja California, see Henry J. Burke, *Olive Industry in Lower California, Mexico,* U.S. Foreign Agricultural Service, Foreign Agricultural Report No. 85 (Washington, D.C.: U.S. Government Printing Office, 1955).

13. Graydon K. Anderson, *The Port of Ensenada. A Report on Economic Development* (San Diego, California: Economic Research Center, Department of Economics, San Diego State College, 1964), pp. 26 and 42.

14. For the PAN views of the 1959 elections in Baja California see Carlos Ortega C., *Democracia Dirigida con Ametralladoras. Baja California: 1958–1960* (El Paso: Talleres La Prensa, 1961); *Mas Sobre el Caso de Baja California, Partido de Acción Nacional,* (México, D.F.: Editorial Jus, 1959). The PAN weekly, *La Nación,* had several articles on the issue in Vol. 36, 1959.

15. For comments on this election, see "México: Historia de Dos Ciudades," *The Economist para América Latina* (London), Vol. 2, No. 14 (July 10, 1968), pp. 12–13.

16. For a study of the Catholic Church in Mexico, see Rutilio Ramos et al., *La Iglesia en México. Estructuras Eclesiásticas* (Friburg: Oficina Internacional de Investigaciones Sociales de FERES, 1963).

17. These observations coincide with the estimates made by one of the local pastors.

2
Organized Labor Groups

ORGANIZATIONAL CAPABILITY OF THE LABOR CLASS

The official national statistics for 1964 show that only 10.5 percent of the total economically active population in the country was unionized.[1] In the municipality of Ensenada, as estimated in Table 6, 40.1 percent of the working class belonged to labor groups in 1960; if we add the unionized bureaucrats to the unionized workers, then close to 30 percent of the municipality's total active population is organized in the labor movement (not including the *ejidatarios*). The higher stage of economic development and urbanization of the municipality may be in part responsible for the difference. Contact with urban, industrial areas in the United States also may have promoted a general awareness that organizations are necessary for developing a modern society. William D'Antonio and William Form in their study of Ciudad Juárez (Chihuahua), another border town, characterized the labor movement there as active, perhaps even more so than its counterpart in the neighboring city of El Paso, Texas.[2]

There are 101 labor organizations in the municipality, excluding the small coalitions of workers. The number of organizations is not the only indicator of the organizational life of a community; others are size of the organizations, how actively members participate, actual performance, and overlapping affiliations. Although the high number of labor organizations does not in itself mean an effectively organized labor movement in Ensenada, during this study field observations of the labor groups in the municipality strongly suggest that most of them, perhaps as many as 90 percent, are active, hold regular meetings, and perform their functions fairly well.[3]

LABOR UNIONS AND ASSOCIATIONS

In Mexico the labor movement is hierarchically organized. The unions at the local level are the basic units. Generally, they combine into several local federations, each of which in turn joins with federations from other cities to form the state confederations. Several state confederations form the national confederations. Figure 2 shows the organization of a labor confederation.

The federal labor law established the following five types of unions: (1) Guilds *(gremiales)*[4] a category that includes many of the associations of self-employed workers. (2) Industrial unions *(industriales)* and (3) Unions of a firm *(de empresa)*, which for the present purpose, are similar; they consist basically of all workers of a factory who have a collective contract with the firm. (4) National unions *(nacionales),* trade unions having their locus of power in Mexico City. The local branches of the national unions have double organizational ties, one to the local federation and one to the national head-quarters; decisions affecting the local unions are generally made by the latter. (5) Unions of workers of several trades *(oficios varios).* Theoretically, these

TABLE 6

ESTIMATED PERCENTAGE OF WORKING CLASS ORGANIZED IN
LABOR MOVEMENT IN MUNICIPALITY OF ENSENADA (1960)

Activity	Total Working Force[a]	Number of Workers Organized[b]	Percent Organized
Agriculture and fishing[c]	7,300	2,136	29.3
Manufacturing	2,762	1,420	51.4
Construction[d]	1,044	913	87.5
Transportation	936	680	72.6
Services[e]	2,389	969	40.6
Utilities[f]	202	–	–
Commerce[g]	206	206	100.0
Unspecified	949	–	–
	15,788	6,324	40.1

[a]Estimated from the national census of 1960. Estados Unidos Mexicanos, Secretaría de Industria y Comercio, *VIII Censo General de Población, 1960. Estado de Baja California* (México, D.F.: 1963). The estimate was calculated from Tables 21, 22, and 23.

[b]Including labor federations, fishing cooperatives, the CNOP unions, and the independent unions. Data obtained from each organization.

[c]This item presents some problems because of the peculiar nature of the *ejido* system and the several associations of farmers grouped within the CNOP. The national census of 1960 has an error in the number of *ejidatarios* in the municipality of Ensenada. According to the census there were only 62 *ejidatarios* in Ensenada, an unlikely figure considering that there were 17 *ejidos*; there were approximately 2,000 *ejidatarios* in 1960. The *ejidatarios* and the CNOP independent farmers are not included among the organized working force, although in many respects they are organized.

[d]Reliability about the number of construction workers is minimal due to the constant fluctuations within the same year, depending on the time of the year and the available resources for public works.

[e]Including domestic servants, none of whom is unionized.

[f]No information available.

[g]Including street vendors only.

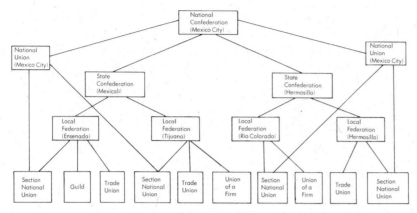

FIGURE 2.
SCHEMATIC ORGANIZATION OF A LABOR CONFEDERATION

unions are to be formed by workers of several trades or guilds when the membership of each is too small for it to have a separate union. In practice, frequently *oficios varios* are composed of construction workers.

Integration of Salaried and Independent Workers

Five national labor confederations have local federations in Ensenada: the Confederación Revolucionaria de Obreros y Campesinos (CROC), the Confederación de Trabajadores Mexicanos (CTM), the Confederación Regional de Obreros Mexicanos (CROM), the Confederación Revolucionaria de Trabajadores (CRT), and the Confederación General de Trabajadores (CGT).[5] In addition to the national federations there are two large independent unions and several small independent coalitions of workers.[6] Table 7 presents membership in organized labor with a breakdown by urban and rural areas and also by unions and associations.

A distinction should be made between labor unions and labor associations. Members of unions work under a contract. Members of associations are self-employed laborers who nevertheless are organized and are affiliated with the labor federations.

Generally, studies of the Mexican labor movement have included neither cooperatives nor the workers' associations that have been incorporated into the Confederación Nacional de Organizaciones Populares (CNOP) of the PRI.[7] Strictly speaking, these laborers do not work under contract.[8] However, this study of the labor movement revealed that the cooperatives and the workers' associations of the CNOP are ideologically identified with the labor

TABLE 7
ORGANIZED LABOR FORCE IN ENSENADA, 1967 (MEMBERSHIP BY LABOR FEDERATION)

| Federation | Number of Unions and Associations | City[a] | | Rural[b] | | Total Members |
		Union Members	Association Members	Union Members	Association Members	
CRT[c]	5	40	38	240[d]	–	318
CGT[c]	3	83	32	–	–	115
CROM[c]	10	272	170	175	–	617
CROC[c]	30	1,514	192	879	29	2,614
CTM[e]	27	622	675	951	–	2,248
Subtotal	75	2,531	1,107	2,245	29	5,912
Independent[f]	2	230	–	–	–	230
CNOP[g]	10	–	258	–	–	258
Fishing Cooperatives[h]	14	–	60	–	594	654
Total	101	2,761	1,425	2,425	623	7,054

[a]Including nearby town of El Sauzal.
[b]A few of the unions and some of the fishing cooperatives operate outside of the municipality and outside of the state of Baja California.
[c]Data elicited from federation officials.
[d]Including part-time workers.
[e]Data from official labor census, Municipal and Federal Labor Boards of Conciliation, Ensenada.
[f]Not including small coalitions of workers.
[g]Data from the CNOP files.
[h]Estimate.

movement and have a sense of belonging to the same socioeconomic stratum.

Also, a large number of the workers in the labor federations—1,136 out of 5,912—were nonsalaried workers who labored under organizational conditions similar to those of members of the cooperatives and CNOP associations. There was, for example, no difference between the working conditions of the CROC Association of Street Musicians and the CNOP Association of Street Musicians, or between the CTM Association of Street Peddlers and its counterpart in the CNOP. From a functional point of view the federations of cooperatives and the CNOP associations could be categorized as labor federations.[9]

The fact that the labor federations are formed by union and association members is important to understanding the Mexican labor movement. It suggests that the labor movement is not exclusively a force opposing managerial groups. The labor movement has a secondary role: to represent self-employed laborers and to organize these persons—members of the lower socioeconomic groups—into associations. Association and union workers are brought into daily contact through the federations, and thus have an opportunity to study jointly such common problems as the increasing cost of living, deficiencies and limitations of social security,[10] and housing and school shortages. In formulating proposals to improve their lot, in mutually attempting to solve these problems, in trying to obtain political patronage, the association members and the union members act as one group.

In the city of Ensenada, then—and within the political context of the municipality—the five labor federations, the federation of cooperatives, and the several labor groups of the CNOP constitute the organized labor movement. The peculiarity of the situation in that the labor federations are a mixture of salaried and independent workers cannot be overemphasized. As shown in Table 7, the CTM, for example, has more nonsalaried workers than salaried workers in the city.[11]

Association and Union Members as Employers

Of particular interest is the fact that association members themselves are sometimes employers of laborers. Taxi owners are a case in point. They are members of one of four associations, which are affiliates of the CROC, CTM, CRT, or CROM. They usually hire drivers for the second and third shifts, and sometimes also for the first shift. In accordance with a Mexican tradition, the hired drivers share half their income with the owners.[12] Truck owners in the three teamster associations in the municipality follow similar practices. Street vendors *(vendores ambulantes),* licensed by the municipality, frequently have a friend, relative, or employee selling for them; some have been able to obtain multiple licenses from City Hall through political patronage and have become small entrepreneurs in this profitable tourist-supported business. During a session of the CTM Association of Street Vendors one of the members fiercely attacked the new statutes of the association because they openly permitted members to hold more than one license apiece. He believed this would lead to abuses and to the exploitation of their employees by the members of the association, thus creating a group of bosses *(patrones)*.

Paradoxically, the workers who are employed by other workers are not organized. They are neither protected by the labor law nor covered by social security. When a secretary general of the CRT was asked about this situation, he replied quite simply that, under this system, two people could earn money, the holder of the license and his employee, and that two wage earners were better than one. A secretary general of the CTM explained that it was a matter not of exploiting the employees but of giving them a fair share, 50 percent of the profits, and that, in addition, the employer helped his employee in various other ways. At the same time, however, he said he would favor association membership for these employees.

A common practice is for the associations, which are empowered by the Secretary of Communication and Transportation to handle the port loading and unloading operations and to transport the cargo to warehouses, to hire laborers themselves. These associations, characterized by one labor leader as "privileged," hire hundreds of extra hands during the winter months when the export of cotton bales to Japan is at its peak. All equipment, tractors, trucks, and the like are owned by the associations and are bought through regular loans. A former secretary general of the Unión de Cargadores y Similares Progreso, CROC, said that the entrance fee for its association was 50,000 pesos, a sum that represented the estimated prorated value of the capital equipment. (When one of the members leaves the association or dies, he or his family is reimbursed the entrance fee.) No new members have entered the association in the last several years because of the high fees, and at any rate the membership is reluctant to admit new members, even if they could pay the fees, because there are slack months during which there is not enough work for the existing membership.

There is no difference between these organizations and the cooperatives. Both are franchised by the government, both frequently obtain government loans for the acquisition of equipment that is jointly owned by the workers, and both have business-type contracts, the cooperatives with canneries and the dock workers with shipping lines, agencies, and brokers.[13]

Some labor leaders are very much aware of this anomaly in the Mexican labor movement. A former secretary general of the CROC said: "When workers take over the management of a business they are worse than the original bosses . . . they place themselves at a higher level than the rest of the workers, they become *patrones* . . . and this is very bad for the labor movement." In a case that made headlines in the local newspaper, one of the officers of the executive committee of the CTM was called before the labor authorities by his new employees in a gas station. The employees accused him of exploitation *(negrero)* and violation of several articles of the federal labor law.[14]

In sum, two significant characteristics of the labor movement in Ensenada are: (1) It is integrated by salaried and independent workers who think of themselves as forming one unified social group, and this—as will be shown—in spite of considerable economic differences among them; (2) it is not an uncommon practice for workers to hire other workers and to earn a profit from the labor of the others.

These factors have multiple effects on the political and social system. Power becomes diffused in the struggle between labor and management. The labor federations are concerned not only with obtaining benefits and improvements from management but also with satisfying the needs of members who have no bosses. Demands such as better living conditions, reduction of taxes, and control of licenses often can be satisfied only through political patronage and governmental favoritism.

Union workers do have broader perspective and can better understand their society and its complexities because of their opportunity to mingle with other workers from different occupations and backgrounds. Many are acquainted with workers who are, in their own way, small but successful entrepreneurs, so that they observe economic mobility at close quarters. Those who employ other workers experience the problems of management, and can be expected to oppose radical extremists. On the other hand, the worker-manager has frequently abused his position and has thus contributed to a sense of alienation in the labor movement. There is little doubt that these conditions operate as a braking mechanism within the society and that they reduce the intensity of the struggle between classes. The labor movement is itself a microcosm of society.

Autonomy of Local Unions

The unions and associations in Ensenada are not puppet groups of the federations. With the exception of the small CGT Federation, the unions enjoy almost complete autonomy from the local federations in handling their internal affairs. As a CROM labor leader put it:

The autonomy of the unions is respected. The federations can only give guidelines, orientations, give some help, try to convince that one way of doing things may be better than another, but we as members of the federation cannot impose our will. We can ask the union to take into consideration our recommendations, but we can never say to the union: do this, do that. The unions are completely independent.

In support of the truth of this statement is the ease with which unions shift alliances from one federation to another. In the last decade three CROC unions moved to the CRT, and one of them returned to the CROC several years later. Two unions affiliated with the CTM left that federation to become members of the CROC. The CROC lost one union to the CGT, as did the CROM. The CRT received one union from the CTM but lost another that finally decided to be independent. One of the CROC unions also became independent. The changes of affiliation have seldom produced frictions in the labor movement. They are viewed as failures of the parent federations to retain the dissatisfied unions rather than as maneuverings by the recipient federations.[15]

The large federations can afford to lose a few unions, which will in turn be replaced by newly organized groups. As one author has indicated, this process guarantees the independence of the unions and a fair treatment of the unions by the federations.[16] The existence of several labor federations also tends to reduce their potential bossism.

There is an important exception. Evidence suggests that the local chapters of the national unions are controlled by their national headquarters. The secretary general of the CRT national executive committee wrote to the Ensenada federation:

In regard to [the crooked maneuvers of] . . . tell the Executive Committee of the Association of Truck Drivers that if they fall in his trap and become a national union they will regret it. These unions are like the ones that Pedro directs from here, something like the Unión de Palas Mecánicas and Terraceros of the CTM. The contracts will be drawn here, and they will lose their autonomy. I have always maintained that the workers of Baja California should handle themselves and their unions there.[17]

The remote-control direction that the national unions can exercise on local sections is illustrated by the case of the ghost union organized by a cannery in 1967. The cannery had signed a collective contract in Mexico City with a national union affiliated with the CGT. Four cannery workers had signed the contract. In the meantime, the other 296 workers had organized a local union affiliated with the CROC. A bitter labor conflict ensued. The firm had signed the contract in Mexico City in order to move the locus of negotiations away from the workers, preferring to deal with the labor leaders in Mexico City.

The independence of the unions from the local federations is further guaranteed by the fact that the ruling body of each local federation is its general assembly, composed of several secretaries and a number of representatives, usually three or five, from each member union. The approval of a resolution requires a legal quorum and a majority vote. Observations of several assembly meetings and study of the official meeting minutes for the last three or four years of three federations suggest that the meetings of the assemblies are free gatherings, with high participation, and that members attending have few inhibitions about speaking out. Even highly sensitive topics are freely discussed at the labor meetings. One set of minutes reads:

In the same way, it was indicated that according to the Statutes of the Confederation of Mexican Workers, all members had to belong to the PRI. Accordingly the Secretary General urged the Secretary Generals of each organization to affiliate their members to the party as soon as possible. To which one of the fellows *(compañeros)* said that Mexico was a free country and, consequently, it couldn't be demanded of anybody to belong to any party . . . because the unions should be kept out of politics and their task was to help the workers. In this respect other people said that the point at stake was not the limitation of free thought or belief, but the enforcement of the statutes of the federation . . . [18]

In March 1965 Carlos Madrazo, then president of the national central committee of the PRI, visited the city. Leaders of the CROC were uncertain as to whether members of the federation could be requested to participate in the welcoming rally. The matter had to be brought to the assembly meeting for discussion:

The arrival of Lic. Carlos Madrazo was discussed by the Assembly, and after long debate it was agreed by vote to make it compulsory for members of the federation to attend the mass reception. . . .Each Secretary General was made responsible for his union. Then the Assembly moved to discuss the speakers for the reception. Among others the name of——was proposed but it was argued that this *compañero* had been a member of the National Liberation Front. It was said that that didn't mean he was a member of the Liberation Front for the rest of his life. The motion was passed to propose his name to the Party as the person chosen to deliver the keynote speech. [19]

At the request of the PRI, candidates for elective office such as municipal councilmen and state and federal deputies are also selected by each federation following the procedures of majority assembly vote. Practically all important financial issues and labor problems are decided in the same fashion.

UNITY AND CLEAVAGE IN THE LABOR MOVEMENT

One finds an economically heterogeneous group of workers in this labor movement. A handful of workers drive Ford Galaxies; a considerably larger number have refrigerators, televisions, and other modern appliances and live in well-built homes; other workers—and they constitute by far the majority—can barely make ends meet. These economic disparities are readily observable.

One local labor leader commented: "How could there not be differences if some workers like those of Alba Roja make seventy dollars a week and others don't even make a minimum wage?"[20]

In general, members of associations that hire workers are the wealthiest. The dock workers' and taxi drivers' associations employ workers and their members are relatively quite wealthy. Members of technicians' unions, such as radio and television technicians, are also relatively wealthy. Some members of fishermens' and divers' unions are also well off, because special salaries are paid in those occupations; divers can make between 30,000 and 50,000 pesos per season gathering algae.[21] In the middle of the economic continuum are the unions of factory workers and the unions of agricultural workers. At the low-income end of the continuum are the construction workers, whose major problem is shortage of work, and members of associations whose incomes depend on seasonal work, such as the street musicians and porters.

Cooperation among Labor Leaders To Gain Ends

The economic differences, which are very noticeable to observers, and the organizational differences between unions and associations do not seem to keep the labor movement from being solid and well integrated. The numerous cleavages and conflicts between and within unions and federations heal fast whenever concerted action is needed to protect some of their mutual interests. The labor movement has shown a capacity for common action when defending the interests of the lower socioeconomic strata of the community and acting as their representative, and also in matters of political support for the state and federal regimes.[22]

One case in point occurred in the summer of 1967. The Secretary of Industry and Commerce franchised a private association of car dealers for the import and sale of second-hand vehicles. The five labor federations of Tijuana promptly called a meeting to study ways in which to stop the monopoly on auto imports. The CNOP associations of workers joined them immediately. The combined labor organizations began the protest by sending urgent telegrams demanding immediate revocation of the franchise to the President of the Republic, the secretaries of Interior and of Industry and Commerce, the state governor, and several minor officials. The labor federations protested that the franchise would hurt the interests of the workers and of the lower social classes in that these groups would have to pay higher prices for cars that they themselves could otherwise import from across the border. The labor federations of Mexicali and Ensenada supported these demands, and a massive state rally was scheduled. A few hours before the rally, when the temper and patience of the workers were beginning to show alarming signs, news arrived from Mexico City that the demands of the workers had been acceded to.

Inability of the Labor Federations To Cooperate in Labor Matters

The labor movement has never acted as a group, however, on issues related to labor-management conflict. In the city for example, no federation has ever joined another in solidarity strikes or protests even in cases in which the labor groups seemed to have a common cause.

In 1967 one of the CTM agricultural workers' unions called a strike against a vineyard. The strike was declared illegal by the labor authorities, but the union complained that the authorities had acted fraudulently in accepting signatures of nonunionized workers in the official count.[23] At the same time, the firm brought a criminal suit against the secretary general of the CTM of Ensenada, claiming that he had been a trespasser and had damaged private property. The criminal court dismissed the case for lack of evidence.[24] At no time during these incidents did any of the other four local labor federations express publicly moral support, sympathy, or backing for the CTM. This has usually been the practice.

The Ensenada labor federations constantly complain about the inefficiencies of the Mexican Institute of Social Security (IMSS),[25] yet the local federations have never been able or willing to establish a common front against the IMSS. Instead, each federation presents its own demands to the local IMSS. If they are not met, it then goes to its own national central committee in Mexico City, which in turn presents the demand to the national board of the IMSS. The labor movement might increase its bargaining power with the IMSS if the five local labor federations acted together and expressed their demands directly to the national IMSS. For example, if the local CROC were to feel that the local IMSS needed more personnel to provide adequate service to the workers, it could convene a general meeting of all the federations to discuss the problem. Then a common resolution could be formulated and forwarded to the national IMSS.

Labor unity of this kind could be expected to increase the bargaining power of the movement in labor matters before management and government.

Perspectives for the Unity of the Labor Movement

The labor federations have similar formal organizations, minimal statutory differences, and parallel goals and ideologies. At the local level they are very pragmatic. One secretary general commented, "We are all the same under different names," a thought he repeated on several occasions. One of the most knowledgeable local labor leaders used almost identical words: "Today there are no differences between the labor federations, just different names." Rank and file members share their leaders pragmatism. One CRT construction worker, waiting for an opening in a cannery that had a contract with the CGT, responded to a question about his CRT membership by saying that since he was a part-time worker in the cannery it did not matter to what federation he belonged. "In fact," he added, "I used to be in the CTM before I came to Ensenada. What matters to me is that I have work, not what federation I belong to."

If the differences are so minimal, then why have the federations failed to cooperate more with one another in dealing with labor problems? Although some leaders have begun to complain about the increasing number of federations, no one wishes to have only a single large federation. The belief that several can do the job better than one seems to be accepted. The government, for obvious reasons, has no desire to see a merger of labor groups into one gigantic federation. One labor leader shed some light on this attitude:

The unity of the Mexican labor movement has gone through several phases. . . .Now we have the Labor Congress *[Congreso Obrero]* whose objective is to unify the force of the workers; this is very good because, without depriving the federations of their autonomy, it will strengthen the power of labor. During the Congress it was agreed that delegates would visit the municipalities, but so far this has not been done. The unity in Ensenada has to come from outside. Someone from outside has to do it, because here *there is a great deal of individualism, and a lack of training in labor matters. We don't have a class conscience.* [Emphasis added]

"Individualism," for this labor leader, meant the unwillingness of the worker to make any special kind of effort for the benefit of his fellow workers; in this sense the speaker thought of labor as having no class conscience. This is a major limitation of the labor movement in Ensenada, and is reflected by members' reluctance to pay dues and other fees for needed projects.[26] The labor groups have the potential for far greater effectiveness.

There is no question that labor leaders desire greater unity,[27] but also undeniable is their clumsiness in working toward that goal. The mayor has tried several times to persuade the federations to march together as a symbol of unity in the May Day parade,[28] but leaders of the large federations are unwilling to undermine their own prestige by fraternizing with leaders of less powerful groups. Some labor spokesmen also have suggested that the labor federations put off attempts to unite until each has achieved internal unity, a goal that is itself still distant.

Perhaps, also, local labor leaders decline to take action toward unity because they are waiting to see what direction the labor unity movement will take in Mexico City. They know that, unless the unity of the labor movement is achieved on a broad base, cooperation among local federations would accomplish little. For example, the federations in the municipality and the state have proven that they can organize impromptu alliances when threatened by other local groups, but they know that, even united, they would be powerless to affect major labor problems like unemployment and inflation. Then, too, structural and organizational problems facing the local labor federations can be solved only by policies at the national level. Until definite steps toward unity are taken by the national organizations in Mexico City, alliances such as the Bloque Unido Obrero (of the CRT, CROM, and CGT), the Confederación Nacional de Trabajadores (of the CRT and CROC), and the Labor Congress of the five federations will continue to mean little at the local level.

ORGANIZATION, BEHAVIOR, AND OPERATIONAL POLITICS IN LABOR

Organization and Behavior in Labor

There are no sociological studies of the Mexican labor movement and it is not now possible to reach any definite conclusions regarding correlations between organizational variables and behavioral traits of the labor groups. Nevertheless, it may be interesting to examine a few observable behavioral differences that, on analysis, seem to suggest the existence of correlations.

At the local level, small federations seem more prone to corrupt leadership than do large federations. The CGT in Ensenada is a prime example, with a high correlation of the two variables. The CRT, the second smallest federation in size, also has had its share of corrupt leaders, although at present this is not the case. The leaders of large federations would be expected to have greater opportunities for dishonesty than the leaders of small federations; small federations have fewer contracts and fewer members, handle very small amounts of funds, and receive smaller subsidies from the government. Yet it is the small federations that, for the most part, have corrupt leadership.

Perhaps this can be explained as follows. First, the leaders of small federations find cases of collusion relatively easy to conceal; if the leaders of large federations were systematically to try to deceive their followers they would be caught sooner or later. Second, small federations are less powerful; for that reason the best workers, who can choose, join the large federations. It is easier to deceive and manipulate the less trained, less capable, and less interested workers. Corrupt federation officials therefore seem to have difficulty retaining positions in large federations, but survive in smaller ones. The large federations have built-in cleanup systems that are apparently quite effective.

There are also clear behavioral differences between the CROC and the CTM, the two largest federations in the municipality. The CTM has elected the same secretary general for the past ten years. The CROC, on the other hand, has never allowed the same man to be in that office for more than one term (a year), with one exception, a leader who was reelected to the general secretariat several times but always after an interval of several years' absence. This has happened only twice during the last ten years. In addition to leadership continuity, the CTM seems to be less democratic internally than the CROC; this is observable in the way its meetings are conducted, the way records are kept, and some aspects of internal organization. These differences may be partly explained by several factors.

1. Terms of office in the CTM are two years, in the CROC, one year. CTM leaders thus come to exercise tighter control because of their longer tenure.

2. The national executive committee of the CTM has had the same chairman for the last twenty years. By statutory law, however, the national executive committee of the CROC cannot be reelected for a second consecutive term (a term is four years). It is quite possible that the national committees influence the local ones.

3. The CTM has 10 national unions, of a total membership of 27 unions and associations. The CROC has no national unions. The CROC claims 192 association members, of a total membership of 1,706, whereas the CTM claims 675 association members, of a total membership of 1,297 (Table 7, "City" data). In a sense the national unions have double organizational ties— one to the local federation for articulating demands to local and state government and some political demands to the PRI; one to the union national headquarters, for articulating labor demands. Therefore, the local sections of the national unions have weaker ties with local federations than do the other unions, and they are understandably less interested in local federation affairs.

4. The CTM has a larger proportion of rural workers than does the CROC, and most of the CTM rural workers are farmers, whereas the CROC has a majority of industrial workers in the rural areas.

It might be suggested that farm laborers are more manageable than industrial workers (item 4), and that union workers are more active in the federation than are association members (item 3); consequently, the CROC would have more hard-core members than the CTM. This fact, along with items 1 and 2, suggests that bossism and continuism could take root more easily in the CTM than in the CROC.

At present it is difficult to know more precisely how these patterns of membership relate to behavioral traits; it is obvious that the membership composition of the local labor federations is different. More research is necessary before more definite conclusions can be reached. In the meantime and by the way of summary it can be suggested that the behavioral differences between the two largest federations, the CROC and the CTM, may be caused by different terms of office, different behavior on the parts of their national executive committees, differences in membership (the CTM having more agricultural workers and a larger percentage of association members than the CROC), and the presence of several national unions in the CTM and their absence in the CROC. If, as seems likely, these organizational characteristics do indeed influence the behavior of the leaders, then the *caciquismo* (bossism) concept of leadership loses its validity. The organizational characteristics indicate the kinds of limitation imposed by the group on the leader; the behavioral differences of the groups seem to be based more on structural differences than on the personality traits of leaders.

Political Continua of the Labor Federations

Operational differences exist among the local labor federations, but they are not like those observed by some authors on the national level. Figure 3 presents four continua along which the local federations have been placed according to their operations in the municipality. The continua are strictly qualitative and are based on responses elicited from labor leaders and from the study of official records.

FIGURE 3.
CLASSIFICATION OF LABOR FEDERATIONS IN ENSENADA

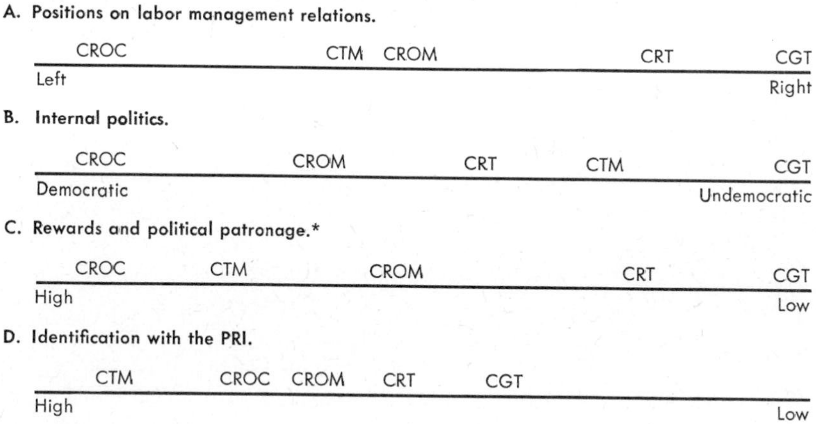

A. Positions on labor management relations.

CROC	CTM CROM	CRT	CGT
Left			Right

B. Internal politics.

CROC	CROM	CRT	CTM	CGT
Democratic				Undemocratic

C. Rewards and political patronage.*

CROC	CTM	CROM	CRT	CGT
High				Low

D. Identification with the PRI.

CTM	CROC CROM	CRT	CGT
High			Low

*In Ensenada rewards and political patronage went to labor federations in direct proportion to their size.

Frank Brandenburg and Robert E. Scott in their analysis of the Mexican public respectively distribute the labor federations in political continua as follows:[29]

CGT	CROC	CRT	CTM	CROM
Radical Left	Independent		Revolutionary	Toward Right
(Anarchists)	Left		Left	

Brandenburg

CROC	CRT	CTM	CGT	CROM
Left				Right

Scott

These observations contrast with our findings in Baja California. In Ensenada, for example, there is overwhelming evidence to support the position of the CGT at the extreme right end of continuum A in Figure 3. The secretary generals of the other four federations agreed unanimously that the CGT was a "white federation," a collaborator with and tool of management.[30] "These are the labor organizations we should fight against," commented one leader. The CGT leaders were notorious for their dealings with management and for organizing ghost unions.

The fact that the CGT is low in continuum C does not by any means indicate that it opposes the government. It receives little political patronage because of the conversion factor: low capability to support the government because of low membership equals low benefits and little patronage. This point is illustrated by the following two examples.

1. In 1959 the CGT in Ensenada sent a letter to the municipal committee of the PRI; in it, the CGT boasted that it had 300,000 members nationwide, that all of them were members of the PRI, and that it had 814 local members. The letter continued:

We believe that within the PRI we should have the same rights as the other federations CTM, CROM, and CROC, because our members have helped to carry out the programs of our Institutional Party as much as the members of the other federations. Consequently, we ask that our organizations have the same number of delegates to the party convention as the other labor federations.[31]

2. During the 1966 PRI campaign of affiliation, the CGT local committee refused to affiliate its members in Ensenada, deciding to affiliate in Mexicali instead, because of personal enmity between the secretary general of the CGT and one of the members of the municipal committee of the PRI. The local PRI wrote to the CGT national executive committee, explaining that the regulations issued by the PRI central committee required affiliation through local headquarters and urging the national committee to ask the local CGT to follow these regulations. The national CGT apologized in writing for the behavior of the local secretary general. The letter added:

We would like to inform you that the Confederación General de Trabajadores which we represent has sent instructions to all the groups affiliated to the federation to the effect that each and all the workers who belong to our organizations should be affiliated to the Institutional Revolutionary Party of which we are a part.[32]

The instructions received by the Ensenada CRT Federation from its national headquarters indicate how similar the federations are:

The Executive Committees of each union and of each organization member of the CRT will be responsible for affiliating to the PRI all the members of its group. Consequently, the Executive Committees will be responsible for filling out all the forms given by the PRI. . . . We recommend that this work of affiliation be completed as soon as possible, and it should include not only the workers of our unions and associations, but also all relatives who are of age. This is according to our conviction and ideology that organized workers strengthen the Institutional Revolutionary Party as the representative of the progressive forces of the Mexican Revolution.[33]

The other three labor federations receive similar reminders from their national committees to affiliate with the PRI and to carry out other political activity organized by the party. In 1967, a few months before the federal deputy elections, the CTM secretary general addressed the general assembly of the CTM Federation with these words:

It is mandatory that we follow the directives of the National CTM Executive Committee and that we affiliate all our members and relatives to the PRI. For this reason the CTM's Secretary for Political Affairs should continue to be a member of the PRI Municipal Committee. Through him our Federation will be told the instructions of our party . . . [34]

On February 23, 1964 (a few months before the national presidential elections), the state CROC Confederation convened a political convention in which the following was approved:

That in all political campaigns the CROC supports the PRI candidates. To implement this objective the Confederation will organize campaigns of orientation for members of the CROC during the political campaigns. That the CROC organizes a campaign to affiliate to the PRI the CROC members who are militant in other parties.[35]

At present, it is difficult for a labor federation to survive without making overtures to the PRI because of the low stage of industrial development, the lack of union training among workers, and particularly the dependence of the judiciary and labor authorities on the Executive.[36] Even the now extinct local Unión General de Obreros y Campesinos Mexicanos (UGOCM) had to play by the rules of the game. In 1959 Alfonso Corona del Rosal, then president of the national executive committee of the PRI, visited Ensenada. The PRI municipal committee invited the UGOCM to attend a reception for him. The invitation was accepted with the approval and blessings of its regional leader, Jacinto López, an avowed Communist.[37]

Two conclusions emerge from observations made during this study. In the first place, whatever the ideological tendencies of some of the national leaders in Mexico City, it is clear that these tendencies are diluted by the time they filter down to a provincial town. The rank and file members of the labor federations do not necessarily share the ideological positions of the national leadership, but join whichever group can offer them work. Second, the left-to-right political continuum does not seem to be unidimensional. The CROC is the most aggressive federation toward management, yet it accepts whole-heartedly the PRI and its middle-of-the-road stand. It should be emphasized that the differences presented in Figure 3 are extremely thin, and that the data suggest that they are produced more by organizational diversities than by different ideological positions. In the final analysis, the classifications of the labor federations at the national level along a left-to-right political continuum do not necessarily reflect the situation at the local level.

LEADERSHIP RECRUITMENT AND TRAINING

Selecting Leaders

All the sociological techniques used to identify leaders in a community or in complex organizations have their shortcomings, and it was not easy to decide which technique or combination of techniques would elicit the most reliable information in this study, with its limited research resources.[38] A list of current officeholders was at first expected to give a fairly complete inventory of labor leaders, but it soon became evident that some persons who had been pointed out by respondents and the press as labor leaders were not included on the lists of those holding office in the federations at the time the research was carried out. The leaders were finally identified by using lists of officeholders of the five labor federations and the state confederations since 1960,[39] talking with past and present officeholders, informally meeting with workers, and studying the records of the federations. A clear pattern of recruitment emerged. The identified leaders and the recruitment pattern were ultimately checked against each other to verify the findings.

Labor leaders were defined as *those persons within the labor movement who influenced labor policy decisions in the community;* in other words, those workers who were most frequently consulted about labor problems or whose advice was most often sought by other workers and by the unions. (Consultants and advisers outside the labor movement, such as labor lawyers and politicos, were deliberately excluded, since it was clear that they were consulted on a limited range of matters only.) This definition supports at base the observations of Amitai Etzioni, who suggests that the concept of leadership should be defined by each researcher "in the manner most helpful to his work," and that "so long as he uses it consistently . . . there is little room for argument."[40] One of the characteristics of the labor movement in Ensenada is that its leaders have little power. The power is held by the group, the unions or the federations. It would have been self-defeating to define leaders as the holders of power in the decision-making process.[41]

The recruitment process for labor leadership is simple. Workers are first exposed to positions of responsibility within labor groups at the union level as members of one of several committees, such as finance committees, justice committees, or *ad hoc* commissions. At times these men may be called on to moderate meetings or to represent the unions before the federation. The resourcefulness and skill of a worker in handling these appointments is informally but explicitly appraised by his co-workers. If the evaluation is favorable, then his chances for election to a union office are high. Holding an office in the union (most terms are for one year) is the second step toward achieving leadership status.

It is not difficult for a willing and capable person to win a union office. The executive committees of the unions have several offices, rotation of offices is high, and generally the membership of the unions is not very large. Holding a union office implies that the officer has to give some time to the union—writing minutes, keeping accounts, arranging meetings, or attending most of the ordinary and extraordinary assemblies. These tasks are non-salaried and many of the workers understandably do not care for them, while others are handicapped by illiteracy.

At this level the worker begins to know people outside his own union, and, if he is also successful in this position, after one or more years he may be elected to the offices of the federation. Tables 8 and 9 show that many workers hold federation offices only once. This may depend on the individual's own interest; for reasons already indicated, many do not wish additional involvement. Ability shown while in office also influences markedly a member's number of terms in office. It is not possible to generalize, because terms of office differ from federation to federation, as does the number of times a worker generally must be reelected to office before he becomes a leader under our definition. In the case of the CROC, for example, those who had been elected three or more times to office during a ten-year period were the labor leaders. Most of them had also been elected to the executive committee of the state federation, had been municipal councilmen, or had occupied offices in City Hall. Some had represented labor before the federal and local labor authorities or had held office in the PRI.

TABLE 8
EXECUTIVE COMMITTEES OF ENSENADA CROC FEDERATION (1959-68)

Secretariats	1959	1960a	1961	1962	1963
General	N. Bojórquez (5)b		N. Bojórquez	S. Montoya (1)	F. Morales
Interior	F. Morales (3)		J. Moreno (5)	J. Moreno	N. Bojórquez
Exterior	J. Rincón (1)		J. Moreno	J. Muñoz (2)	J. Torres (2)
Acts	A. Aguilar (1)		J. López L. (1)	E. Moreno (1)	Z. Domínguez (3)
Treasurer	R. Palos (3)		E. Peralta (1)	M. Crespo (2)	O. Campos (1)
Labor	A. Carrillo (6)		J. Núñez (1)	N. Bojórquez	J. Muñoz
Agreements	R. Cortés (1)		A. Medina (1)	A. Carrillo	A. Carrillo
Organization	R. Ramírez (2)		A. Carrillo	V. Cárdenas (1)	J. Bambrila (3)
Cooperatives	—		—	—	—

Secretariats	1964	1965	1966	1967	1968
General	N. Bojórquez	E. García	J. Moreno	P. Ventura	J. Bambrila
Interior	E. García (3)	J. Moreno	P. Ventura (2)	J. Bambrila	R. Ferniza (1)
Exterior	J. Torres	F. Morales	G. Rodríguez	J. Jacinto (1)	R. Zamora (1)
Acts	N. Flores (1)	J. Granados (1)	M. Catro (1)	J. Nava	J. Rodríguez S. (1)
Treasurer	A. Carrillo	S. Argueta (1)	G. Castillo (1)	M. Murillo (1)	R. Palos
Labor	J. Moreno	G. Rodríguez (2)	E. García	E. Peraza (1)	A. Amaya (1)
Agreements	M. Crespo	D. Bravos (1)	E. Bastida (1)	R. Palos	C. Meza (1)
Organization	R. Ramírez -	G. Zepeda (1)	J. Nava (2)	A. Carrillo	V. Sanabria (1)
Cooperatives	Z. Domínguez	S. Godina (2)	A. Azuela (1)	Z. Domínguez	S. Godina

Summary:

Number of times in office	Number of persons
6	1
5	2
3	5
2	8
1	29

aNo information available.
bNumbers after the first appearance of a name indicate the number of times that person has held office in the 1959-68 period.
From files of the CROC Federation.

TABLE 9
EXECUTIVE COMMITTEES OF ENSENADA CTM FEDERATION (1959–69)

Secretariats	1959-61	1961-63	1963-65	1965-67	1967-69
General	A. Díaz (5)a	A. Díaz	A. Díaz	A. Díaz	A. Díaz
Labor	Q. Hurtado (3)	C. Alvarez (1)	D. Velázquez (4)	S. Castellanos	S. Castellanos
Organization	S. Castellanos (4)	S. Castellanos	J. Ibarra (2)	Q. Hurtado	J. Hernández (1)
Cooperatives	A. García (1)	J. Peralta (1)	F. Buelna (1)	H. Maldonado (1)	F. Ramírez (1)
Acts	B.Estrada (1)	R. Palos (1)	V. Romero (1)	B. Alfredo C. (1)	D. Velázquez
Education	–	T. Guerrero (1)	L. Pimentel (1)	L. Martínez (1)	Q. Hurtado
Treasurer	–	L. Hernández (1)	J. E. Marín (2)	V. Poncio (1)	J. E. Marín
Social action	–	–	J. Aguero (1)	G. Galindo (1)	R. Martaín (1)
Political action	A. Leyva (1)	D. Velázquez	A. Sánchez (1)	D. Velázquez	J. Ibarra
Statistics	–	–	C. González (1)	F. Ruíz (1)	D. Acosta (1)
Feminine	J. Cota (1)	A. Castañeda (1)	M. Rosales (1)	–	I. Figueroa (1)

Summary:

Number of times in office	Number of persons
5	1
4	2
3	1
2	2
1	28

aNumbers after the first appearance of a name indicate the number of times that person has held office in the 1959-69 period. From files of the CTM Federation.

Socialization of Leaders

Also of importance is what kind of experiences workers have as they advance toward leadership positions, their training and socialization. By the time they become leaders, workers will have attended hundreds of meetings and have led orderly public discussions.[42] They will have learned to talk and to listen at meetings. They will have met public officials and political candidates. They will have traveled rather extensively to other cities and probably will have attended several national conventions in Mexico City. They will have come to know the national labor leaders of their federation and other regional federation leaders as well. They will have studied contracts. They will have sat at the bargaining table with management. They will know the labor law backward and forward and will have been consulted in labor problems on many occasions. The following biographical account was obtained from the files of the PRI and describes the history of a labor leader.

José was born in a small village in the southern part of Baja California in 1913. At the age of eleven he was an orphan with two younger sisters whom he had to support by working as a clerk in a food market. At the age of fifteen, searching for higher wages, he took a job in a mining company and joined a labor union. Since then he has been an active member of labor federations. His grade school education was completed at night school. In 1938, when he was twenty-five, he organized a successful cooperative store for the miners. When he left the job and the town, his share in the cooperative was given to his *compañeros*. In 1939 José was asked to serve on a commission founded to study the economy and minimum salaries in the municipality. At thirty-one he was elected to represent labor before the Federal Labor Board of Conciliation in Guaymas, Sonora. When he came to Ensenada five years later, José was elected once again to represent labor, this time before the Municipal Labor Board of Conciliation. In 1950 he served on the City Hall's advisory board, and for an interim period he headed the Federal Mining Agency in Ensenada. As head of the Federal Mining Agency he stopped several abusive and corrupt practices. He was elected three additional times to the state commission to study minimum salaries in the municipality. During one period he occupied the presidency of the PRI's local municipal committee. He was elected secretary general of his union, federation, and state confederation several times. The report ended with these comments: "The militancy and honesty of this modest worker in the labor movement is beyond question. After thirty years of dedication to his fellow workers he does not even own the poor house where he and his family live."[43]

Electoral Procedures and Elections

There are several procedures for electing officers of labor federations. The two most common are the *terna* and the *planilla*. In the *terna* system, each union of the federation presents three members as candidates to offices of the federation, and each officer is elected separately and by a simple plurality. A union can propose a member for secretary general; if he is not elected, the union can present his name for a different office. In the *planilla*, or slate, system, three or four slates are registered before the election. Each union then has one vote for the slate of its choice, and the slate with the most votes wins the election.

In some cases elections are heated contests, and nobody knows beforehand which candidates will win. This is presently the case in the CROC, CRT, and CROM. As one of the labor leaders said, "In our federation nobody has ever imposed the Executive Committees on us. When the Committee is to be elected there are people who favor so-and-so, others prefer somebody else. So far there have never been impositions. Who knows the next time, but I don't believe so. The decision is made by the workers." This seems to be a fair judgment of the electoral procedures.

In the case of the CTM, one slate is probably prepared by the officers before the assembly meets, and then proposed for approval. Some bargaining and politicking take place beforehand in order to have a fair representation from the most important unions on the executive committee of the federation, a practice that helps to guarantee approval of the slate.

Many of the labor leaders are aware of the evils of continuism. The younger leaders see, perhaps more clearly than their elders, the problems that will plague the system if it becomes less mobile or less open. One of them with a great sense of practical wisdom commented:

Once I was reelected as secretary general of my union, and then I realized that that was not good. It is necessary to give the opportunities to the rest, to let them have offices of responsibility so that they learn the functioning of the union. And I had the statutes changed to make reelection impossible and when my term was over I told the fellows: And now, *compañeros,* according to the new statutes no one of this Executive Committee can be reelected for next year, find somebody else!

The following conclusions emerge from the above observations. Leadership recruitment is very selective, and the labor movement makes the selections. Leadership is achieved, not assigned. The labor movement, as an organizational system, allows for great internal and upward mobility, a fact of paramount importance to understanding the political and social integration of the community. The labor system is also an open system; all workers are allowed to seek office, and rotation of officers is a common practice. Only a few workers have the will, perseverance, ambition, energies, intelligence, and dedication to want to go higher. The legitimacy of the leaders as representatives of the rank and file is based on recognition and acceptance of the leaders' success. A leader is, above all, a labor expert whose knowledge of labor problems is admired and sought. The leaders are self-made experts, a product of the labor movement, and from this fact derive their second base of recognition and legitimacy.

CORRUPTION OF LABOR LEADERS

Corruption among labor leaders is not very unlike corruption elsewhere in Mexico. The two most common sources of money for labor leaders are the contacts they have with the municipal and state government and the subsidies they receive from firms for services rendered in solving labor problems. By Mexican standards, neither of the two situations is dishonest per se, although at times each becomes so.

An example of abuse of the first type would be a labor leader's purchase of land on the outskirts of the city at a very low price because the title is not clear—a frequent situation in Baja California. He might then get the title cleared with the help of government officials he knows, and sell the land at a good profit. At other times, labor leaders appointed or elected through the PRI to public offices are placed in positions that allow them to behave unethically. The office of local price inspector, for example, is frequently assigned to a labor leader. If a store owner is caught selling at excessive prices, the inspector can take a wide range of action. He can overlook what he saw for a cash bribe; he can ask the store owner to bring the prices down to the official level, for which he may receive a compensation; he can fine the owner, as is his duty in the first place. In the Mexican ethical system, the second choice may not be considered dishonest.

Similar observations can be made regarding collusion with management. Labor leaders help the unions to draw up contracts and to present complaints. Through personal conversations with management, they learn how far the union can go in its demands. Honest leaders may want to know the position of management in order to expedite signing a contract and avoid useless delays that, in the end, hurt the workers more than the firms.[44] Management may reward the good faith of the leader with a cash gift. This does not necessarily imply that the leader was in collusion with the firm.

It is very difficult for a labor leader caught in corrupt practices to keep his office in the federation. The CRT, for example, ordered one of its secretary generals to account for missing funds: 1,224 pesos from one of the unions, 5,400 pesos from one of the industries (to help federation representatives attend the national congress in Mexico City), and a 1,500-peso subsidy from the municipality. He refused to do so and was subsequently expelled from the federation.[45] An extremely capable, intelligent, and ambitious young person, after his expulsion he continued to advise some unions on labor matters. Cases of this type do occur, but it is difficult to become rich by pilfering a few dollars here and there; the federations operate in the red and the budgets are very small.[46] It is obvious that, at the provincial level, federation offices are not a Mecca for labor workers.

In summary, there are a few corrupt leaders, a few more who are unscrupulous, and many who are honest. Federation offices are not money-makers. In Ensenada, petty corruption is much more frequent at the union level, where secondary leaders can occasionally pocket money.[47] The labor movement is aware of the corruption where it exists, and workers consider it a disgrace. Honesty is one of the ideal or normative qualities of leadership, and dishonest leaders or potential leaders have to be extremely careful to conceal their derelictions.

PERFORMANCE OF THE LOCAL LABOR FEDERATIONS

Federation Assistance to Unions

Although, as has been indicated, the unions act independently of the local labor federations in handling their internal affairs, the labor federations do perform important functions for them.

When a union needs assistance in dealing with a labor problem, its leaders generally go to the local federation. The union may, for example, want to exert some pressure on the state labor authorities or the governor. The federation will, on behalf of the union, present the demands to the labor board or the governor; if the case is important enough, the federation will ask its national executive committee in Mexico City to put pressure on state authorities from above. The national committee may decide that the situation is not grave enough to merit its intervention and therefore do nothing about the request; on the other hand, it may ask the governor for an investigation or for fair treatment for the union. In some cases the national executive committee will ask all the federations in the country to send wires to a reluctant governor demanding fair treatment for the union. In extreme cases, representatives of the national committee will go in person to see the governor. This is a power game, and each side knows the strengths and weaknesses of the other and how to use its own political weapons. The state labor confederations and the PRI do not intervene.

On one occasion, for example, the secretary general of the CRT received a wire from his national executive committee, requesting that the local federation in Ensenada send a wire to the governor of the state of Aguascalientes to remind him that it was a right of the Mexican worker to unionize and to demand that the governor stop harassing one of the CRT's newly organized unions in Aguascalientes. It is likely that another labor federation in Aguascalientes was urging the governor to deny official registration of the CRT union. The CRT secretary general in Ensenada immediately consulted several sections of the labor law and sent a well-written message. It is difficult to assess the impact of the fifty or sixty wires, received within several hours of one another, on the governor. At any rate, it can be assumed that the telegrams had a symbolic impact. These are common, almost everyday practices in the labor movement.

A somewhat more technical function of the labor federations is advising local unions on legal matters. Work contracts are usually renewed every two years, and at the time of the negotiations individual unions have legal consultations with their federations. Some of the large unions hire their own labor lawyers or consult an expert labor leader, who may not be a member of the executive committee of the federation. Drawing up a collective contract is difficult and requires experience and knowledge of the labor law, and an expert negotiator can obtain better terms for the union.

Federation help for the unions is also important in strikes. The federation is the channel through which funds to help the strikers are collected. The funds never amount to much, even though some out-of-state unions send contributions. On the local level, the federation may be asked for help with picket lines *(turnos de guardia)*. Sometimes picket lines have to be maintained 24 hours a day, because many firms have in the past taken advantage of night hours, when workers were not guarding the premises, to break the official seals and remove the expensive equipment that was to be impounded. Since small businesses such as restaurants and gas stations have only a handful of employees, it is physically impossible for the strikers to keep the long picket hours without help from the federations. These are small services but very important at the present stage in the development of the workers' organization. The unions could hardly survive in their struggle against management without federation help.

The federations provide minimal social services in a society where social services are practically nonexistent. In addition to continually filing complaints with the IMSS, the federations help free union members who have been jailed arbitrarily, assist drivers in settling traffic violations, and write letters of recommendation for workers who are planning to move to other parts of the country. In one of the CTM meetings the secretary general reported that it was becoming increasingly more difficult to get *compañeros* released from jail because the police were refusing to cancel fines. He did add: "The street vendors should be more careful and not insult the police, because then it is really hard to get them out of jail."[48]

Political Activity of Labor Federations

The federations play a significant and effective role in the Mexican political system. At the local level they are one of the very few centers of political communication for a large segment of the population. This is the way it works: When the executive branch of the federal government wishes to increase support for an issue that it thinks might be unpopular, it contacts the national executive committees of the labor federations and explains the situation. The committees forward the instructions to the local federations, and the matter is brought up at one of the local meetings. The unions receive their information directly from the local federations, and they, in turn, read the materials at their own meetings.[49] For example, when President Adolfo Ruíz Cortines devalued the peso in 1954, letters were sent to the local federations explaining the need for the devaluation and the need to minimize the measure's effect on the low-income classes. The federations distributed the information to the unions. Similar procedures have been used in other instances in the past by the Federal Executive when it wished to build up a reserve of mass support. The Federal Executive in this way has capitalized on accomplishments in international relations—as in the return of El Chamizal to Mexico—and has also strengthened popular support for governmental policies in such international problem areas as the desalinization of the Mexicali Valley or the intrusion of Guatemalan fishing boats into Mexican territorial waters.[50]

The PRI frequently uses the communication system of the labor movement to (1) build support for its candidates, (2) recruit new members, (3) recruit actual candidates for some offices, and (4) implement its policies during political campaigns. Figure 4 presents schematically the movement of political communication.

It could be argued that the communication functions of the labor federations are of limited importance since the government has fairly good control over the mass media, which are being used more and more by the lower socioeconomic groups. Clearly, the mass media, particularly radio and television—the workers are more inclined to listen and look than to read—are powerful, fast, and effective. On the other hand, communications released through the federations may have a greater personal impact, and they enjoy the legitimacy of the labor movement.[51]

The labor federations expect something in return for the support they give

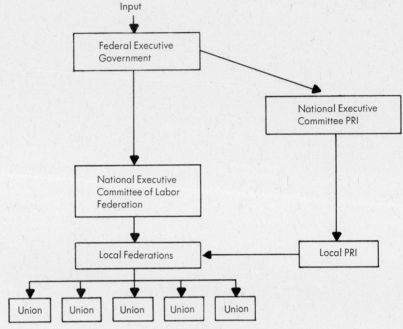

FIGURE 4.
DOWNWARD FLOW OF POLITICAL COMMUNICATION
THROUGH THE LABOR MOVEMENT

to the government, and the government reciprocates with political patronage and economic benefits. The local federations are the key units for distribution of benefits and patronage, which may be in the form of small subsidies from the governor or mayor, cancellations of fiscal debts, land grants for new headquarters and for new housing for workers, grants for different types of permits, licenses, and franchises, or appointments to offices such as labor inspector. At times the federations themselves receive the rewards.

The secretary general of the CRT commented that the government must be on good terms with the labor unions because of their power, and continued:

The government has to give in to some of the demands of the labor groups in the same way that the labor groups have to give in to some of the demands of the government . . . when the government asks for support in some political matter, or for backing for some of the candidates . . . Of necessity the labor federations have to back the government, otherwise at the hour we need help from the government they would screw us *(nos dan en toda la madre)*.[52]

During an assembly of the CTM Federation the following was urged:

... the CTM councilman should get close to the Municipal President and obtain from him some subsidies which could be used as collaterals in obtaining a loan from the bank to complete the construction of the headquarters of the Federation ... some members of the Federation object to the subsidy, but the Secretary General reminds the Assembly that the subsidies are necessary and that other federations receive them too. He said that the CROC is subsidized by the Municipal President and by the Governor.[53]

The clandestine nature of some of the government subsidies to the federations have at times caused internal conflict. During one CROC assembly the secretary general read aloud a letter he had written to the governor, in which he had asked him to clarify the nature of the subsidy to the federation:

We have the knowledge that since the times of Governor Esquivel (1959–64) the labor federations have been given financial help in the form of subsidies. This federation was among those with a monthly subsidy of 2,000 pesos. Up to this day we don't know to whom it is given. The total amount of the subsidies is considerable, but so far it has been of no benefit to this Federation. Consequently, we would like to ask you to order an investigation at the State Treasury to find out who is the person who is receiving the monthly subsidy, because our unions are asking us to clarify the matter.[54]

In the municipality there are several small towns in which union members and their families constitute the majority of the population. In these communities the union assumes the right to propose candidates to the municipal president for the office of municipal delegate. In 1964 in the town of Isla de Cedros, for example, the incumbent municipal delegate was scheduled to be transferred. The municipal president mentioned this to the CROC Federation, which wrote to the union in Isla de Cedros about the future vacancy. The union selected three possible successors and sent their names (the *terna* system) to the federation in Ensenada; the federation presented the names to the municipal president, who made the final decision.[55] Many other cases also seem to indicate that the federations are the organizational units through which the government dispenses benefits to the unions.[56] The flow of rewards is shown in Figure 5.

It was not possible to tell from observing only the local scene whether the national executive committee of the PRI was used by the federal government to distribute some benefits. Given the power of the labor federations in Mexico City, it is doubtful that it was frequently used, because the federations prefer to deal directly with the federal government. An exception might be cases in which the structure of the PRI is used for political patronage, but the distribution of political patronage has not been institutionalized in the Mexican political system, and therefore it is difficult to know how frequently the PRI is used. Those wishing to hold political office do not know the best way to go about obtaining it. For example,

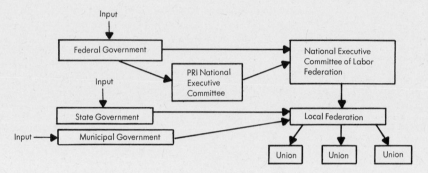

FIGURE 5.
FLOW OF REWARDS IN THE LABOR MOVEMENT

someone who wants to be municipal president will not know whether to be an active member of the local PRI and win an important office there, to cultivate the friendship of the governor, or to look for higher *padrinos* in Mexico City and thereby get closer to some high PRI official or executive of the federal government. In some instances the governor can impose his choice for municipal president in one or several cities of the state; in others appointments are made from Mexico City. Some powerful municipal presidents can hand pick their own successors if the state governor is politically weak.

In the distribution of political patronage, as shown in Figure 5, the state labor federations and the local and state PRI offices have no influence. Political patronage is generally distributed by government officials and by some high PRI officials in Mexico City.

CONCLUSIONS

The first components of the organizational structure of the community begin to emerge from the previous analysis. The results are presented in Figure 6.

The following represent this study's findings:

1.   The lower socioeconomic classes in the municipality consist of two groups:

   (a).   *The organized labor force.* This group with a membership of 7,000 workers (not including the 2,000 *ejidatarios*), is well integrated and its members have a definite sense of identification with one another. The group has multiple channels for demand articulation and its members enjoy a generally   favorable   economic   position,   although   with

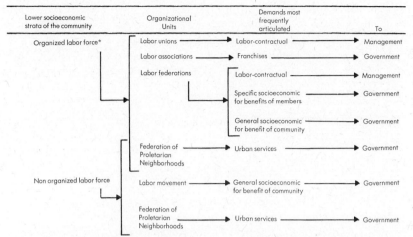

* Independent farmers and *ejidatarios* are not included. They articulate demands through organizations such as the Assocation of Vegetable Producers and through the CNC sector of the PRI.

FIGURE 6.
DEMAND ARTICULATION OF LOWER SOCIOECONOMIC
STRATA OF COMMUNITY

considerable differences from the highest to the lowest. Almost all members have a steady source of income. They are enrolled in the social security program and receive at least the minimum wage. They all receive benefits provided under the labor law. The wide variety of their occupations and their division between associations and unions causes the members of this group to be politically moderate.

(b). *Nonorganized workers.* This group numbers between 8,000 and 12,000 persons, one-third of whom live in the city and the rest of whom live in the rural areas of the municipality. They do not have proper channels for demand articulation; as it will be seen in Chapter 6, they have only one other organizational channel for the articulation of their demands in the city—the Federation of Proletarian Neighborhoods (Federación de Colonias Proletarias, FCP) of the CNOP, a political organization that coordinates demands for such urban services as water, drainage, transportation, electricity, schools, and sanitation. In this sense, they are marginal (outside of the system.) With few exceptions, they are economically underprivileged. They have neither social security nor protection under the labor law, and most do not

earn the minimum wage. Their work is unsteady. Some would
like to become union members, but can find no work; others
would like to join unions but are afraid that if they do so they
may be fired by their employers. Some simply do not care one
way or the other. Although there are not sufficient data to
substantiate this, it could be argued that the majority of this
group is politically indifferent; that many do not vote; and
that those who do vote do so at random or without knowing
what they are doing. They do not have any strong sense of
group identity. The labor movement partially articulates their
demands, and for that reason they do feel some slight sense of
identity with the movement. This group of unorganized
workers exists, is large, is economically and politically
marginal. Currently, it does not constitute a threat to the
established regime. Little else can be said about it.

2.   The basic unit for labor-management relations is the union, whose
function is limited to defending the interests of its members when dealing
with management. On the other hand, the basic unit for articulating
economic demands to the government is the local federation. At the state
level, political and economic patronage for the working class are funneled
exclusively through the local federations. Contrary to what might be
expected, the state labor confederations and the local PRI do not play an
important role in the performance of these functions.

NOTES

    1. Cited in Pablo González Casanova, *La Democracia en México* (México, D.F.: Ed.
Era, S.A., 1965), p. 114.
    2. William D'Antonio and William Form, *Influentials in Two Border Cities* (Notre
Dame: University of Notre Dame Press, 1965), p. 80. The data for this study were
gathered ten years earlier than the data for Ensenada.
    3. Robert E. Scott observed that the lower classes throughout Mexico are unable to
take collective action. Trends in Ensenada, in Baja California, and in other northern
states do not support this contention. Robert E. Scott, "The Established Revolution,"
Political Culture and Political Development, edited by Lucian W. Pye and Sidney Verba
(Princeton: Princeton University Press, 1965), p. 352. The author refers specifically to
workers who have migrated from the rural areas to the cities. Since most of Ensenada's
workers are rural migrants, one would expect his statement to be particularly true there.
This is one of many riddles, and points out the desirability of more regional studies for a
better understanding of the Mexican social system. Nevertheless, it should be indicated
that many students of traditional cultures in Mexico have reported high participation in
secondary organizations. Kenneth Cooper, describing a village in Morelia, observes that:
"Customarily, there is a regular turn-over of personnel in these offices (political and
civic) so that a fair proportion of local male citizens hold one or other of the posts in the

course of their lives." Kenneth Cooper, "Leadership Role Expectations in Mexican Rural and Urban Environment" (unpublished Ph.D. dissertation, Stanford University, 1959), p. 80. For a list of ethnographic reports of indigenous communities with high participation in political offices see: Pablo González Casanova, *op. cit.*, pp. 92 ff. Different reporting is presented by Professor Foster and his students in several studies of transitional villages in the central states of Jalisco, Michoacan, and Morelia. See, in particular, May N. Diaz, *Tonalá: Conservatism, Responsibility, and Authority in a Mexican Town* (Berkeley and Los Angeles: University of California Press, 1966); Theron A. Nunez, "Cultural Discontinuity and Conflict in a Mexican Village" (unpublished Ph.D. dissertation, University of California, Berkeley, 1963), and Cynthia Nelson, "The Waiting Village: Social Change in a Mexican Peasant Community" (unpublished Ph.D. dissertation, University of California, Berkeley, 1963). These studies seem to have internal inconsistencies. On the one hand they report a fairly large number of local political, religious, social, and civic organizations, work groups, cooperatives, communal lands, committees and commissions, and at the same time they emphasize the inability of the people to work together.

4. Article 233 of federal labor law. The Article explains the breakdown with more detail. The Spanish term for association is *unión* or *liga.* The latter term has been used since medieval times to refer to the unions of artisans or guilds. The Spanish term for union is *sindicato.*

5. For a historical background of these confederations, see Victor Alba, *Politics and the Labor Movement in Latin America* (Stanford, California: Stanford University Press, 1968); and Alfonso López Aparicio, *El Movimiento Obrero en México* (México, D.F.: Editorial Jus, 1958).

6. One of the independent unions is the Union of Workers of Fábricas Monterrey with 200 members. Fábricas Monterrey is the most modern industry in the city and it is a subsidiary of the Garza Sada industrial complex. For a description of this private industrial complex, see Frank Brandenburg, *The Making of Modern Mexico* (Englewood Cliffs: Prentice Hall, 1964), pp. 265–66.

7. Roberto L. Mantilla Molina, *Derecho Mercantil* (México, D.F.: Ed. Porrúa, 1956), explains the legal and organizational characteristics and the development of the cooperative movement in Mexico.

8. Several of the fishing cooperatives work under business contracts which *de facto* are very similar to labor contracts. The cooperatives contract with canneries for sale of produce, terms for loans, fringe benefits, and so on.

9. From the political point of view these groups belong to the popular sector of the PRI. As it will be seen in detail in Chapter 6 this is one of the many incongruities facing the sectors' organization of the party.

10. Some of the association members are covered by social security, and others are not. To see in detail the coverage consult Alberto Trueba Urbina and Jorge Trueba Barrera, "Ley del Seguro Social," *Ley Federal del Trabajo Reformada y Adicionada* (México, D.F.: Ed. Porrúa, 1967), pp. 297–340.

11. From this study it is not possible to assess the extent of this phenomenon throughout the entire nation. However, it seems to indicate that caution should be exercised in the use of statistics, particularly in cross-national comparisons, in ratios of striking workers to the total labor force, and so on.

12. In the rural areas, for instance, sharecroppers are allowed to keep half of the produce for themselves. This practice is still in existence, particularly among ritual and blood kins, but it is rapidly being replaced by the system of peonage.

13. The legal status of the labor associations is not well defined by the Mexican labor law. In some instances the labor authorities have denied registration to some of the

associations. Some fishing cooperatives were not considered to be organizations of workers. See the decision made by Dirección General del Trabajo, Departamento de Registro de Asociaciones, Federaciones y Confederaciones, "Oficio 5-11-4369, Expediente 245(30)/-4" (México, D.F.: October 20, 1962). On the other hand, the National Supreme Court ruled that the associations of dock workers, which, as has been indicated, are *de facto* cooperatives, are to be considered labor unions (Alberto Trueba Urbina and Jorge Trueba Barrera, *op. cit.,* p. 248). Labor leaders themselves are not very sure about what to do with some of the associations. For example, the secretary general of the central committee of the CRT ruled that the Ensenada CRT Association of Taxi Drivers was to become a business firm society. Comité Nacional CRT, "Carta al Comité Local de Ensenada" (México, D.F.: July 3, 1967). However, the local federation never implemented this ruling.

14. *El Mexicano* (Ensenada), June 9, 1967, p. 1.

15. On one occasion this was not the case and the change of affiliations produced ill feelings in the labor movement. The CRT Federation reported to the national headquarters that "A new organization has been formed with 19 CTM and 5 CNOP truck drivers. Our success produced some discontent but the differences have been smoothed over." Comité Local CRT, "Oficio 450" (Ensenada: March 9, 1966).

16. Vincent Padgett, *The Mexican Political System* (Boston: Houghton Mifflin Co., 1966), pp. 98 and 100.

17. CRT Comité Ejecutivo Nacional, "Oficio no. 1691" (México, D.F.: June 26, 1967).

18. Federación CTM, "Libro de Actas" (Ensenada: meeting minutes of October 29, 1965).

19. Federación CROC "Libro de Actas" (Ensenada: meeting minutes of March 12, 1965). For a perceptive presentation of the leftist movement Liberation Front, also known as the National Liberation Movement, see David T. Garza, "Factionalism in the Mexican Left: The Frustration of the MLN," *Western Political Quarterly,* Vol. 17 (September, 1964), pp. 447-60. The Liberation Front gained many supporters in Baja California among union workers, *ejidatarios,* and some intellectuals. Former Governor of Baja California Braulio Maldonado (1953-1959) was very influential in the growth of the movement in the state.

20. The minimum salary in Baja California for the 1966-67 period was 35.70 pesos per day, about $3.00 U.S., and it was the highest in the nation. During the same period the minimum salary for the metropolitan area of the Federal District was 25 pesos.

21. Interview with Jesús Sánchez, secretary general of Sindicato de Pescadores y Similares de Baja California, CRT, and also treasurer of the CRT Federation, June 8, 1967.

22. For example, this was the case during the political crisis of the first elected governor of the state of Baja California, Braulio Maldonado. The labor federations of Ensenada en masse supported him against the attacks of the managerial groups and the U.S. press, which accused him of being a Communist. See a most interesting and biased autobiographical account of his six years of government: Braulio Maldonado, *Baja California* (México, D.F.: Ed. Costa Amic, 1960). In other states the labor movement has served as a force against the state and local government and has helped to oust the governor or mayor.

23. According to Article 264 of the federal labor law, the union can strike only when the majority of the workers favor the strike. The labor authorities have the duty to count the workers in favor and those against the strike movement. At this point manipulations by the authorities favoring either position are possible.

24. Angel Díaz, "Informe del Secretario General al Décimo Congreso General de la CTM de Ensenada" (Speech delivered to the CTM of Ensenada on April 1, 1967), p.1 (mimeographed).

25. In every local and state congress this problem is brought up. See for example Federación CROC, "Acta del Tercer Consejo Confederal Estatal del Estado de Baja California, Circular 70" (Mexicali: March 29, 1966), in particular proposals number 5, 6, 8, 10, and 14 of this document.

26. Pursuing this line of analysis invariably leads to cumbersome problems related to the culture and collective psychology of the Mexican society.

27. See Angel Díaz, *op. cit.*, which confirms the idea that unity would have to be imported.

28. Federación CROC, "Libro de Actas" (Ensenada: meeting minutes of May 14, 1963, April 17, 1965, and April 12, 1966).

29. Frank Brandenburg, *op cit.*, pp. 119 ff. The CROM is not categorized at this time by the author but from the context in other parts of his work, it would be safe to assume that he would place it next to the CTM. Robert E. Scott, *Mexican Government in Transition* (Urbana: University of Illinois Press, 1964), pp. 162 ff.

30. *Central blanca, central patronal,* and *sindicato blanco* are terms used to refer to unions that are under the control of management. Belligerent unions are called *sindicatos rojos* or *sindicatos de resistencia.*

31. Comité Ejecutivo de la CGT, "Expediente" (Ensenada: n.d.). The claim that in 1959 the CGT had 814 members in Ensenada was probably exaggerated, although in the decade of the fifties the CGT had many more members that in the sixties, as one of its unions had a labor contract with the construction company that built the harbor.

32. Comité Ejecutivo Nacional CGT, "Oficio no. 268/66" (México, D.F.: November 3, 1966).

33. Comité Ejecutivo Nacional CRT, "Circular" (México, D.F.: June 7, 1966).

34. Angel Díaz, *op. cit.*, p. 6.

35. Federación CROC, "Libro de Actas" (Ensenada: meeting minutes of February 23, 1964).

36. This does not apply to the two large independent unions in Ensenada, but only to federations. It is known that several federations of politically independent unions exist in Mexico, particularly in Monterrey. These isolated cases were organized by the managers of large industrial complexes, who were willing to pay high fringe benefits in exchange for docile unions.

37. Comité Ejecutivo UGOCM, "Carta" (Ensenada: March 6, 1959). The UGOCM of Ensenada fell apart not too long after the federation decided to oppose the PRI candidate for governor in the election of 1959.

38. The reputational method of Floyd Hunter or some of its adaptations were considered inadequate because of the low educational level of most workers.

39. The federation of fishing cooperatives was not studied because of time limitations.

40. Amitai Etzioni, *A Comparative Analysis of Complex Organizations* (New York: The Free Press, 1961), pp. 115-16.

41. For Etzioni's definition of leadership and elites, see *ibid.*, pp. 89 ff. The idea that labor leaders do not hold power in the unions is shared by Henry A. Landsberger. Referring to the Latin American labor leaders he makes this comment: "... labor as a whole exerts tremendous influence on certain decisions without any of its leaders being close to the decision making process. ... It is in this sense that we have called labor's influence impersonal and 'faceless.' " "The Labor Elite: Is It Revolutionary?" *Elites in*

Latin America, Seymour M. Lipset, ed. (New York: Oxford University Press, 1967). p. 260.

42. The union meetings are orderly in conduct and have an agenda. The moderators do their jobs well and pound the gavel with energy when necessary.

43. Comisión Política del PRI, "Biografía Política" (Ensenada: April 14, 1959). This document, in addition to pure description, has interesting insights into the ideal or normative type of leader in the Mexican system.

44. In one case the signing of the contract was delayed for several reasons and the executive committee of the union decided to bypass the adviser and go directly to the bargaining table. During the conversations the two sides lost their patience and strong words were exchanged. During the flareup, the representatives of the firm indicated that they would not make any decision without first consulting the union's adviser who was also, the firm said, "our adviser." Sindicato de Trabajadores de Astilleros Rodríguez, S.A. Ensenada, "Oficio al Comité Ejecutivo de la Federación CROC" (Ensenada: May 30, 1966).

45. Federación CRT, "Libro de Actas" (Ensenada: meeting minutes of August 30, 1966).

46. In 1965 the CTM owed 44,375 pesos for rent. Federación CTM, "Libro de Actas" (Ensenada: meeting minutes of December 10, 1965). The CROC owed the State Government 19,090.70 pesos in fiscal debts. Federación CROC, "Libro de Actas" (Ensenada: meeting minutes of August 3, 1965).

47. It is understandable that in very large unions in other parts of the country the amounts handled could be very large and the possibilities of making good money for corrupt officers higher.

48. Federación CTM, "Libro de Actas" (Ensenada: meeting minutes of January 28, 1966). Street vendors can easily get into trouble with the police because they may not have at hand their license or permit or may be selling in some off-limits zone.

49. Most unions and associations meet once a week. Attendance is generally high; an estimate would be between 50 and 70 percent of the membership. Some unions have stiff financial penalties for members who are absent from meetings without a valid excuse.

50. For a theoretical treatment of government capabilities, see Gabriel A. Almond and G. Bingham Powell, *Comparative Politics. A Developmental Approach* (Boston: Little Brown and Co., 1966). The authors present Mexico as a country that built strong reserves of support and used them for economic development. *Ibid.,* pp. 200-201.

51. There are no studies of the Mexican political communication system, and political scientists—thus far—have seldom referred to this topic. It is too speculative on the basis of the available data to debate the effectiveness of one means versus another.

52. Interview with secretary general of the CRT, June 10, 1967. During the 1964 campaign the PRI convened a mass rally for the closing of the campaign and urged all the labor federations to have all the workers present. The meeting minutes of June 23 of the CROC Federation read: "The Secretary General puts before the consideration of the Assembly the problem related to the participation of the Federation in the last political act that the PRI will celebrate to conclude the campaign . . . the Secretary General argued that from his point of view it would be impossible not to reach a favorable resolution which would call for accepting the PRI invitation. To act otherwise would cause serious damage to the CROC because the unions of the Federation are constantly asking favors from the government . . . "

53. Federación CTM, "Libro de Actas" (Ensenada: meeting minutes of March 18, 1966).

54. Federación CROC, "Libro de Actas" (Ensenada: meeting minutes of December 15, 1965).

55. Secretaría Municipal de Ensenada, "Expediente" (Ensenada: November 10, 1964).

56. The meeting minutes of the federations contained an innumerable number of examples of rewards. Here are a few. In 1966 the CROC Federation owed the state of Baja California 26,850.76 pesos in property taxes. The debt was reduced to 8,696.94 pesos and the federation decided to ask the governor to cancel the debt (meeting minutes of June 6, 1966). The CROC Union of Distributors of Distilled Water asked the federation to send wires of protest to the governor because of the six new permits granted to another union (meeting minutes of March 8, 1966). The CROC union of taxi drivers asked the federation to mediate before the governor urging him not to give 30 new taxi permits (meeting minutes of August 27, 1965). The articulation of demands and the flow of rewards are the same in all labor federations in Ensenada. An exception should be made for the several associations of workers within the CNOP. The statutes of the CNOP do not allow associations within the CNOP to federate because the CNOP is theoretically a federation for the bureaucrat and white collar unions, and professional associations and other groups. This amalgamation is too artificial and does not work. The workers of the associations of the CNOP became aware instinctively of the need for a functional federation for the articulation of their demands and organized their own federation, the Asociación Proletaria Liberal de Ensenada (APLE). The state CNOP chiefs first admonished the APLE leaders, and then ordered them to disintegrate the federation because it was irregular, but the federation was kept. Their position is a little different from that of the labor federations, and weaker. Interview with Enrique Acevedo, secretary general of the CNOP of Ensenada, August 27, 1967.

3

Solving the Labor-Management Conflict

ORGANIZED MANAGEMENT

The Chambers

In Ensenada there are five chambers: Commerce (Cámara Nacional de Comercio, CANACO), Tourism, Industry of Manufacturing (Cámara Nacional de la Industria de la Transformación, CNIT, organized in 1965), Construction, and Fishing Industries. The last two can be disregarded because they are so disorganized; the Chamber of Fishing Industries, for example, disappeared almost entirely when the Chamber of Tourism and the CNIT were organized in the city. The fishing canneries joined the CNIT, and the large and important Association of Commercial Sport Fishing (Asociación de Armadores de Pesca Deportiva) joined the Chamber of Tourism. The changes were motivated by desire for higher prestige and better national contacts, available through the newly organized chambers.[1] A few owners of commercial fishing boats, however, remained in the Chamber of Fishing Industries, which still has offices in the city.

The local Chamber of Tourism is of recent origin (1960), and is primarily concerned with promoting tourism, one of the city's basic industries. The chamber organizes and sponsors such tourist activities as the pre-Lenten Carnival, the Newport-Ensenada Yacht Race, and the Redondo Beach-Ensenada Caravan of the Air. Under the leadership of a young and capable engineer, it is attempting to make the city a convention center for the northwest of Mexico, with the hope that some North American groups will also hold meetings there. The chamber works very closely and apparently harmoniously with the local state delegation of tourism on matters like elaborating specific programs and printing and distributing tourist propaganda. The specific goals of the Chamber of Tourism make it

52

independent and free of political and ideological ties. This chamber is not concerned with labor-management problems.

The local Chamber of Commerce has specific goals that require no detailed explanation. All merchants with invested capital of more than 2,500 pesos ($200 U.S.) have to affiliate with it by law. In this sense the chamber is not a voluntary association. However, the chamber has among its members on a voluntary basis many businesses such as tourist camps, hotels, motels, restaurants, construction firms, canneries, fishing boats for commerce and sports, mechanical repair shops, one taxicab company, agricultural firms, real estate offices, accounting firms, private hospitals and laboratories, and several of the largest industries. The official catalog for 1966 lists 670 businesses.[2] The unusual composition of the Chamber of Commerce can best be understood by going back to 1917 when it was first given official status in Mexico and began to assume functions similar to those of associations of employers with a clearly defensive attitude toward government and labor.[3]

In the last few years the Chamber of Commerce in Ensenada has modified its defensive functions against labor substantially and has dedicated its efforts to its most specific goals, promoting trade and commerce. The new statutes, approved in 1967, have eliminated all functions similar to those of associations of employers.

A Voluntary Association: The Centro Patronal

The shift in the Chamber of Commerce functions was caused by the appearance in the city of a new voluntary association of businessmen, the Centro Patronal de Ensenada, affiliated with the Confederación de Centros Patronales de la República Mexicana (COPARMEX).[4] Ensenada's Centro Patronal has grown startlingly. Organized in 1964 by a group of 40 prominent local businessmen and managers, the Centro had 164 members by mid-1967, and the firms and businesses of its members employed a total of 2,623 workers, or slightly more than 50 percent of the total union membership of the municipal labor federations.

Its organizers were motivated primarily by the need for a common front against the increasing aggressiveness of the labor sector. They saw that the increasing complexity of modern industrial life required them to have a specific, functional interest group through which to articulate demands and exert pressure on the government. The businessmen previously had used the Chamber of Commerce for these purposes, and, as a consequence of its multiple functions, the chamber had become an ill-defined organization. The Centro organizers believed that the Chamber of Commerce should concentrate on fostering trade and commerce, and that a new organization totally independent of the government should be organized for demand articulation and defense of self-interests.

The COPARMEX had drawn its declaration of principles from the economic philosophy of the Catholic Church, but the Ensenada Centro drew members from different ideological backgrounds. Even among the founders there were members of the several chambers, members of the Masonic lodges, Knights of Columbus, PRI and PAN members and partisans, and several foreigners. The membership became even more pluralistic ideologically as the organization grew. The manager of the Centro Patronal made it quite clear that the organization's cohesiveness was based on the need to defend common interests against labor and government: "The Centro was organized as a necessity during a time of great labor unrest which was favored by the Governor. For reasons of political expediency he lashed the unions into strikes and the peasants into land invasions."

The Centro also organized lectures, conferences, workshops, panel discussions, and seminars as part of its program to improve the quality of employers and productivity of firms. A provincial town without a center for higher education, Ensenada welcomed these activities. Experts and professors of business administration delivered lectures in the city for the first time. With rapidly increasing prestige, the Centro Patronal has become involved in other community issues and has expanded its influence to areas outside the field of labor-management relations.

Management Unity

In spite of their increasingly specific goals, the Centro and the several chambers have many common problems, some stemming from the labor federations, some from the action or inaction of the government. Profit sharing, social security, working conditions, commodity prices, competition of street vendors against established stores, and other such issues, raised by the lower socioeconomic groups, also affect the upper socioeconomic groups that make up the different chambers and the Centro.[6] Matters of common concern to the upper economic groups are fear of intervention by the federal government in key areas of production or commodity distribution, the unpredictability of the government in the control of imports and exports and in changes of the status of the Free Zone, and the failure of the government to make necessary infrastructural investments in the municipality or its tendency to make the wrong type of investment.

The Ensenada data suggest that the number of chambers and voluntary organizations has not fragmented the businessmen as a group. On the contrary, challenged by labor and government, business leaders have made common cause and have strengthened alliances across organizational, ideological, and political lines. The Centro Patronal has played an important leadership role in organizing the business community, and has become the most important business group in the community.[7] The president of the Chamber of Commerce said:

The Centro Patronal is going to be the most important pressure group in the community. It has a very important role to play in the future because it is a private organization and gathers persons of several activities. Because of the semi-official status of the chambers, the government has been able to reduce their bargaining power by splitting them into many chambers. Now in Mexico we have the Chamber of Manufacturing Garments, the Chamber of Bakeries, and so on.

The members of the upper socioeconomic groups in Ensenada are well organized in a variety of functional interest groups.[8] There is no competition or conflict among these associations, which cut across ideological and political preferences, because the organizations have specific and different goals. Leadership is exercised through the offices of these organizations, very seldom through personal channels. In spite of personal enmities, managers and businessmen, like members of the labor force, have shown the ability to organize and work together. In addition, this sector of society shows signs of fairly high integration.

THE NATURE OF THE CONFLICT

Confrontation

In his penetrating analysis of labor-management relations, Robert Dubin suggests that the two groups confront each other privately through the bargaining process and publicly through the exercise of pressure on the government in attempting to solve their conflicting interests.[9] This double confrontation can be represented in the following manner:

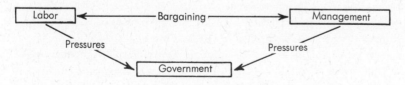

The same scheme is applicable to labor-management relations in Mexico, with some important exceptions. First, the bargaining process in Mexico is not always private; one or both of the conflicting parties frequently ask the governor to mediate, or he may volunteer to mediate. The federal labor law specifies many cases in which private bargaining must become public; for example, it has a proviso that labor authorities must declare publicly the legality of the strike. Consequently, direct, private confrontations between labor and management become more restricted. This may in part account for the absence of violent conflict between labor and management. In the few isolated cases of violence resulting from labor disputes (almost none in Ensenada), the struggle has been between the unions and the government or between opposing unions. However, these factors do not necessarily minimize privacy in the bargaining process. Second, because the labor movement in Mexico includes self-employed individuals and because of the special semiofficial nature of the several chambers, the labor-management conflict is a conflict not only between employees and employers but also between the self-employed who are members of the labor federations and their competitors who are members of the chambers. Figure 7 describes the confrontation between labor and management in Ensenada.

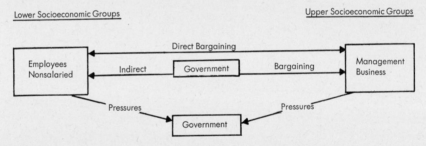

FIGURE 7.
THE BARGAINING PROCESS BETWEEN LABOR AND MANAGEMENT

Polarity of classes has long been a part of Mexican life. The revolution of 1910 reduced it but did not remove it entirely. One might ask: Why has this polarized conflict not disrupted the social system more frequently? How is it that a fairly well-organized labor force has not used its potential force in more radical ways?[10] The traditional response to such questions has been to point to the meek subjection of labor leaders to the establishment and to the obvious buying-off of labor leaders at the national level.[11] These explanations are only partially satisfactory and leave much unexplained. In Chapter 2 it was pointed out that class tensions are reduced by the presence of the self-employed within the labor federations. In this chapter we can observe that the tensions are further reduced by the institutionalization of conflict and collective bargaining through a system of political and legal mechanisms.

Interaction between Labor and Management

The first reaction of organized labor to the Centro Patronal in 1964 was alarm. A letter sent by the secretary general of the CTM to the executive committee of the CROC explained that the new association of employers had been organized in the city, and continued:

I have used all possible influences to see that the legal status of this association not be granted. Because of these influences the registration of the association is still pending. It is very important that your Executive Committee also exerts pressure on the labor authorities so that under no circumstances the Centro Patronal be registered. It will be a menace to all free and organized workers. Already and as a consequence of the first steps taken by the managers to organize against us, I inform you that they have created the first white union which they will use to protect the interests of the Centro Patronal . . . All this means that, in the future, the managers properly organized will foster other white unions to guarantee their own interests and to protect themselves against the established federations . . . The white union has already been duly registered. I believe that to counteract its actions we have to be completely united. In regard to the Centro Patronal I would like to suggest that if you have the opportunity, send a wire to the State Board of Conciliation, special group number 1, asking not to register the Centro Patronal . . . [12]

The fear expressed by the letter was understandable; the hegemony of the labor federations was being seriously challenged by a management organization for the first time in the history of the city. But later developments showed that the Centro Patronal was not at all interested in competing with the federations and organizing the workers in white unions. Many of the members of the Centro Patronal clearly preferred to work with "red unions." "It is easier and less expensive," commented one manager. He went on to explain that the unions could demand only a few fringe benefits here and there, a couple of pesos more or less, or a day off now and then. Whether the unions were right or wrong was not relevant, according to him; what was important to him was avoiding time-consuming conflicts that could end up with a union writ of *amparo* (request for protection) in Mexico City.[13] His argument in brief was that it was pointless to argue with the unions when their demands could so easily be met at a low cost.

The Centro Patronal began a campaign of approach to the labor federations, designed to decrease tension and misunderstanding between labor and management and to provide a climate of trust. Its first overtures were not well received by the labor leaders. On May 1, 1965, the secretary general of the CROC, one of the most radical leaders in the federations, denounced publicly the president of the Centro as "an exploiter of the workers" and referred to the activities of the Centro as "nothing other than the dark activities of a group which represents the grand trust of the North [the United States] to bribe bureaucrats and destroy the rights to unionize and to strike."[14]

The managerial principles of the Centro Patronal were sent to all members in bi-weekly installments through bulletins and news releases. At the same time the Centro made efforts to improve its public image. The executive board wanted to show that the organization was something more than a group of wealthy businessmen attempting to make more money at the expense of the working class and in opposition to the government. A campaign to project a more positive picture was launched, and a series of advertisements was placed with the news media to remind managers and businessmen publicly of their obligation toward the workers and to remind the government that it should pay promptly the full IMSS dues: "Managers who do not pay minimum wages are violating legal dispositions. In fact, what they do is to exploit the workers to enrich themselves. A business firm which, for whatever reason, has not had the foresight to modernize and secure sufficient profits to pay minimum wages should disappear. This firm is a negative asset for the country."[15] The article insisted on the need to pay minimum wages and quoted a recent survey by the National Commission of Minimum Wages showing that in Mexico City 25 percent of the working force was not receiving the minimum wage and that in the rest of the country the percentage rose to 40. The labor leaders welcomed some of these ideas. Many of their past conflicts with management had been caused by irresponsible businessmen. On the other hand, the policy of approachment and good will did not please the more conservative members of the Centro. One member said, "I do not pay my dues to the Centro to have it tell me what I have to do, but rather to defend my interests. It may be time to get out of the organization."

In 1967, after tireless effort on the part of the energetic young manager of the Centro Patronal, representatives of the CROM and CGT federations attended for the first time a general assembly of the Centro. During the reception that followed, the labor leaders were asked to address the gathering. The news bulletin of the Centro stressed the importance of this occasion, on which management, labor, and government had met on amicable terms.[16] The labor federations reciprocated, and by January 1968 even the CROC had representatives of the Centro Patronal at its annual general assembly. As a consequence, a better understanding between labor and management is slowly evolving in the city.

Value Positions of Labor and Management

Experts in industrial relations have suggested that management has two major self-images in respect to its role, one of itself as a defender of free society through the free enterprise system, the second as the defender and promoter of the welfare of its workers. It has also been suggested that organized labor views itself as the instrument of social justice and the protector of the worker against management.[17] These descriptions apply to Ensenada so well as to suggest that the value positions of labor and management in Mexico are like those of their counterparts in the rest of the Western world. The declaration of principles of the Centro Patronal, for example, clearly presents the two images previously mentioned, and labor leaders frequently represent themselves as seekers after social justice. In an address to the general assembly, the local secretary of the CTM Federation declared:

We would like to reaffirm that the CTM seeks the achievement of social justice. We are not simply looking forward to the day when the wealthy are less wealthy and the poor are less poor; this is only the economic aspect of the problem. Social justice for us is a way of life in which the individual can achieve well-being in all his activities. We believe that there is no social justice when the courts do not provide prompt and expeditious justice, there is no social justice when the right to strike is attacked, and the right to unionize is denied. When a poor old man drags along the streets of the city an ice cream cart to make a meager living by selling, and he is harassed by the police, at that moment there is no social justice. Then, we should ask ourselves, should our participation in the political arena be limited to remembering and to praising to the point of boredom our dead heroes? Should it be confined to the political campaigns at which time we can make a show of our knowledge of the history of Mexico? We don't believe so. We should be active in learning about and finding solutions to these problems. This is what we understand by social justice.[18]

The emotional tone of relations between labor and management groups is a consequence of their value positions. Labor and management know that their interests conflict, and labor views the conflict as part of the class struggle. Labor's view is that employers and businessmen are unscrupulous profit seekers who have resources, and that the labor unions should try to get as much as possible from them; that the labor organization and the labor law—which should be improved—are the only means available for stopping money-hungry employers; that workers who are not unionized are consistently exploited. There is no ideology or philosophy behind these principles, but rather the experience of many years of relations with employers. Nevertheless, it does not necessarily follow that workers and managers regard each other as arch-enemies.[19] On the contrary, as will be explained later, labor and management are neither friends nor foes. They compete with and distrust each other, but expediency has brought them to cooperate with one another more often than to maintain mutual antagonism. The political system has provided mechanisms for interaction that also have enhanced the spirit of cooperation.

THE BARGAINING PROCESS

Labor Demands

Henry A. Landsberger, after analyzing the only three available attitudinal surveys of the labor movement in Latin America, concluded that these studies confirmed each other in the sense that labor leaders "chose economic objectives as their most important," and said, "Our aim has been to show that those most directly involved in labor-management relations see the unions chiefly as a tool to obtain economic benefits through collective bargaining."[20] Data obtained in Ensenada by methods different from Landsberger's corroborate these findings. Reading the minutes of labor group meetings and official documents showed that the main concerns of the unions are higher salaries and better living standards.

Minimum wages are specified by law, and there can be little argument about this topic between labor and management at the bargaining table. Although wage laws also regulate some of the specialized workers' salaries, most specialties do not come under the wage law. Since there is an increasing number of specialized workers in industry, wages continue to be one of the central issues in collective contract bargaining. In construction and cannery work it is customary to pay by the job, but payments per unit of production also have to be negotiated.

Differences in wage scales are not large, but in a tight economy a few extra pesos are very welcome to the workers. The list of wages for 1966–67 for workers at the cannery Conservas del Pacífico is presented in Table 10.

TABLE 10
WAGE DIFFERENTIALS IN A LOCAL CANNING INDUSTRY,
ENSENADA, 1966 (in pesos)

All general work	35.7 per day[a]
Belt lines	35.7 per day
Machine operators	40.0 per day
Mechanic helpers	40.0 per day
Special machines	42.0 per day
Mechanics	50.0 per day
Hand preparing anchovies	5.5 per 20 kg. box
Machine preparing anchovies	1.7 per 20 kg. box
Hand preparing sardines	1.3 per 20 kg. box
Canning anchovies	6.0 per box of 48 cans of 1 lb.
Canning sardines	1.2 per box of 48 cans of 1 lb.
Canning anchovies	3.5 per box of 100 cans ¼ Club

[a]Official minimum wage for 1966-67.
From Empresa Conservas del Pacífico, "Tabulador de Salarios" (Ensenada: February 7, 1966).

Besides wages, several other important economic questions have to be settled during labor-management bargaining. The overall importance of collective bargaining can be understood best by looking at the complex working conditions in such industries as canning, fishing, tourism, and agriculture, the basic industries in Ensenada, which are seasonal and extremely dependent on weather conditions. The canneries, for example, do not have refrigeration plants. Perishables have to be processed immediately upon arrival. Manpower needs and working schedules thus become day-to-day variables during the season and extremely unpredictable at other times of the year. The issues quickly arise: Which workers are to be given preferred job opportunities? How is full-time employment to be defined in order to extend many of the benefits and fringe benefits required by law? How should yearly vacations and weekly days of rest be scheduled? These and similar questions can be answered only by a consensus of the contractual parties. Some of the large hotels have threatened to close down during the winter months unless the unions permit them to reduce staff enough to operate without high losses. Again the questions arise: How long is the winter season? How many employees should be released? Should they be compensated in some way? Are they to have job preferences during the next season? These questions too can be settled only by bargaining.

Collective bargaining deals also with benefits not included in the labor law. A good relationship between the two parties may motivate a firm to go one step beyond the minimum requirements. Labor leaders try very hard to secure extra benefits that will enhance their leadership status, such as a few hundred pesos to cover expenses for conventions; help to the family of a deceased worker above the IMSS insurance benefits; payment of the worker's share of the IMSS fees, if the worker has not been fully employed for lack of raw materials; compensation for voluntary retirement; fellowships for workers' children[21]; a system of small loans at no interest.[22] Firms frequently comply with some of these requests. One manager commented:

It is good relations. I don't mind giving a few hundred pesos here and there for something or the other. It makes them happy, and when there are some problems it is easier to work them out. I always make the checks out to the union or federation to make sure that the money doesn't go into anybody's pocket.

Improved working conditions and better treatment by overseers are frequent demands:

This union asks the management to call the attention to the overseers, foremen, and wardens to stop shouting at the workers, and to stop ridiculing or degrading their dignity by the use of gross expressions . . .[23]

This union demands the firing of overseer so-and-so because of his behavior with the workers. He is a slave driver and only lacks the whip . . .[24]

According to the talks held with the management, it was clearly specified that the union would be the only agency for employment of workers. Consequently, the overseers should stop their practice of hiring people at their will ... [25]

Many overseers are former workers or persons of the lower socioeconomic groups who show little empathy and understanding for the unions.

Labor Tactics

Labor leaders know that there are different types of management, and follow various policies in presenting their demands. Violence is never regarded as an effective means for improving the laborers' condition. Good, open relations has proved to be the most successful avenue in dealing with large firms. Labor has called strikes against large firms very seldom and with reluctance, preferring a certain amount of give and take. The labor force is both conservative and moderate, and does not approve of any direct action that might antagonize large firms or the government. In 1962 the secretary general and two other members of the executive committee of the CROC Federation joined the leftist radical movement, Movimiento de Liberación Nacional. They were asked by the general assembly to resign immediately. Such affiliations are simply believed to be too radical. In 1965 the secretary general of the same federation was asked to resign after initiating seven strikes against major industries. His leadership as a champion of direct action against management was not accepted. One worker commented: "He was a catastrophe."[26]

The policy of good relations with management does not mean that the workers will be satisfied with any offer. They fight tenaciously for their rights and benefits and seek legal protection when necessary. The yearly report of one of the federations includes the following:

In the revision of one of the contracts it was necessary to threaten to strike to obtain the wage increase. And it took two months to obtain the agreement for a 10 percent increase in salaries and other social and economic benefits. Our great victory was the acknowledgment from the representative of the firm, an American fellow, that it was the fault of the company that had caused so many violations of the contract. He promised that in the future the offices of the manager would be opened to the union and that the problems would be studied immediately. It is our satisfaction to affirm that this offering has been fulfilled and that at present the relations between workers and management— if not friendly—have a basis of a better understanding ...[27]

The unions have been less hesitant to strike against small firms than against large ones, in part because small-business managers have little experience to bring to the bargaining table. Their businesses are often bankrupt, and the workers strike in hope of compensation. Strikes against small firms are due in part also to the less complex nature of small labor disputes; negotiated settlements are generally much quicker.

Management Responses

Data gathered in this study suggest that relations between labor and management are in a transitional stage. The Centro Patronal is in part responsible for a developing climate of confidence and trust, a goal that is still distant. The fluidity of the situation makes it difficult to build a typology of businessmen's behavior and even more difficult (although it would be extremely interesting) to relate the types to other business variables such as success, productivity, and degree of cooperation with labor.

A survey of cases filed with the Municipal Labor Board from 1953 to 1966 shows that small businesses are more likely to be denounced by labor than large ones. Hardly any of the threat-to-strike actions were taken against the larger industries, whereas 13 percent involved cleaners and bakeries and 53 percent involved the tourist industry through such small businesses as hotels, motels, restaurants, and night clubs (see pp. 66-67). Small farms were also frequently involved in this type of dispute. Demands against large firms (arbitrarily defined as having more than 20 employees) were more frequently directed at those owned and operated as family businesses than at those operated by professional people and generally owned by stockholders which were a part of larger national commercial or industrial complexes.[28] The trends observed are summarized tentatively in Table 11.

TABLE 11

TRENDS IN FREQUENCY OF LABOR CONFLICTS AND BUSINESS FAILURES, BY SIZE OF FIRM, ENSENADA (1953–66)

Size of firm	Management	Attitudes Toward Labor	Frequency of Labor Conflicts	Frequency of Business Failures
Small firms (fewer than 20 employees)	Family	Negative	Very high	High
Large firms (20 or more employees)	Family	Mixed	High	Medium
	Professionals	More positive	Low	Low

In a representative case, a large family firm's business failure and conflicts with labor were reported by a farm labor union, which complained that the owner was hiring free workers instead of union workers, and listed his violations of the labor law and the collective contract: (1) Workers were not paid for the seventh day of the week, as stipulated by Article 93 of the labor law. (2) Overtime was not paid at the rate of 100 percent over regular wages (Article 92 of the labor law). (3) Workers were paid only every three or four weeks, whereas Article 87 required at least weekly salary payments. (4) Contrary to the collective contract, management failed to provide proper medical care for the workers and their families. (5) Contrary to the collective contract, management failed to provide a water tank for workers; as a result they had to walk more than half a mile to bring water to their dwellings.[29] The managerial history of this businessman shows an astonishing number of losses in labor disputes. Several of his businesses had been closed down by strikes. The Centro Patronal refused to look into his problems,[30] and other managers simply characterized his business behavior as foolish and lacking common sense.

Professional managers view labor's demands with a certain ambivalence. On the one hand, they recognize the legitimacy of many of the demands and are willing to provide fringe benefits beyond those required by the federal labor law. On the other hand, they believe that increasing labor demands must in time be met with a corresponding increase in performance by the workers if the development of the local industry is to have a solid foundation. In this light the managers believe that some labor demands are unrealistic and will do more harm than good to the labor force in the long run. A manager explained the difficulties:

I just spent several hours with the representatives of the union. But, what can I do? The workers in Ensenada are asking for higher salaries than our workers in Monterrey but their productivity is lower because they don't have the training. Our quality control lab shows that the number of defective units of production is very high. Our only alternative is to reduce the number of workers and to increase the number of supervisors . . . I know that it has been hard for the workers to adjust to production lines, to the idea that you have to be on time to work, that you don't miss work because one of your *compadres* is having a birthday party . . . I don't know why but the workers here are not as responsible as the workers in Monterrey.

A similar predicament was expressed by a factory owner. "I don't know whether I should sell the factory, close it, or diversify future investments." His firm was having many difficulties with the union, and he feared unfair competition from the government. His concluding remark was "I feel extremely insecure."

The following conclusions emerge from Ensenada.

1. Even large firms are concerned about a possible imbalance between labor's demands and productivity.

2. Large firms are better able to overcome temporary crises and to meet some of labor's demands without serious conflicts because they have larger resources and are fairly well managed. Although they also have better political contacts with the Federal Executive in Mexico City, which at times they have used to settle labor conflicts, the key to their success is professional management. Large firms with nonprofessional management have been prone to business failures and labor conflicts.

3. Many small entrepreneurs have serious difficulty in accepting the idea that labor is a well-organized, competitive force that knows how to exercise its rights, and difficulty in adjusting their managerial roles to the needs of a fast-growing and modernizing society. Consequently, legal claims against them are very frequent.

4. The labor force is conservative and will not use violence to settle labor disputes.

5. Open hostility does not characterize labor-management disputes. The participants approach each other with a certain measure of fear and distrust, but also with the understanding that accommodations have to be agreed upon either at the bargaining table or before the labor authorities.

LEGAL MECHANISMS: THE BOARDS OF CONCILIATION AND ARBITRATION

Organization of Labor Boards

The labor authorities are basically administrative boards empowered with judicial authority.[31] The federal labor law establishes two distinct areas of jurisdiction: (1) the federal jurisdiction, empowered to mediate and arbitrate all cases in the federal territories and in the Federal District as well as cases dealing with certain industries specified by the labor law; (2) the state jurisdiction empowered to mediate and arbitrate all cases not specifically included under the federal jurisdiction.[32] In the municipality, the fishing canneries, harbor activities, and cement and mining industries (with a total of twenty-six unions) come under the federal jurisdiction. The state jurisdiction is under the organizational control of the state government, which also makes all appointments to the state labor administrative boards.

The federal and state labor authorities are organized into two boards, the Board of Conciliation and the Board of Arbitration. The function of the first is to reconcile the two parties; if this action fails, then the second board arbitrates between the litigants. The Board of Arbitration corresponds to an appellate court; its decisions are binding, and there is no higher labor board of appeal. A disputing party can, however, file a writ of *amparo* (request for protection) with the federal circuit court (the circuit court having jurisdiction over Ensenada is in Tijuana).[33] The circuit court judges the validity of the writ and either accepts or rejects it. If the writ is accepted, the grantee takes his petition to the national Supreme Court. This action automatically suspends the decision of the Board of Arbitration on the grounds that there has been a breach of the national constitution.[34] When the Supreme Court rules on cases brought to it by the writ of *amparo,* it is in effect ruling on a matter of constitutionality, not specifically on the labor dispute. The Supreme Court creates *de facto* a precedent binding on the Boards of Arbitration. Since use of the writ of *amparo* is a common practice in resolving labor conflicts, the Supreme Court is producing a fast-growing body of precedents through which the labor law is reinterpreted.

Ensenada's State Board of Conciliation, known as the Municipal Board, has territorial jurisdiction over the municipality. The Federal Board of Conciliation with offices in Ensenada has territorial jurisdiction over the state of Baja California and the municipality of Rio Colorado in Sonora. The organization of these boards is very simple. The president of the Municipal Board is appointed by the governor, who has the authority to remove him at will. The president of the Federal Board is appointed by the national Secretary of Labor, and he also can be removed at any time. The presidents function as judges. Until very recently all presidents of the Municipal Board were former workers; in 1966, a labor lawyer was appointed to the office for the first time.[35] The president is assisted by a secretary, who has always come from the ranks of labor. His functions vary from clerical chores to acting as president of the board. Each board also has secretarial assistants, whose functions are primarily clerical. Labor and management each elect one representative to the boards to support their interests. In the past, these representatives have been labor experts.

Types of Legal Action

Three types of legal action may be used to bring a case before the Board of Conciliation: the ordinary action, the threat-to-strike action, and the strike.[36] Ordinary actions result from the demands of a group of workers, a union, or, frequently, an individual worker who alleges that some violation of the labor law has resulted in an economic or physical injury. In all such cases financial compensation is sought.

Threat-to-strike actions are usually preliminary moves by a union demanding approval of a new contract or revision of an old one. Sometimes the unions also use threat-to-strike actions when they feel that some clauses of the collective contract have been violated. The action presents management with a deadline for accepting or rejecting the union's proposals. The understanding is always that rejection of labor's proposal will result in a strike. In the time between the presentation of the threat and the deadline, labor and management engage in serious collective bargaining, independently or with the assistance of the board. In some large industries or when the problem is particularly serious, the governor may be called in by either one of the parties to mediate. The bargaining period is at times extended by the petition of either union or management or in some cases by the direct action of the governor.

The threat-to-strike action is viewed by the unions more as a means to pressure a firm into serious bargaining than as a first step toward a real strike. Threat-to-strike actions have very seldom developed into strikes. Through private bargaining and mediation, labor and management usually settle their differences and reach mutually acceptable agreements. Sometimes, receiving a promise of partial fulfillment of its demands, the union withdraws the action; this may occur before or shortly after a strike begins. The official record of the Municipal Board of Conciliation shows that between October 1966 and September 1967, forty-eight threat-to-strike actions were filed,[37] with the following outcomes:

Withdrawal of action before strike	26
Agreement before strike	13
Withdrawal of action after strike	7
Strike (declared illegal)	2

Threat-to-strike actions are used by some union executives to pressure firms into paying them to withdraw the action. It is difficult to assess the extent of this practice because it is covert. Some union executives have been caught in collusion with management and expelled from office after being tried by a union commission of justice. The rank and file and their honest leaders are alert to this danger, and demand a clear accounting of all transactions.

If a strike is declared in favor of the workers by the Central Board in either Mexicali or Mexico City, the firm has to pay wages lost by the workers since the beginning of the strike. Since the decision of the Central Labor Board can be suspended by filing a writ of *amparo* and the losing litigant will probably use this recourse, solution of the conflict may be further delayed. Most firms do not have the economic reserves to pay wages lost during a long strike. There are only two hopes for survival for a firm involved in such a dispute: that the Central Labor Board or the Supreme Court may rule against the union (very improbable, since recognition of the legality of the strike generally implies that the union has a legitimate action), or that the firm may be able, through political maneuvering, to force the union to withdraw its action. In the municipality all legal strikes have resulted either in the permanent closing down of the struck firm and a corresponding loss of jobs without full compensation, or in a rapid settlement of the dispute.

Large firms are more often determined to fight the strike all the way to the Supreme Court than are small ones. They have resources to pay legal fees, and at times also to bribe labor authorities to slow down the legal process with the aim of forcing the union to withdraw the demand because of its members' desperate need to return to work. The workers have never had to withdraw a demand for this reason. Strikes against small firms have generally been solved within months. These firms for the most part had been bankrupt even before the strike, and the owners had no reason to fight the case. The workers have frequently been given the businesses as part payment of the wages lost since the beginning of the strike.

A strike is equally disastrous economically for the workers, particularly members of the large unions. The unions do not have funds to support their members during a strike, and the small contributions that come in from the local unions and union members of the national confederation are insufficient. The workers are understandably reluctant to strike unless a firm flagrantly and frequently violates the labor law or the labor contract; even then, the union may choose to file an ordinary action and seek financial compensation.

Characteristics of Labor Boards

Two particularly important characteristics of the Boards of Conciliation are easy accessibility and procedural simplicity. The informality of the boards can be fully appreciated only by direct observation. The cost of redress is low, and since the plaintiffs are always workers, the boards are very important for the labor sector. The large number of cases adjudicated by the boards attests to their ability to provide rapid and substantial redress for labor claims.

Figures 8 and 9 present the number of cases of ordinary and threat-to-strike actions brought before the Federal (1955-66) and Municipal (1953-66) Boards of Conciliation. Complete figures for economic compensation paid by defendants were not available. Partial figures were obtained at the Municipal Board of Conciliation, and the monthly payments were computed over a period of seven years (1961-67) by using the complete figures for forty months. The amounts of economic compensation calculated in this way show the very high figure of 126,374.38 pesos or approximately $10,000 U.S. per month. To this amount should be added the compensations obtained through the Federal Board.

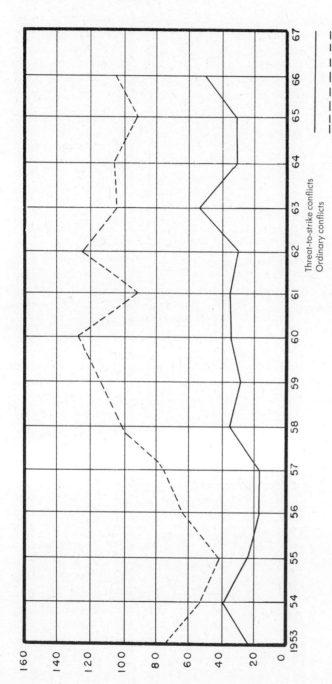

FIGURE 8.

NUMBER OF THREAT-TO-STRIKE AND ORDINARY CONFLICTS BROUGHT BEFORE MUNICIPAL BOARD OF CONCILIATION, ENSENADA, 1953-66 (ABSOLUTE FIGURES)

Threat-to-strike conflicts
Ordinary conflicts

Source: Official register, Municipal Board of Conciliation, Ensenada.

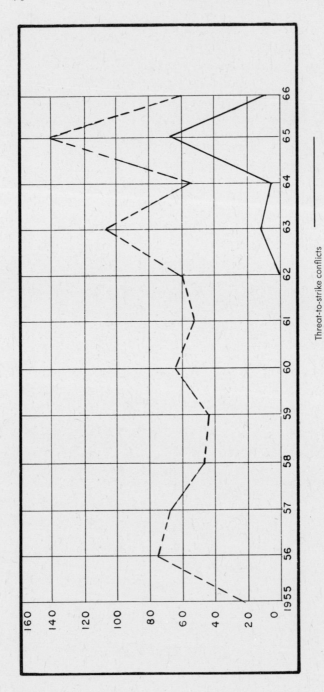

FIGURE 9.
NUMBER OF THREAT-TO-STRIKE AND ORDINARY CONFLICTS BROUGHT BEFORE FEDERAL
BOARD OF CONCILIATION, ENSENADA, 1955-66 (ABSOLUTE FIGURES)

Source: Official register, Federal Board of Conciliation, Ensenada.

The Federal Board of Conciliation in Ensenada has jurisdiction over most of the industries that have large unions, such as the fishing industries and canneries, the cement plant, and the firms that operate in the harbor. The threat-to-strike actions of the large unions at times require a considerable amount of bargaining, and frequently the local Federal Board of Conciliation, with its limited conciliatory powers, cannot solve the conflict. In such cases the actions have to be transferred to the Board of Arbitration in Mexico City. Transferring causes delay, and many unions prefer to start the threat-to-strike action directly at the Board of Conciliation in Mexico City, by-passing the local board. Then if necessary the action can be transferred from conciliation to arbitration without delay. For this reason Figure 9 shows a very small number of threat-to-strike actions before the local Federal Board. Until 1963 no threat-to-strike actions had been registered with the Federal Board in the city.

The labor boards were originally organized to provide fast and inexpensive redress to workers in labor matters. Some authors have pointed out that the need of the workers to go to Mexico City to expedite their cases contradicts the spirit of the labor tribunals. These writers are particularly concerned with the ever-increasing jurisdiction of the Federal Boards; they maintain that all jurisdiction should return to the State Boards, and furthermore that the local boards should be given powers of arbitration.[38] In Ensenada the fact that the Federal Board has jurisdiction over many of the large unions is a factor limiting the efficiency of the labor boards.

The labor federations have frequently complained that the conciliation process is too slow. The Ensenada CROC Federation presented this motion before the second state council:

That the Boards of Conciliation are extremely slow in processing the cases. The working class is generally the plaintiff and suffers most from lack of speediness. It is proposed that through the State and the National Executive Committees a petition be forwarded to the proper authorities to increase the personnel of the local Federal Boards . . . [39]

Relation between Government Policies and Number of Labor Conflicts

It was reported consistently during conversations with knowledgeable business people that the first elected governor of Baja California (1953-59) had followed a disastrous policy toward the business community, siding with labor, urging workers to take legal action against management, and urging peasants to invade private property. His successor (1959-64), businessmen agree, alleviated the situation somewhat, yet there was still the widespread feeling that the governor was siding with labor at the expense of the business community.[40] The incumbent governor (1965-) has begun to create a climate of confidence, which businessmen consider necessary to attract new investors and new industry to the region.

In Figure 8 the curve representing ordinary conflicts at the Municipal Board climbs fast and steadily from 1955 to 1960, during the term of the pro-labor governor. In 1960 it begins to decline, in spite of industrial growth. The threat-to-strike curve slopes downward from 1954 to 1957, then takes a slight upward trend with a few moderate ups and downs. Figure 9 shows the ordinary conflicts before the Federal Board in Ensenada declining from 1956 to 1959, then beginning to slope upward with pronounced peaks in 1963 and 1965.

The short span of time analyzed and the lack of any economic studies of the region make the following interpretations of the curves extremely tentative: (1) There seems to be no correlation between the actions of labor and changes in the Federal Executive (1958 and 1964). (2) There seems to be no correlation between the number of ordinary conflicts before the Federal Board and the labor policies of the governors, perhaps because the Federal Board is beyond the political control of the governors. (3) There seems to be some correlation between the governors' labor policies and the number of ordinary conflicts before the Municipal Board; the more prolabor the governor, the higher the number of conflicts, perhaps because of the possible political control of this board. (4) There seems to be little correlation between the governors' labor policies and the number of threat-to-strike conflicts before the Municipal Board.

Why this is so is not clear. It could be argued that the more favorable the governor is toward labor, the higher are the pressures of labor on management; then the two curves in Figure 8 should be roughly parallel. It could be suggested also that management will be more inclined to accept labor demands without the need of the threat-to-strike action during the term of a prolabor governor. On the other hand, Figure 10, which presents the main causes of threat-to-strike conflicts, suggests that this type of conflict is more independent politically than is the ordinary conflict. The curves in Figure 10 are erratic; when a firm violates a contract, a union will make a demand, regardless of who is in power. Contracts have to be revised, and the peaks of this curve coincide with the even years, when minimum salaries were officially changed. Contracts are signed whenever new businesses are organized or the unions convince the employees of a business that unionization will be to their advantage. For example, the CTM campaigned heavily among agricultural workers in 1961 and 1966, and this accounts for the peaks in those years. It can safely be assumed that many of these actions will take place independently of the governor's position in labor-management conflicts.

In spite of the governor's interference in solving labor conflicts, there is

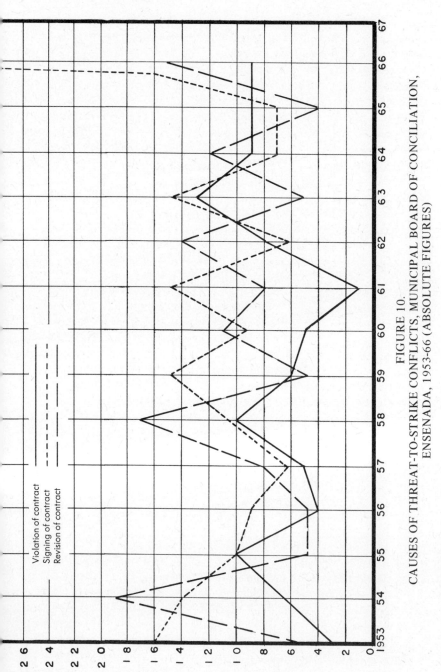

FIGURE 10.
CAUSES OF THREAT-TO-STRIKE CONFLICTS, MUNICIPAL BOARD OF CONCILIATION,
ENSENADA, 1953-66 (ABSOLUTE FIGURES)

Source: Official register, Municipal Board of Conciliation, Ensenada.

little doubt that the local labor boards are active in mediating disputes between unions and managers. They also mediate disputes between nonunionized workers and their employers. To assert, as some authors have, that the labor boards are merely instruments of the government or rubber stamps for the demands of the workers is to oversimplify the facts and misunderstand the function of the boards.[41] The official yearly report of activities of one of the local boards in Ensenada, presented in Table 12, gives a fair idea of its mediatory functions.

TABLE 12
ACTIVITIES OF MUNICIPAL BOARD OF CONCILIATION,
ENSENADA (August 1, 1962—July 31, 1963)

Ordinary conflicts	
Ended by opinion of the board	61
Ended by mutual agreement	21
Ended by withdrawal	51
Total	133
Threat-to-strike conflicts	
Ended by conciliation	19
Ended by withdrawal	29
Pending	6
Total	54
Activities	
Official letters (*oficios girados*)	584
Agreements sanctioned (*convenios sancionados*)	214
Commissions performed (*despachos diligenciados*)	235
Certificates and affidavits issued (*actas levantadas*)	831
Resolutions formulated (*acuerdos dictados*)	1,290
Notices served (*notificaciones personales*)	721
Schedules served (*cédulas notificatorias*)	325
Orders (*instructivos*)	297
Court appearances (*comparecencias*)	604
Statistical forms (*formas de estadística*)	126
Summons (*citatorios*)	462
Grievances presented (*razones asentadas*)	392
Attachments (*embargos*)	67
Amparos	16
Payments ordered (*cantidades pagadas*), in pesos	1,201,868.00

From Junta Municipal de Conciliación de Ensenada, "Informe de Labores" (Ensenada: August 1, 1962 to July 31, 1963).

In spite of their operational deficiencies, the Boards of Conciliation should be seen as successful empirical mechanisms. They help to bridge deep social cleavages that in other societies have produced violent confrontations. In a way, an evolution similar to the one that took place in labor-management relations in the United States, from overt violence to a peaceful routinization of the process of solving labor conflicts, is slowly taking place in Mexico. The comments of Robert Dubin about these events in the United States are particularly illuminating, after observing the Mexican system in Ensenada:

Failure, through negotiation, to solve the dispute typically leads to intervention by a government agency to conciliate or mediate the differences . . . The recent history of strikes indicates a remarkable standardization of this form of emotionally toned group behavior . . . There is no advantage in secretly calling a strike and then springing it on management . . . Similarly, there is no special advantage to overt violence in industrial disputes, or to the use of novel tactics like the sit-down strike and mass picketing. These devices once had important functions as tactics of conflict . . . Overt conflict has become systematic—it has been institutionalized.[42]

LEGAL MECHANISMS: THE MIXED COMMISSIONS[43]

The Mexican political system has developed several legal mechanisms, other than the labor boards, through which capital and labor are forced to accommodate conflicting demands under government surveillance. At the local level two are of particular importance: the Special Regional Commission of Minimum Wages and the Profit Sharing Commissions, the latter formed by workers and management in each firm. The mediatory functions of the government through these commissions should not obscure the fact that labor and capital again are brought together in a process of interaction that can be described only as indirect bargaining. New avenues of communication are opened between the two groups.[44] Figure 11 is a schematic representation of indirect bargaining through the minimum wage commissions.

The minimum wage is one of the basic issues in the labor-management conflict. Labor organizations frequently debate it and it is always discussed at their conventions.[45] Management is equally concerned with minimum wages, but for different reasons: members of the Centro Patronal and of the chambers have a common interest in keeping the increases in minimum wages as low as possible and in obtaining compensatory price increases. Local managers frequently discuss this and other important issues with the headquarters of their national organizations. The channels for the articulation of their demands are clearly outside the political party system. These groups never use the PRI or other parties to voice their demands. They do, however, have access to the Federal Executive through their national headquarters. Trips to Mexico City by businessmen are very frequent, and good contacts there are business assets. The PRI is used only indirectly, by individuals; that is, a businessman may use an important PRI member, such as an important sen-

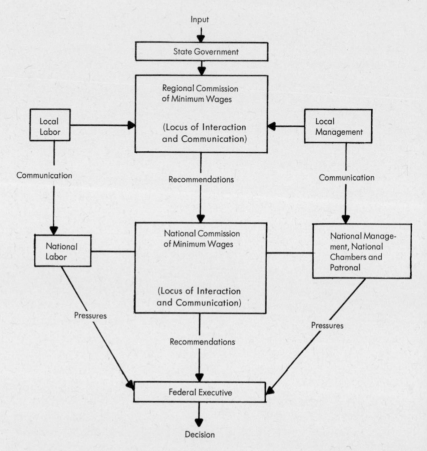

FIGURE 11.
INDIRECT BARGAINING BETWEEN LABOR AND MANAGEMENT
THROUGH THE MINIMUM WAGE COMMISSIONS

ator or a high-ranking party official, as a contact with the Federal Executive.
This practice is seldom used by organized groups, which have more or less
institutionalized access to the Executive. After national conventions, for example, it is customary for business leaders to visit some of the secretaries or
general directors of national agencies. When federal officials visit the state,
organized business groups hold receptions for them and talk about the problems and needs of business. An example of these practices was reported by
the Centro Patronal:

The Manager informed us that during the national convention of Centros
Patronales in Mexico City directions were given to the representatives of
capital before the Regional Commissions on Minimum Wages . . . He also in-

formed us about the visits of the delegates to Lic. Sealtiel Alatorre, National Director of the Mexican Institute of Social Security, and to Lic. Gilberto Loyo, Director of the National Commission on Minimum Wages. The delegates spent two hours with each of the Directors, presenting the views of the managerial groups. Particularly important was the conversation about the possible increase of the IMSS fees, and about its financial situation.[46]

The Regional Commissions on Minimum Wages and the other mixed commissions perform advisory functions instead of the decisional ones assigned to them by law. Clearly the locus of decisions is the Federal Executive in Mexico City. The relevance of these commissions lies in the opportunity they provide for conflicting sectors of the community to air their views and demands in each other's presence, to carry on a dialogue, and to feel that at least to some degree they participate in the decisions made by the National Executive.[47] In other words, the importance of these commissions is based on the interaction they generate between labor and management.

Students of organizations have shown that the degree of cooperation between the leaders of an organization determines the level of effectiveness of that organization.[48] That is, greater cooperation in the leadership of an organization leads to a more effective organization. If a community is viewed as an organization, then the principle can be applied to this study. The means of interaction and communication between labor and management are provided by the various legal and political mechanisms that the political system has institutionalized. In Ensenada the interaction between labor and management does not produce antagonism. On the contrary, it has forced them to cooperate; precisely how much or how well cannot be determined, but the positive tendency is established.[49] New groups, such as the Centro Patronal, seem to have helped to develop cooperation between the groups and consequently improved the total effectiveness of the system.

POLITICAL MECHANISMS

The nature of the State Labor Boards allows some political maneuvering by the state executive. This opportunity is welcomed by the governor, for he can use his influence as a political tool or as a means to protect the economy of the state. His freedom is limited, however, by the federal labor law and the economy of the state. Within these limits he can find ways to favor either labor or management according to his preference or to the dictates of politics. He can hasten or delay a case, complicate or simplify procedures, lose or misfile official documents. He can call labor leaders and drop hints of subsidy reductions or cancellations. He does not have to remind them that franchises can be granted to more willing and cooperative labor groups. He can call in the state police to disperse picket lines. Management also knows well that it is difficult to oppose him, and prefers to give in now and then in order to prevail in other matters. In other words, each of the contenders, labor, management, and the governor, is involved in a political game in which all factors have to be carefully considered.

Frank Brandenburg has aptly characterized the Mexican political system as Machiavellian.[50] The governor, in spite of his apparent power, has to know how to establish by peaceful means and skillful negotiations equilibrium between the demands of labor and management.[51] Failure to do so will relegate him to a political limbo,[52] for the misuse of force is the road to political obscurity. Although the use of force is sometimes viewed sympathetically when the primacy of the PRI is being contested by the PAN or other political forces, it is not viewed with approval in many other situations. The state police have been summoned by the governor only three times in Ensenada during the past decade; each time they dispersed picket lines, using no force, and violence did not erupt.

The state executive tries, through conversation and personal meetings, to convince labor and management of the economic advantages to them of following a middle-of-the-road policy: Employers have to have attractive reasons for investing capital in the city; commerce and industry generate jobs and taxes, and both are necessary for the labor federations and for the state; the business sector of the community can pressure the governor into restraining labor's demands by threatening to reduce jobs and thereby revenues. The governor will, in a way, be the intermediary and explain to the unions the need to moderate their demands. He is persuasive because he can control the State Labor Board and the distribution of subsidies. On the other hand, he cannot afford to lose the political support of the labor force. Too many restraining orders create unrest among the workers,[53] and they will then take their complaints to the Federal Executive and to the national executive committees of their own federations. As a result, the governor may be pressured from above to grant their demands.

In order to minimize possible imbalances the governor is forced to create a system of political mechanisms. In Baja California this is the commissions of consultation. During the governorship of Braulio Maldonado (1953–59) it was called the Consejo de Planeación Económica y Social (Council of Economic and Social Planning), and during the governorship of Raúl Sánchez Díaz the Dirección de Promoción Económica Industrial (Board of Economic and Industrial Development).[54] These boards are supposed to create channels of communication and interaction between labor, management, and the state government, study common problems, and find solutions for them. At times conferences are organized involving all three sectors.

Informal consulations among the governor, labor, and management are also common. When a major labor conflict erupts, management and labor will appeal to the governor before going to the labor boards. The governor will sometimes summon them to a round table discussion of possible solutions to conflicts. If no solution is in sight after several meetings with the governor or one of his top aides, then the case will go before the labor boards. The governor has enough time to mediate in only a few of the labor conflicts, which he chooses for their economic or political importance.

In spite of their usefulness as devices for communication and interaction, the political mechanisms also leave room for favoritism, and sometimes arouse distrust because of this. In 1963, one of the unions of the CROC Federation struck one of the large local motels. Immediately after the union declared the strike, the workers wrote letters to the other CROC unions asking for moral support and requesting that they send telegrams to the governor and the labor authorities in support of the striking union's claim that the walkout was caused by management's refusal to sign a collective contract. The specific problem that the union was facing in this case was that the manager of the motel was the son of the municipal president, who had previously been president of the PRI Municipal Committee. The union expressed its fears thus: "The many political influences of the manager are well known, and we fear that he may be able to manipulate and have the Labor Board declare the strike illegal."[5 5]

NOTES

1. Interviews with Lic. Ricardo Bienvenida, president of the Chamber of Fishing Industries and of the Board of Municipal Collaboration (Junta de Colaboración Municipal), September 12, 1967 and Alejandro Mondragón, former president of the Commercial Sport Fishing Association and municipal treasurer, August 16, 1967.

2. Cámara Nacional de Comercio de Ensenada, "Directorio" (Ensenada: August 1966).

3. Alfonso López Aparicio, *El Movimiento Obrero en México* (México, D.F.: Editorial Jus, 1958). In 1917 the statutes of the confederation were reformed and also the law granting the confederation legal personality. The chambers began to operate as unions of employers electing the representatives of capital before the Boards of Conciliation and Arbitration, p. 192.

4. By a peculiarity of the Mexican labor law, the Centro Patronal had to be formally organized as a union of employers. Article 232 reads: "Union is the association of workers or employers of the same or similar professions, trades or specialties organized for the study, betterment and defense of their common interests."

5. Raymond Vernon, *The Dilemma of Mexico's Development* (Cambridge, Mass.: Harvard University Press, 1965), pp. 165–66. Some of the basic principles of COPARMEX can be briefly outlined without attempting to summarize the total philosophy: (1) Harmony between the factors of production. The Marxist concept of class struggle is outdated because labor and capital need each other. Exploitation of the worker is not only morally evil, but also economically ruinous. The happy worker is the most productive worker. (2) Scrupulous observance of the law. (Of course, loopholes

should be carefully searched for.) (3) A positive attitude towards business profits. Such profits are a healthy sign and the just reward for the efforts of the managerial class. Profits should be reinvested to open new sources of work and wealth. (4) The elimination of competition between the government and the private sectors. In some key industries the government should be in partnership with private enterprises. Preferably, however, the government should devote its resources to the development of the economic infrastructure.

6. Whenever one of the organizations considers that the matter may also affect or may be of interest to other organizations, the group will solicit their support in presenting the demand to the government. The reading of the minutes suggests that this procedure has been institutionalized.

7. Some animosity between the Centro Patronal and some of the chambers at the national level has been suggested by Raymond Vernon, *op.cit.,* p. 169. In Ensenada the organization of the Centro Patronal did not produce cleavages among businessmen, and there was no animosity between the Centro and the Chamber of Commerce. In fact, the two are located in adjacent offices and share some of the same office equipment; their relations are most cordial. Most of the members of the Centro Patronal retained their membership in the Chamber of Commerce. When in 1967 the Chamber of Commerce reformed its statutes, the Centro helped to draft the new ones. See Centro Patronal de Ensenada, "Libro de Actas" (Ensenada: meeting minutes of January 17, 1967). The Centro also promoted the organization of the CNIT in the city in 1965. See Centro Patronal de Ensenada, "Libro de Actas" (Ensenada: meeting minutes of September 8, 1965). The minutes read: "And it was agreed to continue insisting in the organization of the Chamber of the Industry of Manufacturing, CNIT."

8. There are several other functional interest associations in the city besides the ones already mentioned. The Asociación Portuaria (Harbor Association) is a small organization of custom brokers, ship line agencies, and in general of maritime business to solve problems concerning the operation of the harbor. The Asociación de Pequeños Agricultores de la Costa (Association of Small Farmers) and Asociación Vinícola (Wine Growers) are two among many more.

9. Robert Dubin, *Working Union-Management Relations: The Sociology of Industrial Relations* (Englewood Cliffs, N.J.: Prentice-Hall, Inc., 1958), p. 238. "Union and management pressure groups operate to gain dominance in the legal social policy decisions . . . Collective bargaining centers social policy making in the private sector of the society."

10. As a counter example, for a well-illustrated case of the use of violence as a radical bargaining tool, see James L. Payne, *Labor and Politics in Peru. The System of Political Bargaining* (New Haven: Yale University Press, 1965).

11. See, for example, Vicente Fuentes Díaz, "Desarrollo y evolución del movimiento obrero a partir de 1929," *Ciencias Políticas y Sociales* (México), Vol. 5, No. 17, (July-September 1959), pp. 326–48.

12. Federación CTM, "Oficio no. 1114. Expediente 1/SG/63" (Ensenada: July 13, 1964). For an explanation of white and red unions see Chapter 2, p. 49 note 30. It should be remembered that according to the Mexican labor law the Centro Patronal is a *sindicato* of employers, and, consequently, it has to be registered before the labor authorities.

13. *Amparo* is a writ that grants legal protection to the petitioner when he alleges that his personal constitutional rights will be violated by the action of the government. The supreme court of the nation enjoins the government's action until its constitutionality is established in court. The role of the writ of *amparo* in labor conflicts is explained in p. 66.

14. *El Mexicano* (Ensenada), May 3, 1965.

15. Lic. Roberto Guajardo Suárez, president of COPARMEX, in *Boletín Empresarial* (Organo de Difusión del Centro Patronal de Ensenada), year 2, No. 8, January 14, 1967. Here are a few more samples of the Centro's ideas: "We would like to reaffirm that the main activity of the Centro Patronal de Ensenada is not to mediate in labor conflicts but to prevent them. We believe it to be important and urgent to find avenues for a better understanding between the factors of production . . . " *Boletín Empresarial,* year 1, No. 2, September 13, 1966. "In a few days a commission of the IMSS will be in town to help managers and workers in carrying out their obligations to the IMSS. As you may recall, the IMSS has recently cancelled the tours of inspection with the healthy purpose of creating a climate of confidence among managers, and with the expectation that they will correspond and freely accept their obligations to the IMSS. The announced visit will be limited to correct certain anomalies, and there will be no sanctions or fines of any type. We believe that it is necessary on our part to correspond to the confidence of the IMSS, and to fulfill our obligations to the IMSS. Without any doubt, this will be the best sign of respect towards the rights of the workers." *Ibid.,* year 1, No. 1, October 31, 1966.

16. Centro Patronal de Ensenada *Boletín Empresarial* (Organo de Difusión del Centro Patronal de Ensenada), year 2, No. 12, April 15, 1967.

17. Arthur Kornhauser, Robert Dubin, and Arthur M. Moss (eds.), *Industrial Conflict* (New York: McGraw-Hill Book Company, 1954), pp. 18 ff.

18. Angel Díaz, "Informe del Secretario General al Décimo Congreso General de la CTM de Ensenada" (speech delivered to the CTM of Ensenada on April 1, 1967), p. 6 (mimeographed).

19. For contrasting views, see William D'Antonio and William Form, *Influentials in Two Border Cities* (Notre Dame: University of Notre Dame Press, 1965), p. 94.

20. Henry A. Landsberger, "The Labor Elite: Is It Revolutionary?" *Elites in Latin America,* Seymour M. Lipset, ed. (New York: Oxford University Press, 1967), pp. 272 ff. The three studies are: the study of conflict and consensus in Venezuela by the Centro de Estudios del Desarrollo of the Universidad Central de Venezuela, with the collaboration of Frank Bonilla; the Alex Inkeles' study of Chilean labor unions; and Landsberger's own study, also of Chile.

21. Article III, Sec. 21, makes it compulsory for firms with more than 400 workers to provide a fellowship for one of the workers or for a worker's son, and for firms with more than 2,000 to provide three fellowships. Smaller firms may, however, voluntarily do the same.

22. Several local canneries have loan systems paying generally 150 pesos per week during the off-season months.

23. Sindicato de Trabajadores de la Compañía Empacadora Baja California, "Oficio no. 560" (Ensenada: April 19, 1966).

24. Federación CROC, "Libro de Actas" (Ensenada: meeting minutes of July 13, 1965).

25. Sindicato de Empresa de Trabajadores de Conservas del Pacífico, "Oficio no. 5" (Ensenada: August 22, 1966).

26. Students of group leadership have shown that generally leaders conform to group values. See George C. Homans, *The Human Group* (New York: Harcourt, Brace and World, Inc., 1950), pp. 141 ff.

27. Federación CROC, "Reporte Anual" (Ensenada: January 7, 1965).

28. Local examples of these firms are: Empresas Longoria (Subsidiary from Monterrey), Fábricas Monterrey (Subsidiary from Monterrey), Olivares Mexicanos (of the

Nacional Financiera), Cementos California (controlling stockholder General Clark), the Abelardo Rodríguez group that was bought by the Banco de Fomento Cooperativo, a decentralized government agency, during the summer of 1967, and several firms owned by North American groups.

29. Federación CTM, "Libro de Actas" (Ensenada: meeting minutes of February 3, 1965).

30. Centro Patronal, "Libro de Actas" (Ensenada: meeting minutes of April 19, 1966).

31. A considerable amount of material on this topic has been written by labor lawyers. The historical development of this institution is well presented in some of the works. See, for example, Mario de la Cueva, *Derecho Mexicano del Trabajo* (México, D.F.: Editorial Porrúa, 1959); Alberto Trueba Urbina, *El Nuevo Artículo 123* (México, D.F.: Editorial Porrúa, 1962); and Arturo Valenzuela, *Derecho Procesal del Trabajo* (México, D.F.: Editorial Porrúa, 1959). There are no sociological studies of the functions and performances of these boards.

32. Title 8, Articles 334 to 401 of the federal labor law presents the structure and formal organization of these boards.

33. For a detailed explanation of the writ of *amparo* in labor cases, see Jorge Trueba Barrera, *El Juicio de Amparo en Materia de Trabajo* (México, D.F.: Editorial Porrúa, 1963). The writ of *amparo* has a much broader application and it is an important and little-studied aspect of the Mexican political system.

34. For Baja California the writs of *amparo* of the State Labor Board cases are reviewed by the fourth court of the supreme court of justice of the nation in Guadalajara (Jalisco), while the federal cases go to the supreme court in Mexico City.

35. The Federal Board of Conciliation was transferred from Tijuana to Ensenada in 1958. It was not possible to establish the background of former presidents of the board. The incumbent was an economist.

36. Strictly speaking, the threat-to-strike is not a legal action, but a prerequisite for establishing the legality of a strike. It cannot be compared to the cooling-off periods provided by other labor legislation. In practice, however, the threat-to-strike has become an action and it is understood as such by the workers and by the boards. Furthermore, the threat-to-strike action has to be officially registered with the labor boards. See Article 265 of the federal labor law.

37. Junta Municipal de Conciliación, "Expediente de Huelgas" (Ensenada: October 1966-September 1967). The Board gathers and issues the yearly official figures before the governor's State of the State message, which generally takes place sometime during the summer or early fall. For this reason January to December figures were not available.

38. For an interesting discussion about this topic, see Luis Castellano de la Torre, "La Función Jurisdiccional de los Tribunales Laborales de Arbitraje" (unpublished *licenciatura* thesis, Universidad Autónoma de Guadalajara, Facultad de Derecho, Guadalajara, 1966).

39. Federación CROC de Ensenada, "Ponencia al Segundo Consejo Estatal" (Ensenada: September 22, 1965).

40. The governor died eleven months before the termination of his term. An interim governor was elected by the state congress for the remainder of the term according to Article 46 of the state constitution. *Constitución Política del Estado Libre y Soberano de Baja California* (Mexicali, Baja California: Editorial Congreso, 1953).

41. See Frank Tannenbaum, *Mexico: The Struggle for Peace and Bread* (New York: Alfred A. Knopf, 1962) and Lesley B. Simpson, *Many Mexicos* (Berkeley and Los Angeles: University of California Press, 1967), p. 333: "All labor legislation, as Daniel Cosío Villegas observed in his melancholy *La Crisis de México* (1947), had only one

purpose: to favor the worker; *with few exceptions the courts always decided for him;* and, thus protected by the state and the courts, the worker lost all sense of responsibility and perspective, and looked upon the public as a source of spoils, while the employer came to feel that the courts were merely instruments of vengeance and coercion, and that he could not hope for justice from them." [My emphasis]

42. Robert Dubin, *op. cit.,* p. 250.

43. The term mixed commissions *(comisión mixta)* is used in Mexico to refer to a commission formed by representatives of the private and public sectors.

44. The structure and functioning of these commissions appear in Articles 401-A to 401-I, and 414 to 428-Y of the federal labor law. Other legal mechanisms that will not be treated in this study are the mixed commissions of health and security and the mixed commissions of the IMSS, the former to study safety labor conditions and the latter to oversee the proper treatment of workers by the IMSS.

45. See, for example, Confederación Estatal CROC, "Convocatoria, 18 Consejo Confederal Estatal Ordinario" (Tecate, Baja California: September 1967) and Confederación Estatal CROC, "Convocatoria, Segundo Consejo Confederal Estatal Ordinario" (Ensenada: September 1965). The meeting minutes of the conventions of the other federations show that minimum wages, profit sharing, and cost of living are always among the topics studied.

46. Centro Patronal, "Libro de Actas" (Ensenada: meeting minutes of June 14, 1965).

47. Generally, the National Executive resolves the conflicting demands for minimum wages with a compromise. In this sense, the Executive is sensitive to the demands. Thus, if labor is asking for 36 pesos per day and management is willing to pay 30, the official minimum wage will be established somewhere in between.

48. Amitai Etzioni, *A Comparative Analysis of Complex Organizations* (New York: The Free Press, 1961), p. 94.

49. In addition to the evidence already presented, many other references could be introduced. Among a few: "The union hopes that the demands would be heard because we like to have, now and always, good relations with management avoiding frictions and achieving a greater understanding and coordination." Sindicato de Empresa de Trabajadores de Conserva del Pacífico "Oficio no. 5" (Ensenada: August 22, 1966).

50. Frank Brandenburg, *The Making of Modern Mexico* (Englewood Cliffs, N.J.: Prentice-Hall, Inc., 1964), pp. 141 ff.

51. The governor is directly responsible to the National Executive for his administration. It is known that in a few states strong men rule with limited control by the Federal Executive. The state of Guerrero is probably the best example. Clearly, this is not the case in Baja California.

52. This is what happened to Lic. Braulio Maldonado, the first elected governor of the state of Baja California (1953—59) because he sided too often with labor, thereby creating unrest among businessmen and merchants. He also allegedly pocketed four million dollars. However, his political failure was due to his misuse of force and to the unrest he produced among some sectors of the state.

53. Conflicts between the government and the labor federations become tense now and then. In 1966 a serious conflict took place between the Ensenada CROC Federation and the government. The federation alleged that the state government had acted illegally in the handling of a labor dispute. A state convention was summoned by the CROC to study the case. The convention, representing 12,000 workers throughout the state, sent this message to the governor: "After careful consideration of the procedure which was followed by the labor authorities to register the Union of Construction Workers of the CRT, this assembly regards the action to be illegal .... The registration took place

during the time when the state board was in recess, and the special group number one which handles the registrations was not legally integrated. The labor representative in that particular group is a member of the CROC and he had no knowledge of the action. Besides, the whole situation was handled in a secret manner by order of some mysterious public official who works for your government. Our disappointment is a consequence of the high hopes and deep faith we had from the days you became the official candidate for the governorship of the state. We had hoped that the team you would select to govern our state would always act properly and according to the principles of justice. Events as the one mentioned above have betrayed you and the Mexican Revolution. Accordingly, we respectfully beg you to make an effort to avoid similar situations in the future, for if they were to happen again, the labor movement and in particular this confederation would be seriously endangered by the behavior of public officials, whom we believe to be entrusted with the work of making justice without privileges or crooked settlements. Their decisions and judgments are to be according to the laws of the country and of the State." Confederación Estatal CROC, "Pleno Confederal, Resoluciones" (Tecate, Baja California: January 24, 1966).

54. The Consejo de Planeación was organized in Baja California as well as in other states under the initiative of President Adolfo Ruíz Cortines (1952-58). Under the Dirección de Promoción a permanent mixed commission operates the Comité de Programación General y Económica, formed by representatives of the three sectors. It acts as an advisory board to the Dirección de Promoción.

55. Federación CROC, "Libro de Actas" (Ensenada: meeting minutes of September 24, 1963). The strike was declared legal by the labor authorities two weeks later.

4

The Public Sector: Bureaucratic Behavior

ORGANIZATION AND PERFORMANCE OF
RANK AND FILE BUREAUCRATS

Discussion of the rank and file bureaucrats will include organization, performance, ties with the official government party, and opportunities for corrupt practices. In Ensenada it was not possible to deal with all bureaucrats as a group, but was necessary to treat separately the federal, state, and municipal bureaucrats.

The Unions of Bureaucrats

The federal bureaucrats belong to sections or delegations of national unions with headquarters in Mexico City, organized by secretariats or federal agencies. The employees of the Secretary of Industry, for example, form the Union of Workers in Service to the Secretary of Industry. Several unions may be organized within one secretariat or agency that has large subsecretariats or departments. For instance, employees of the telegraph office have their own union, as do employees of the postal department, and both agencies are under the supervision of the Secretary of Communication and Transport. Local sections or delegations communicate their demands directly to their headquarters in Mexico City. The local sections and delegations in the city form the local Federation of Government Workers (Federación de Sindicatos de Trabajadores en el Servicio del Estado FSTSE), which has its counterpart at the national level.[1] Figure 12 shows the organization of the bureaucrats.

It is important to note that the local unions do not use the PRI or even the CNOP to articulate demands. Federal bureaucrats at the local level depend on the Party even less than do the labor organizations. It was mentioned earlier that the local labor federations are the essential political units. In contrast,

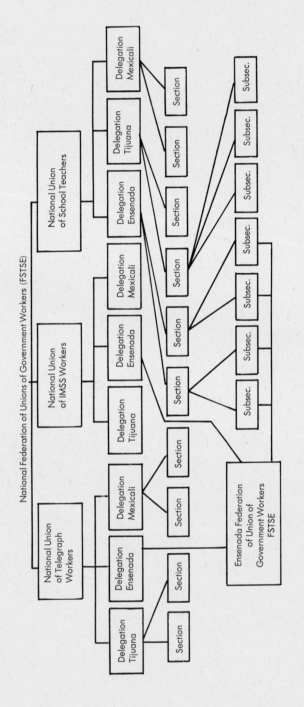

FIGURE 12.
UNIONS OF CIVIL SERVANTS

the local FSTSE has no practical functions. In Ensenada it seldom meets, perhaps once or twice a year; it does not have a local office, and in the past its actions have been very much limited to petitioning for specific wage compensations and the construction of a local hospital for federal employees.[2]

State and municipal bureaucrats belong to one state union, which has four sections, one in each municipality of the state. The organization of the union and its relations with the state and municipal governments are specified by the State Civil Service Law.[3] These bureaucrats' demands are also articulated outside the CNOP. State and municipal bureaucrats are the only group that makes a monthly contribution to the PRI (not to the CNOP), and these contributions are considered nonvoluntary because they are automatically deducted from the workers' salaries by the municipal and state cashiers.

Performance

The State Civil Service Law determines which state and municipal employees can be members of the unions and which are to be considered private employees *(personal de confianza)*. In Ensenada the state *personal de confianza* is very small and is limited to the chiefs of the offices and to persons working for the security forces; in Mexicali, as would be expected, the number increases considerably. On the other hand, the *personal de confianza* of the municipal government is large. Table 13 presents the percentages of unionized and nonunionized civil servants by levels of government in Ensenada.

TABLE 13
UNIONIZED AND NONUNIONIZED CIVIL SERVANTS
IN ENSENADA, 1967
(percent)

Levels of Government	Unionized Employees	Nonunionized Employees
Municipality (Total, 271)	27	73
State (Total, 453)	81	19
Federation (Total, 1,166)	92	8

From information obtained from the Ensenada Section of the Union of State and Municipal Bureaucrats (Sindicato Unico de Trabajadores al Servicio de los Poderes Estatales y Municipales) and from each federal office.

A large percentage of the municipal jobs is distributed every three years by the newly elected Municipal Council. These employees can hardly be considered civil servants; they are political protégés whose appointment is a reward for services rendered to the candidates during the political campaign. They are recruited mostly from the lower socioeconomic groups, and are laborers and peasants who are influential among large sectors of the voting population through neighborhood organizations, peasant groups, and labor unions. They do not belong to unions of bureaucrats. These temporary bureaucrats have no training for the white collar or administrative occupations given them at City Hall, and their performance is very low. Conversely, a large percentage of state and federal employees make careers in civil service. With the exception of the chiefs and members of the various police branches, they are unionized. Those of them who enter the bureaucracy by personal favoritism or by political patronage become politically independent when they unionize. They receive on-the-job training. Others, recruited in less personal ways, are professional or semiprofessional and politically independent, and for them the government is just another employer.

Table 14 shows the number of government employees in the municipality by level of government and by service. A large percentage of federal and state employees (77.1 and 75.3, respectively) occupy positions in education, health, or public works. These departments are streamlined, and there is little waste of human resources. The federal and state departments of education, for example, each have one superintendent and one secretary; the rest of their personnel are schoolteachers, some of whom teach two or three sessions because of the shortage of classrooms and teachers. The shortcomings in the school system are due not to poor performance on the part of the teachers but to inadequate facilities such as laboratories, gymnasiums, and libraries, and to the poor teacher training, and, in general, insufficient funds. The federal and state governments have appropriations for teachers' salaries and the construction of new schools, which, when built, consist of the barest essentials—classrooms. The federal government provides textbooks for the grade schools, and there is a poorly organized school lunch program for poor children. All other expenditures have to come from the local community.[4]

In many cases, although bureaucrats in the ranks (such as teachers) perform responsibly and efficiently, services themselves are inadequate because of lack of coordination and foresight by agency administrators or support by government officials. The following case illustrates this problem.

In the fall of 1967, 110 grade school children could not attend school because of lack of space. Parents in this poor neighborhood organized a Parents' Association Committee and sought help from the mayor, who promised to find land where a school could be built but added that he could do nothing to solve the problem for that school year. The Comité Administrador

TABLE 14

NUMBER OF GOVERNMENT EMPLOYEES BY LEVEL OF GOVERNMENT AND SERVICE, ENSENADA (1967)

Service	Federal[a]		State		Municipal		Total	
	Number of Persons	Percent	Number of Persons	Percent	Number of Persons	Percent	Number of Persons	Percent
Education	320	27.4	245	54.0	0	0	565	29.9
Health	300	25.7	74	16.3	0	0	374	19.8
Public Works and Maintenance	277	23.8	23	5.0	74	27.3	374	19.8
Tax Collection	72	6.2	33	7.5	14	5.1	119	6.3
Police and Security	0	0	45	9.9	111	40.9	156	8.2
Communication	65	5.6	0	0	0	0	65	3.4
Administration	0	0	0	0	47	17.3	47	2.4
Other	132	11.3	33	7.2	25	9.2	190	10.0
Total	1,166	100.0	453	99.9	271	99.8	1,890	99.8

[a]Including federal agencies.

The municipal data were calculated from "Ley de Egresos del Municipio de Ensenada, Ejercicio Fiscal de 1966," in *Periódico Oficial, Organo del Gobierno del Estado de Baja California* (Mexicali: December 31, 1965, Vol. 62, No. 36, Sec. 8). The state data were calculated from "Ley de Egresos del Estado de Baja California, Ejercicio Fiscal de 1966," in *Periódico Oficial*, ibid., Sec. 2, and from the official record of the local section of the Union of State Bureaucrats. The federal data were calculated from the official records of the local ISSSTE (the Social Security Institute for Federal Workers) and from visits to several offices.

del Programa Federal de Construcción de Escuelas (CAPFCE), which was the
federal agency responsible for providing the school building, had not foreseen
the situation and could not build the school that year. The parents obtained
the services of three teachers from the local superintendent of federal schools;
the CROC Federation volunteered its assembly hall; the Lions Club bought
desks; the parents organized a rotating team to provide janitorial services and
help the teachers. However, three classes had to share the assembly hall and
the noise level was very high; lighting was poor, and on some days classes had
to be dismissed early to free the hall for union meetings. Teaching effectiveness was greatly reduced. In this case two federal organizations, the Superintendency of Schools and the CAPFCE, were unable to work together to find
a solution for a comparatively simple problem, although the teachers performed ably.[5]

Participation in the PRI

The total number of persons employed by the three levels of government
in Ensenada in 1967 was 1,890 (Table 14). As the estimated active population in the municipality in 1967 was 30,000 persons, approximately 6 percent of the active population was on the government payroll. In terms of
votes at the local level, this figure is negligible. Only 486 of the bureaucrats in
Ensenada were affiliated with the Party, and this number is probably exaggerated; the CNOP official figures do not coincide with the actual affiliation
cards issued by the PRI Municipal Committee.[6] About 10 percent of the
CNOP members are bureaucrats, according to CNOP information. These data
seem to stand in contrast to the observations made by students of the Mexican political system at the national level. Frank Brandenburg says: "By its
very nature in Mexican political life, the FSTSE . . . was solidly committed to
membership in the official party. It became, and remains, the pillar of the
party's 'popular sector. . . .' "[7]
Of particular interest is that, of 565 teachers, only 75 were affiliated with
the CNOP. The schoolteachers do not owe their jobs to the Party and their
services are required regardless of who is in power. The same reasoning probably applies to the small but increasing number of professional degree holders
in the bureaucracy, such as medical doctors, engineers, and geologists, and
perhaps to a lesser degree to semiprofessional employees such as nurses and
topographers. (Medical doctors are being employed more and more by the
Mexican government, not because of political patronage to the medical pro-
fession but because of the trend toward socialized medicine in the country.)
Federal bureaus whose work requires little training, such as the Ensenada
Office of Finance or the Post Office, have a larger percentage of PRI affiliates

than do bureaus with more professional or technical personnel. In the Office of Finance 39 of the 42 employees were affiliated with the PRI, as were 26 of the 39 employees in the Post Office, but only 38 of the 233 employees in the Social Security Institute (IMSS) and 6 of the 23 employees in the Social Security Institute for Federal Workers (ISSSTE) were affiliated with the PRI. And, as previously mentioned, only 75 of the 565 teachers in Ensenada were PRI affiliates.

Unionized civil servants cannot be discharged unless they are guilty of misconduct in office as defined by law. In this sense they enjoy a secure position and they may be completely independent of the Party and the government. The 74 unionized municipal employees in Ensenada care little whether the PRI or the PAN wins the municipal elections. Their union is a functional group and will defend the interests of its members independently of political preference. In Ensenada the municipal employees occasionally have threatened to strike. On one occasion their union filed a writ of *amparo* when the municipal president refused to pay some salary compensations, and the municipality lost the case.[8] The outcome of elections affects the non-unionized municipal employees, but not surprisingly: they usually are replaced by new political recruits, even if the PRI wins the elections.

At the local level, the unionized bureaucrats do not seem to enjoy any special benefits that other workers do not have. Perhaps the main difference lies in the stability of their jobs. Salaries are not significantly different. Of all the state employees in Baja California, for example, 633 earned monthly salaries ranging from 1,250 to 1,500 pesos. This range is slightly above the minimum wage requirement of 1967 for labor. Profit sharing undoubtedly accounts for the difference. Fringe benefits are very much standard in respect to the two groups.

Civil servants regard their employer very much as laborers regard private employers. The bureaucratic chiefs are commonly referred to by the rank and file as *representantes patronales*. The tendency of civil servants to regard themselves as laborers is noticeable in the following statement of the secretary general of the local delegation of the IMSS Union, in a letter addressed to the labor federations:

In order to reduce the deficiencies caused by our Union in the operation of the IMSS we would like to make the following suggestions: (1) The services of the IMSS could be improved *if the users, who are workers like ourselves would receive full cooperation from our part not as employees but rather as unionized workers.* (2) We believe that whenever there is a complaint against the services of the IMSS it should be understood that we are not necessarily the ones to be blamed. It may very well be that the failure lies somewhere else, *perhaps in the lack of organization, perhaps in the shortage of personnel,* or for any other reason beyond the control of the workers. (3) With a desire of mutual cooperation we are asking the labor unions to present complaints first to our Union. This procedure will produce the following advantages. We will study if the complaint has some basis, then in common agreement we will decide whether it is more convenient to bring the complaint to the attention of the *representante patronal,* or to impose upon the person at fault a penalty by the union, which as you know could be more effective. On the other hand, if after the study of the complaint, it was decided that there was no real basis for it, unnecessary complaints will be eliminated. The enemies of progress are eager to point out the negative consequences of the work of the Revolution, as it has already happened in several instances . . . This procedure will also serve *to strengthen the bonds between our unions,* and consequently with the good will of both sides it will be possible to have a better service within the limitations of human possibilities.[9]

In 1966 the employees' union of the local Federal Health Center, an office dependent on the Secretary of Health (Secretaría de Salubridad y Asistencia), protested that they were not being paid the minimum wage.[10] They asked for the moral support of the labor federations and urged them to write on behalf of the Health Center employees to the President of the nation, the secretaries of Health and Finance, the secretary general of the national executive committee of the FSTSE, the secretary general of the national executive committee of the Union of Health Workers, and the grand commission of the National Chamber.[11] The local, state, and federal committees of the CNOP were conspicuously absent from the list, an additional indication that the unions of bureaucrats have no enduring links with the Party and an illustration of the affinity between the unions of bureaucrats and the labor unions. (It is also worth mentioning that the employees of the Health Center did not complain to their local director because they knew that the solution to their problem was in Mexico City; the director could only have waited for the money to come, as the civil servants had to do.)

Conflicts between the unions of federal bureaucrats and the government are few in comparison to conflicts between the labor unions and management. The civil servants rarely strike, with the exception of the union of schoolteachers, which strikes from time to time. The infrequency of conflicts is the consequence not of docility on the part of the bureaucrats but of the extreme care taken by the government to avoid any confrontation, for reasons of prestige.[12]

Opportunities for Graft

The large majority of civil servants hold positions that offer few occasions for dishonesty.[13] Employees of the IMSS or the state hospitals, the several hundred clerks and manual workers, and the schoolteachers can be counted among those with few opportunities to profit from corruption. There is perhaps some pilfering of materials, or a few cases in which a teacher is paid without having done any work, but these are exceptions, and it should be added that corrupt practices take place in private firms as well.

In 1967 the state of Baja California decided to enforce the Law of Job Incompatibilities, which prohibits civil servants from appearing on more than one state payroll without special permission. After preliminary investigation, several abuses were disclosed. One woman teacher was on seventeen different payrolls; several other teachers also held governmental positions, while their names appeared on teachers' payrolls but they did no teaching. In Ensenada the most notorious case was that of a city council member who was at the same time the director of two schools. It was alleged that he had never visited either school since he had been elected to the city council. One of the schoolteachers was doing all his work but receiving no compensation for it. The councilman was publicly repudiated by the schoolteachers' unions, and the abuse was corrected. Such cases of public dishonesty, however, are few, and the dishonesty is, in general, on the part of persons who occupy higher offices.

Those rank and file bureaucrats who do have opportunity for graft are the members of the police and traffic departments and, in particular, the custom employees. The first two groups are open to bribes in exchange for cancellation of fines or to facilitate the issuing of permits, a kind of bribe that can be a very profitable source of income for unscrupulous employees. The police and traffic officers are the lowest paid bureaucrats. The municipality employs 111 persons in the Department of Public Security, 80 of whom receive the lowest possible municipal salary, 1,265 pesos per month. In addition, these employees are not permitted to unionize and therefore do not receive social security or free medical benefits. The same is true of state police officers.[14]

Custom employees have greater opportunities for graft and corruption than do the other bureaucrats. The problem is particularly grave in Baja California, because three of the four major cities are border towns and the fourth, Ensenada, is a port and requires a maritime custom house. Import duties frequently are not collected but are exchanged for bribes. Some businessmen claim that negligence and corruption on the part of the custom officers have been the major causes for their business failures. Large shipments of second-grade eggs and even rejected produce from the United States market is sold at very low prices to Mexican dealers, who in turn market them at competitive prices in Baja California after bribing the custom officers, a practice that brought financial disaster to several poultry businesses that might have otherwise been very successful.[15]

At the local PRI headquarters criticism of the custom officers and other corrupt officials is common. One of the secretaries of the Party commented that the chief of the Federal Highway Patrol had paid 300,000 pesos to get his job but that he had done "good business," and that in the five years he had been in Ensenada he had been able to build a half-million peso home. A high-ranking PRI member criticized Tijuana custom officers who boast about their profiteering, including one man who bragged that his daily "extra income" was never below 1,000 pesos—probably about half his monthly official income.

A local dealer in second-hand appliances complained about the increasing cost of bribes at the customs station, which could be as high as 2,000 dollars, depending on the size of the truck. The bribe was often higher than the value of the merchandise. The anecdotes, stories, and gossip about the corrupt practices of the custom officials are innumerable. The repercussions of their behavior affect the low-income groups, who have to pay higher prices for second-hand articles coming from the United States, and there is a general dissatisfaction in the community with the performance of these civil servants.

THE UPPER RANKS OF THE BUREAUCRACY

In general, the upper level members of the bureaucracy are chiefs and subchiefs of offices, inspectors, supervisors, and a few others, such as judges, who have been invested with particular powers. This definition is not very precise but is sufficient for Ensenada, where the organization of the upper ranks of the bureaucrats is not very complex. Inspectors and supervisors come to the city only on inspection tours, and consequently little attention is given here to those offices.

The salaries of the upper ranks, although very low in comparison to salaries in similar occupations in the private sector, are considerably higher than those of the lower ranks, and in 1967 ranged from 4,000 to 6,000 pesos per month.

In discussing the upper ranks of the bureaucracy it is necessary to differentiate among the three levels of government. Nor are all offices equally important. The Federal Mining Delegation, for example, is an office of little significance. Its chief has few responsibilities and they are clerical only. The supervisor's position in the Federal Cashier's Office (Pagaduría Civil) is also unimportant, consisting mainly of the bimonthly payment of federal employees; computerized checks are sent from Mexico City and the office simply distributes them. Other offices are more important because they do more work or have more employees. The Federal Board of Material Improvements has only seven employees but its chief is responsible for over a million pesos worth of public works every year in Ensenada; the IMSS employs more than two hundred persons and provides medical services for several thousand. There is no need to categorize the bureaucratic offices in terms of their importance. The main consideration to be kept in mind is that some generalizations are unavoidable when referring to the upper ranks of the bureaucracy.

Recruitment and Stability Patterns

Recruitment patterns of bureaucratic chiefs vary. Some offices have a system of promotion, and their chiefs are recruited from the rank and file by seniority. This is the case for the Post Office, the Telegraph Office, and the superintendency of schools. However, the final decision is based on political patronage. When the director of one of the local schools was asked whether the office of superintendent was filled on a seniority basis, he smiled and replied, "Yes, seniority and pull." These positions have tenure and incumbents cannot be removed until the mandatory retirement age of sixty-five. The superintendent does not receive a salary much higher than that of a grade school director, a position that an individual usually holds before being promoted to superintendent. In 1967 a state superintendent had a monthly salary of 4,282 pesos and the directors of grade schools 3,748 pesos. However, the superintendency carries a considerable amount of prestige and other fringe benefits. Each of the two superintendents has organized a private normal school by using most of the facilities of the public schools, and it is to be expected that the normal schools have produced some income.

Chiefs of some other offices are recruited from the rank and file but have no tenure and can be removed from office at the will of higher chiefs. This was true of such positions as the two offices of the Harbor Authorities, the superintendency of Road Maintenance, and one of the offices of the Land Commission. Characteristically, all these offices were occupied by professional people—most of them engineers—and their jobs were highly technical.

The majority of offices is filled by political patronage. Appointments are made by the municipal president, the governor, or some high federal chiefs. It was not possible to determine at what level of the federal bureaucratic structure the appointments for Ensenada were made. The federal appointments originate in Mexico City (the regional offices have no power to make these appointments), but whether the secretaries, the subsecretaries, or in some cases the President of the nation or the powerful Secretary of the Interior had made the appointments could not be determined. The local and regional PRI have no voice in these appointments. It is clear that appointees for federal offices have to have good contacts in Mexico City.

The PRI is a channel to attaining office in one special way. Persons who have the patience and the interest to climb up the political ladder of the PRI on the local level may then make contacts with executives of the bureaucracy at the national and state level. If the Secretary of Industry and Commerce visits the city, the higher officers of the PRI have access to him; when they make trips to Mexico City or Mexicali they have access to other PRI officials who are close to the real power holders in the bureaucracy. One of the PRI officials said frankly, "I am interested in holding office in the party for professional reasons." But this is not the common recruitment pattern of chiefs; it is perhaps more usual to hold office in the PRI after having held a position in the bureaucracy.

An office in the local bureaucracy enables one to make contacts with important officials in Mexicali and Mexico City through which, if his own patron is removed from office, he can obtain another office. In this way the upper ranks of the bureaucracy perpetuate themselves.

The recruitment process is well illustrated by this biography of a former bureaucrat. He was born in a little village in the state of Michoacan in 1900. He came to Baja California as a rank and file federal employee at the age of nineteen, and served for one year in Mexicali, which at that time was a very unimportant border town. The following year, when the municipality of Tijuana was organized for the first time, he was appointed chief of the traffic department and chief of the police force. He occupied those offices for four years. He then entered private business and became a successful businessman in the dairy industry in Tijuana. Thirteen years later his business career was interrupted when Governor Colonel Rodolfo Sánchez Taboada (1937–43) appointed him chief of the special police force at the Agua Caliente race track in Tijuana. He became the protégé of Sánchez Taboada. Two years later, in 1939, he was appointed chief of the security police in Tijuana, a very important job in that particular town.

When Sánchez Taboada became president of the PRI Executive Committee in the Federal District he appointed the former chief of police as his personal secretary. In 1946 the PRI selected Sánchez Taboada to be a special delegate and to lead the presidential campaign of Miguel Alemán in Michoacan. When Miguel Alemán assumed the presidency, he appointed Sánchez Taboada president of the National Executive Committee of the PRI, and Sánchez Taboada brought his protégé in as an auxiliary member. In December 1952, incoming President Adolfo Ruíz Cortines appointed Sánchez Taboada his Secretary of Navy, and Sánchez Taboada immediately appointed his protégé chief of the federal fishing agency in San Diego, California.[16] After the death of Sánchez Toboada the once lowly bureaucrat returned to Ensenada, his wife's birthplace, and went back into private business. In the meantime his two children had become prominent businessmen in Ensenada. In 1959 he entered public life once again. He was appointed president of the PRI municipal committee in Ensenada, and in December of the same year he was appointed chief of the municipal traffic and police departments. In 1962 he was appointed by the party to be the candidate for the municipal presidency and was successfully elected to that office in the same year. In 1965 he went back once more to private business.

It is worthy of note that his political career in Mexico City was subsequent to his bureaucratic career, and indeed followed even his business career. His

PRI appointments in Mexico City and in Ensenada were merely temporary waiting periods. The study of other cases suggests that this is a common pattern, perhaps because there are more people "offering" their services to the government than there are available positions. In many cases the PRI is the exit door from executive positions. It is also important to observe the rapid and easy shifts from public life to private business and vice versa.

There is a tendency to view the Mexican bureaucratic machine as a revolving door through which people go in and out every six years with the changing of the President and the governors. This may be true in Mexico City and in the state capitals, but the data gathered for Ensenada suggest something different. Table 15 summarizes the data and shows that the stability of the chiefs of the federal and state offices is low. Of the 111 federal chiefs, between 1953 and 1967, 69 held office for periods shorter than three years, and 92 were in office less time than the presidential six-year period. Similarly, of 56 chiefs in the state bureaucracy during the same period, 31 headed their respective offices for less than three years, and 46 remained in office less time than the six-year gubernatorial period.

TABLE 15
STABILITY OF CIVIL CHIEFS OF FEDERAL AND STATE GOVERNMENT
OFFICES AND AGENCIES, ENSENADA (1953–67[a])

Years in Office	State Chiefs[b]	Percent	Federal Chiefs[b]	Percent
12 or more	3	5.3	8	7.2
9 to 11	1	1.6	4	3.6
6 to 8	6	10.6	7	6.3
3 to 5	15	26.7	23	20.7
2 or less	31	55.8	69	62.2
Total	56		111	

[a]In 1967 there were 21 state offices in the city. The table is based on the analysis of 15 offices. The same year there were 26 federal offices and 8 federal agencies. The table is based on the analysis of 24 offices and 7 agencies. Two subchiefs of the two most important federal offices were included. One federal office was also included that moved to Mexicali in 1964.

[b]The same person occupying two different offices is considered as two chiefs. Chiefs who left office and returned to the same office after a short period have been considered as serving in one interval. Interim appointments have not been taken into account.
Calculated from information obtained from each local office.

The data in Table 15 also can be used to compare the stability of the federal and state offices. The total number of office years (A) and the total number of chiefs (B) between 1953 and 1967 were calculated, and the stability mean was obtained by dividing A by B. The results are presented in Table 16. The state chiefs average three years in office and the federal chiefs 3.4. If the offices with tenure are not taken into account the stability mean for the federal chiefs is reduced to 2.9 years. The chiefs are not necessarily removed from office in the same year in which the governors and President take office; sometimes they are but no generalization can be made. In Ensenada no pattern in the time of changes could be found for federal or state chiefs. All municipal chiefs are automatically replaced with the change in the municipal administration every three years.

TABLE 16
STABILITY MEAN OF CIVIL CHIEFS OF FEDERAL
AND STATE GOVERNMENT OFFICES AND AGENCIES,
ENSENADA (1953–67)

	State Offices	Federal Offices	Federal Agencies	Federal Total	Federal Total Minus Promotion Offices
A. Total number of office years	168	315	64	379	304
B. Total number of chiefs	56	82	29	111	104
Stability mean (A/B)	3.0	3.8	2.2	3.4	2.9

From these observations and the study of several cases the following conclusions can be drawn.

1. The frequent changes show that demands for these offices are high, and apparently pressure from sponsors to place their protégés is also high. The system of fast rotation seems to be imposed by the need to increase the possibilities for political patronage. The pressures are so great that offices in the Party often are used as waiting stations.

2. The political system has produced a highly unstable bureaucratic directorship.

3. The instability of the bureaucratic chiefs is probably one major cause of the inefficiency of the bureaucracy. For example, over a period of several years, the local director of the National Bank Ejidal was changed every six or seven months. It is hardly conceivable that an institution can be effective under these circumstances.

4. Opportunities for corruption are increased because a new chief can always blame his predecessor for irregularities.

Increasing professionalization of the upper ranks of the bureaucracy does not seem to alter these patterns. In 1967 14 of the 32 federal chiefs and 10 of the 21 state chiefs had university degrees. Engineers and technicians account for the largest number of professionals, followed by doctors and then a handful of lawyers. In the municipal bureacracy there were no degree holders, but this situation was anomalous because there had been two or three professionals in each administration in previous years. Nevertheless, this number is very low and affirms the fact that the municipal bureaucracy is the least professional of the three.

Opportunities for Graft

There is no single answer to the question of why there is such a high demand among holders of professional degrees for these offices. Some of the offices bring high financial rewards, not necessarily in salaries but rather in under-the-table money making opportunities. Municipal chiefs have limited opportunities for graft, state chiefs greater opportunity, and federal chiefs the greatest. As will be pointed out in the next chapter, the municipal budget is small and is closely supervised by some of the local organizations and by the state government. At this level, unexplained discrepancies are detected easily. As a former councilman once commented, "Ensenada is a very small community; everything is known by the people immediately. It is not possible to make money."

Businessmen and merchants seek positions in the municipal administration mainly for reasons of personal prestige and for the important contacts such positions provide that are useful in their businesses. The exception is the office of municipal president, which offers a relatively high salary (10,000 pesos per month, including appropriations for personal expenses) and provides the possibility to make money on the side. A former municipal president answered quite openly the question of why individuals seek the municipal presidency: "There are three reasons which motivate persons to become municipal presidents. The first is personal glory, the second is the possibility to make some money, and the third—in a few cases, in a very few cases—is to be able to do something to help the people."

State offices in Ensenada are administrative units of offices in Mexicali. State chiefs implement policies established in Mexicali and have little policy-making power. (This is also true of federal chiefs, but state chiefs are much more closely supervised by their own chiefs, who are geographically closer than the federal bosses in Mexico City.) The state offices in Ensenada have very small budgets, most of which go for salaries. However, some of the state chiefs do have the opportunity to use their contacts within the Mexicali government for personal profits in private business. It also should be remembered that the local state chiefs are by no means overburdened with work and can find time to work in their own businesses or for other firms.

The federal offices have larger budgets and more remote supervision. In

1967 the Federal Board of Material Improvements built a bridge in the downtown area over the Ensenada River, which is a dry river bed except during the
rainy season. The townspeople were happy with the small new bridge, since
all traffic had had to go over the only other bridge in the city during past
rainy seasons. One week after the bridge had been officially dedicated, unusually heavy rains brought the river to an unprecedented high level and the
bridge collapsed. A large amount of public criticism resulted. Some people
blamed the Board of Material Improvements and others the construction
firm. The underlying suspicion was that somebody had made a crooked deal
and had saved some money for personal use. The board and the construction
firm insisted that the bridge had been built according to specifications and
that the disaster was an act of God. The actual reason for the bridge's collapse
was never determined. Ensenada is far from Mexico City, and the accident
was not important enough to motivate the chiefs in Mexico City to conduct
an investigation.

Some agencies handle relatively large amounts of money, for example, the
several government banks. Others, such as the PRONAF agency (National
Border Program) or the National Housing Institute (INV), carry out large
construction programs. Several knowledgeable professional contractors indicated that it is an established custom in Mexico for the contractor to give
10 percent of the construction cost to the bureaucractic chief. There is no
need to elaborate on the fact that some federal chiefs can make fortunes
through graft at the local level.

Identification with the PRI

One last question about the upper ranks of the bureaucracy has to be
answered, and this has to do with its relations with the PRI. The president of
the PRI municipal committee commented: "Yes, you would expect the
bureaucrats to be very active in the Party, but they are not." In 1966 the
local PRI sent a memorandum to the regional headquarters in Mexicali complaining about the apathy of the bureaucratic chiefs, who had failed to be
present at party functions and activities.[17]

A distinction has to be made among the three levels of government. The
interest of the federal chiefs in local politics is minimal, and so is their
involvement. They seldom take root in the community because their terms in
office are short. Generally they are from other parts of the country, and only
those who have tenure can be considered residents of the community. At the
end of their years in office, the federal chiefs return to their own communities or are transferred to new positions. None of the federal chiefs pays fees
to the Party, and from 1953 to 1967 only four of them have occupied offices
of importance on the PRI municipal committee. Two of these were bureaucrats with tenure. To a lesser degree the same is true of the state chiefs in
Ensenada, although more of them are residents of the state.

Federal and state bureaucrats are sometimes asked to assist the local Party: to serve as members of committees formed to organize receptions for the President of the Republic, for the PRI candidate for the presidency during the campaign tour of the municipality, and for the president of the PRI national executive committee. Such services are considered a privilege rather than a duty. When the President of the Republic visited the city in the spring of 1967, even some wealthy PAN members cooperated by contributing several thousand pesos to pay for the reception.

The case of the municipal bureaucrats is different. The number of members of the PRI municipal committee who have occupied municipal office is very high. This reflects the fact that the municipal offices are generally political rewards given by the PRI to active local members after the local campaigns, or to groups like the unions and *ejidatarios,* which are active sponsors of the local PRI. As previously mentioned, the selection of the councilmen often is made not by the PRI but by the labor federations or the *ejidatarios.* Table 17 summarizes these findings.

TABLE 17

NUMBER OF OFFICERS OF THE PRI MUNICIPAL COMMITTEE WHO HAVE BEEN CHIEFS OF BUREAUCRATIC OFFICES IN ENSENADA (1954–67)[a]

Level of Government	Number
Municipal[b]	24
State	3
Federal	4
Held no office[c]	13
Total	44

[a]The four most important offices of the PRI municipal committee were selected.
[b]Includes 4 substitutes *(suplentes).*
[c]Most of these persons are aspirants to municipal offices and probably will be given offices in future administrations.
From files of the local PRI headquarters and information obtained from informants.

Table 18 summarizes the findings of this section.

TABLE 18

STABILITY, PATTERNS OF CHANGE, AND IDENTIFICATION OF BUREAUCRATIC CHIEFS WITH THE LOCAL PRI IN ENSENADA

Level of Local Bureaucracy	Stability in Office (Mean)	Patterns of Change	Identification with Local PRI
Local	3 years	Regular changes with municipal elections	Very high
State	3 years	No observable pattern	Low
Federal	2.9 years	No observable pattern	Very low

NOTES

1. This does not include the several sections of schoolteachers. The organization of schoolteachers is particularly complex, since state and federally employed teachers comprise one single union that has several sections in Ensenada.

2. Interview with Francisco Ramírez, member of the executive committee of the FSTSE, September 21, 1967. Salaries for federal employees are the same everywhere in Mexico. Cost of living is very different throughout the country, and salaries of federal employees are adjusted by the addition of special compensations. In Baja California bureaucrats receive 100 percent compensation with the exception of Ensenada, where the compensation is only 90 percent above the salary. The Ensenada FSTSE was asking for the 100 percent, claiming that the cost of living in Ensenada was as high as the rest of the state.

3. Gobierno del Estado de Baja California, *Ley del Servicio Civil de los Trabajadores al Servicio de los Poderes del Estado y Municipios* (Mexicali, Baja California: Talleres Tipográficos del Estado, 1959).

4. In one of the poorest *colonias,* for example, the neighbors organized fiestas and raffles during the summer of 1967 to collect 10,000 pesos to pay for adding one classroom to their school and painting the other three classrooms. The money was collected by mid-October, and the work completed before Christmas. These citizens were extremely proud of their achievement, and because of their success were thinking of adding two more classrooms, so that they would not have to send their children to the downtown schools. The service clubs and the Masonic lodges also are active in collecting funds for school improvements, and furnish the poorer schools with desks and materials.

5. The director of one of the local public high schools, in a talk given at a Lion's Club meeting, confirmed the observations that educational or other public service deficiencies cannot be blamed on the local rank and file bureaucrats. He severely criticized the state governors for failing to provide the schools with adequate financing: His school, for example, had been forced to keep the same enrollment for several years, although the number of applicants was increasing every year, and new classrooms were urgently needed. It had become necessary to give entrance examinations to limit the number of incoming first-year students because it was not possible to further overcrowd the classrooms (already used by 50 students per room). He added that some of the parents of the 100 rejected students had complained bitterly to him about the injustice of the system and had expressed disappointment in the Mexican Revolution. The director's own view of the school system was pessimistic. His school needed laboratories, a library, a gymnasium, and other recreational facilities. The school had to ask for a registration fee of 50 pesos and monthly payments of 20 pesos per student to have the school cleaned and to have money for other necessary general expenses—a practice clearly prohibited by the Mexican constitution. The only money they received from the state was for salaries, and the promises of two governors of a monthly allowance of $1,600 to the school had never materialized.

6. The CNOP office claimed 4,251 adult members. Affiliation cards issued to the CNOP were 3,964.

7. Frank Brandenburg, *The Making of Modern Mexico* (Englewood Cliffs, N.J.: Prentice-Hall, Inc., 1964) p. 86. See also, Robert E. Scott, *Mexican Government in Transition* (Urbana: University of Illinois Press, 1965), p. 81: "The government bureaucrats, for example, are one of the strongest units in the Popular sector of the official party, and well they might be, for they receive special benefits from the government far beyond their social or economic contribution to Mexican life. Probably, it would be fair to say that the low-cost housing, special commissary facilities . . . more nearly reflect

their high degree of intensity of political action and consequent contribution to the strength of the revolutionary party."

8. Interview with Juan Arredondo, Secretary of Labor, Ensenada section of the Unión de Trabajadores al Servicio del Estado, December 13, 1967. Conflicts between the state or the municipality and the employees are solved through special boards of conciliation. Demands are very much limited to petitions for wage salaries and promotions.

9. Delegación del Sindicato de Trabajadores del Instituto Mexicano del Seguro Social, "Expediente" (Ensenada, Baja California: October 12, 1965). [My emphasis]

10. This situation was possible because these civil servants had not received increases of salaries since 1959. Since that time the minimum wages for manual laborers had been increased on three occasions, and in 1966 these workers received a minimum wage higher than that of the workers of the Health Department in Ensenada.

11. Sindicato Nacional de Trabajadores de Salubridad y Asistencia. Sec. 42, subsec. 3, "Expediente" (Ensenada: May 1966).

12. These comments were made by Lic. Gustavo Rosas, president of the local Federal Labor Board of Conciliation. Interview, July 17, 1967.

13. The concepts of dishonesty and corruption are relative and to some extent are based on cultural values. Different cultures have different ethical standards. For example, the director of a school could admit the unqualified student to his school without its being considered unfair. A mechanic in one of the state shops will not be considered dishonest for repairing a friend's car in the shop, even during his regular working hours.

14. Inefficiency in the security departments is not related to bribing. Security officers are poorly trained, as are the other civil servants. The departments have practically no resources for investigation of crimes, and the employees often complain that they have neither sufficient gasoline for patrolling the municipality nor sufficient funds for repairing the vehicles they do have.

15. Interview with Dr. Gabriel Galván, Executive Member of the Ensenada Poultry Association, October 15, 1967.

16. The Mexican government has an office in San Diego for granting franchises to fish in Mexican territorial waters.

17. Comité Municipal del PRI, Ensenada, "Oficio 32/66" (Ensenada: 1966).

5

The Functioning of Local, State, and Federal Governments

ROLES OF MUNICIPAL GOVERNMENT

Legislative and Administrative Roles

Observers of the Mexican scene agree regarding the political and economic dependence of local government upon state and federal governments,[1] and, generally, that the subjugation of the municipality to the state is a reflection of the subjugation of the state to the federation. A local commentator wrote in a progovernment newspaper:

Our municipality like the rest of the municipalities in the country receives only a fraction of the state revenues, a participation that should be considered as a mere symbolism. At the same time, the state government is in a similar situation in respect to the federal government which gets the big morsel . . . In short, the fiscal structure should be totally and completely reorganized at all levels, municipal, state, and federal . . . Today's practice of taking the money away from the municipalities and later returning a little to them is the cause of their poverty.[2]

It is no surprise to discover that the municipal government does little that is not of an administrative nature. Although the state law concerning municipalities empowers the municipal council to regulate public services and other activities of the community by issuing statutes and ordinances, the municipal council seldom does so.[3] In the past the council (consisting of the municipal president, one public defender [*síndico*], and five councilmen) has looked with indifference at its legislative responsibilities and has considered such activities outside the scope of its proper concern. Perhaps this situation reflects the fact that only two lawyers have served on the municipal council; nor has the council hired the services of consulting attorneys, an action that it is legally empowered to take.[4] The legislative impotence of the council is illustrated by its inability to issue even traffic ordinances. During the summer of 1967 it decided to issue traffic ordinances for the city, but after several meetings uncovered so many problems that it could not solve that the project was abandoned.[5]

The only community services that the municipal government does provide and administer are the following: (1) The lighting of the main thoroughfares and the downtown area; (2) a bare minimum of street repairs, just enough to keep the streets passable; (3) the posting of traffic signs; (4) street cleaning in the downtown area and in the tourist section of the city; (5) garbage collection; (6) upkeep of two miniparks; (7) upkeep of the civil register; (8) operation of the city's water system, cemetery, slaughterhouse, and public market. The municipality also is responsible to some extent for traffic, police and fire security, and maintenance of the jail. Municipal responsibilities in the rural areas are limited to the appointments of municipal delegates.

Services are few and their quality is very poor. The subhuman conditions in the municipal jail are well known to everyone in Ensenada. There is a saying in town that if one is not a criminal before going to jail he certainly will become one after leaving. The warden and the officers are not professionally trained for their jobs, which they have only because of political patronage.[6] Little could be done to improve conditions at the jail even if the jailers were qualified and trained. The municipal budget appropriates only enough for the salaries of the jailers and three pesos per day per inmate for food. The prison building is in a state of collapse and the cells are filthy, unhealthy, and overcrowded. Some years ago one of the municipal administrations acquired land on which to build a new prison, but the project was abandoned for lack of funds shortly after groundbreaking.

Conditions at the slaughterhouse are not much better. During the summer of 1967 the supervising veterinarian resigned because he had not been paid for several months and because he wanted to protest the poor sanitation at the slaughterhouse. Neighbors had been complaining about bad odors, and the Federal Health Center warned the municipality that something must be done or they would have to condemn the building.

The municipal president explained in August of the same year that the city's water system might break at any time and leave the city without water. The main pipes were more than twenty years old, leaked in several sections, and could not be repaired for lack of money. The diameter of the pipes originally had been calculated for water pressures much lower than those the pipes were under in 1967 due to the growth of the city and its increased water needs. The municipal president, addressing representatives of the most important groups in the city, said that he wanted to let them know about the situation but that there was nothing he could do to remedy it, because there was simply no money available.

Even the police services are inadequate, and some of the neighborhoods hire their own private police to patrol the streets at night. There is often a shortage of money for emergency projects because the accounting system in the municipality does not take into account depreciation expenditures. No administration is in office long enough to be willing to invest money in maintenance and upkeep. They reason that they can always blame previous administrations if something collapses or breaks down. When an administration can somehow scrape together a few extra pesos, it uses the money to build a project as a memorial to itself. One previous administration built the municipal hall, another a small public park; the administration in office in 1967 built the public market.

Municipal Budget

Policy regarding the roles and economies of municipalities in the state are established by the governor. Some governors, for example, may encourage the city council to undertake public projects and to become involved in educational services, while others may discourage such activities.

Figure 13 presents the expenditures of the municipality from 1954 to 1967. Analysis of the figure affirms that the economy of the municipality is under the direct control of the governor. During the term of the first governor (1953-59) the budget grew steadily from four million pesos per year to seven million. The change of municipal president in 1956 does not affect the curve. During the term of the second governor (1959-65) the budget increased by only one million pesos, from seven million pesos in 1959 to slightly less than eight million in 1965; again the change of municipal presidents in 1962 does not affect the curve, which turns sharply at the time the third governor took office in 1965.[7] It seems clear that the municipal presidents have to follow the spending moods of the governors.

For perspective on municipal indigence, one must study the actual expenditures and income of the municipality. Data for 1966 are presented in Tables 19 and 20. In 1966 the budget allowed for expenditures of 9.9 million pesos, and by the end of the year the municipal balance showed expenditures of 8.9 million pesos and an additional one million for transient operations.[8] The balance, unfortunately, does not show the accumulation of the municipal public debt, and consequently it becomes difficult to compare the budget with the actual expenditures. This limitation should be taken into account in the present analysis.

Not infrequently, appropriations are not spent according to the budget approved by the legislature.[9] For 1966 the budget allocated 1.2 million pesos for education, but the municipality spent somewhat less than eight thousand pesos for education. The difference was shifted to the construction of a public market, which had not been included in the budget. The budget allowance for electrical consumption was a little over half a million pesos, but the municipality had paid only one thousand pesos to the Federal Commission of

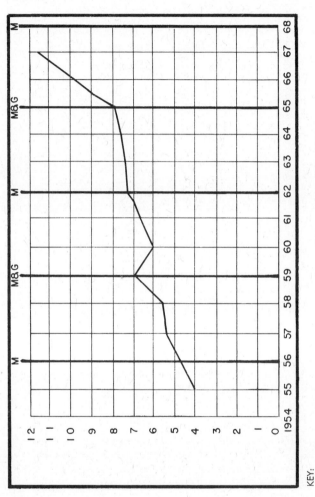

FIGURE 13.
OFFICIAL EXPENDITURE BUDGETS OF MUNICIPALITY OF ENSENADA, 1954-67
(IN MILLIONS OF PESOS)

Source: *Periódico Oficial, Organo del Gobierno del Estado de Baja California* (Mexicali), vol. 67, no. 39, 111; vol. 68, no. 148; vol. 69, no. 184; vol. 70, nos 220, 256, 292, 328, 364; vol. 71, no. 36; vol. 72, no. 36; vol. 73, no. 36.

TABLE 19
EXPENDITURES OF MUNICIPALITY OF ENSENADA, 1966
(in thousands of pesos)

Item	Expenditure Subtotal	Expenditure Total	Percent of Total Expenditures
Salaries		5,072	56.5
Public works		851	9.4
Utilities[a]			
water system	751		
cemetery (estimate)	100		
Total Utilities		851	9.4
Public services			
municipal jail	30		
subsidies to sports	20		
education	7		
electricity	542		
parks and streets	303		
purchase of garbage trucks	202		
Total Services		1,104	13.4
Maintenance and general		1,001	11.1
Total Expenditures		8,879	

[a]Municipal utilities are not operated by a decentralized agency, and therefore, some of the general funds of the Municipality are spent on utilities.

Calculated from Tesorería Municipal, "Corte de Caja por las Operaciones Registradas durante el Ejercicio Comprendido del Primero de Enero al 31 de Diciembre de 1966." Courtesy of Cliserio Gil Brambila, Municipal Treasurer.

Electricity (CFE) by the end of the year, and the difference was supposedly added to the public debt. The saving was used by the municipality to repair and expand the water system and to build the public market. These changes were made with the tacit approval of the governor, since changes in the budget are forbidden by law unless the state legislature approves.[10]

The utilities are not operated as independent public agencies but rather as part of the regular functions of the municipality. The quality of utility services may be affected by the accounting system, because no one can tell whether the utilities are self-supporting, profit-making, or a liability to the municipality. In 1966, for example, the cost of improvements and repairs to the water system was 751,000 pesos and the salaries of the personnel totaled 288,657.[11] The total operation cost has to include other expenses that, in the budget, fall under the general expenses of the municipality. However, even if this amount is very small and is disregarded, at least 1,040,000 pesos were spent on the water system, which in turn produced an income of 1,057,000 pesos. It is probable that several municipal administrations have

TABLE 20
INCOME OF MUNICIPALITY OF ENSENADA, 1966
(in thousands of pesos)

Item	Income Subtotal	Income Total	Percent of Total Income
Taxes			
municipal taxes	1,302		
tax refunds from state	962		
tax refunds from federal government	476		
Total Taxes		2,740	31.1
Licenses, Permits and Franchises		1,717	19.5
Fees		247	2.8
Fines		1,096	12.4
Utilities			
water system	1057		
cemetery	224		
slaughter house	234		
others	199		
Total Utilities		1,714	19.5
Cooperation for public works		277	3.1
Delayed payments from previous years[b]		952	10.8
Others		49	0.6
Total Income		8,792	

[a]Some of the public works are paid for by the persons who benefit from the works. For instance, a traffic light is paid for by the store owners at the intersection. Street pavement is paid for by property owners on the street according to frontage size. The Municipality advances the money for the works, and after completion, the owners pay the Municipality an amount which is called Cooperation for Public Works. Hence, properly speaking, this amount should not be considered as income.

[b]The source does not specify the nature of the delayed payments. Therefore, they could be from delayed taxes or from any of the other entries.

Calculated from Tesorería Municipal de Ensenada, "Corte de Caja por las Operaciones Registradas durante el Ejericicio Comprendido del Primero de Enero al 31 de Diciembre de 1966."

been diverting profits from the water system to other areas of municipal need, thereby depriving the water department of repair funds and reducing the overall quality of the service. The same analysis can be applied to the other utility services.

Perhaps the most outstanding feature of Table 19 is the fact that the largest expenditure, 56.5 percent, is for salaries. As was indicated in Chapter 4, there are 271 persons on the municipal payroll, 74 of whom are unionized and 107 of whom are security force employees, who cannot be unionized. The other 90 jobs are distributed by the city council as sinecures to persons who helped in the political campaign, union leaders, *ejidatarios*, or friends of the new municipal council. Municipal salaries are very low and, in general, municipal bureaucrats feel they are underpaid. Many political appointees do not feel obligated to work very hard, and their presence in City Hall is often symbolic. However, the sheer size of the municipal payroll constitutes a heavy burden on the municipal treasury's scant resources. Little money is left for services and public works. In 1966 the total municipal expenditure for public works and services was 1.9 million pesos, or an average of 20 pesos per person ($1.60 U.S.). This figure in itself is the best indicator of why some services basic to the needs of a modern community do not exist in Ensenada.

Analysis of income sources for the municipality is also relevant. As shown in Table 20, 31.1 percent of the municipal income comes from taxes, about half of this from federal and state taxes that are refunded to the municipality because of municipal participation in indirect taxes and as considerations for the harbor and fishing activities. The second largest source of income (19.5 percent) derives from licenses, permits, and franchises, in reality a type of taxation that, in most cases, affects only commercial firms and businesses. All stores and industrial firms, for example, must pay a license fee, determined by the amount of their capital, for a sanitation permit, and an additional fee for an operation permit.

It is striking that 12.4 percent of the municipal income derives from fines. About one-fourth of this income is from fines imposed by the treasury for delayed tax payments. The remainder of the fines are issued by the police and traffic departments. Traffic fines are very high and the chief of the traffic department is urged to issue as many fines as possible because of the much-needed income it produces for the municipality. If the income from the traffic department is lower than expected, the municipal council suspects the chief of dishonesty.[12]

As a result, the people view police authority and police regulations as something other than the means for maintaining law and order. Persons who are fined understandably look for all possible ways to have the fines reduced or cancelled. The importance of the councilmen as group representatives can be better appreciated in light of these circumstances. If a truck driver is fined, he will go to a union leader, who in turn will take him to the labor representative at the municipal council, who can cancel or reduce the fine. At the office of the councilmen in City Hall or the office of the traffic department, these manipulations are part of the everyday routine. It can be stated without exaggeration that this is one of the main functions of the councilmen.

The 1.3 million pesos in municipal tax collected in 1966 was received from firms with capital up to 15,000 pesos.[13] All in all, the commercial and industrial firms are the only true contributors to the municipal purse. The more affluent segments of the community view the municipal government in its present condition as a political evil, since a large part of their taxes is used to pay the salaries of employees who do little for the city. This situation produces a conflict between the public sector and this particular segment of the private sector.

PERSPECTIVES ON LOCAL GOVERNMENT

Proposal by Business Sector

Several proposals to make the municipal government more effective have come from various individuals and local groups. One of the proposals advocated reducing wage expenditures in the municipality by decreasing the number of employees and by making some of the offices honorary, with the savings to be used for public works and services. This proposal was particularly attractive to some members of the business sector, who realized that the state government would not favor an increase in revenue for the municipality under any circumstances. A former president of the Chamber of Commerce suggested publicly that councilmen should not be paid salaries, as the work they did was insignificant and the resources of the municipality were scarce, and that the offices of councilmen should be honorary only.[14] Many businessmen sided with him.

It is hardly conceivable that the state government would consider improving local government by reducing municipal personnel, because leaders of the labor federations, the *ejidatarios,* the fishing cooperatives, and some of the CNOP organizations—groups whose members are by and large the recipients of the offices—would strongly oppose the idea.[15] The Party has to satisfy the demands of these leaders in exchange for political control of the groups that they lead. The objections to this proposal reflect the political conflict between the business sector of the community, which is the main taxpayer, and the public sector. The former demands more efficient use of its money. The latter cannot provide it because it is determined to obtain its legitimation at the polls under democratic appearances and in order to do so must reward labor and peasant leaders with offices in exchange for the votes of their followers.

The political nature of the conflict was explained by a former councilman who is also a member of the upper class:

The selection of persons for municipal offices is made by Party groups. These groups demand representation in the municipal government, and the Party has to satisfy their demands. Consequently, the persons selected by the Party are not always the best. There are many other persons who are better qualified and more competent, and they have to be left out. The process of selection of Party candidates has disillusioned many people, and many times it has driven the best from politics.

Proposal To Increase Municipal Revenues

There have been several variations of this proposal. The simplest is to raise taxes. Under the present municipal organization and political system this measure would be criticized harshly by most sectors of the community. There is already a general distrust of the government. For the majority of taxpayers higher taxes would seem to increase graft opportunities and the mishandling of funds in municipal offices, which are held by incompetent functionaries because of the recruitment process.

Some local politicians favored the creation of a municipal endowment in order to increase the revenues, with the aim of giving the municipal government greater economic power and therefore more decision-making power. According to one former municipal president, it would be necessary to provide Ensenada with an endowment to carry out public works worth at least six million pesos per year:

Otherwise you can do nothing. During my administration I was able to obtain for the city from President Ruíz Cortines the waterfront lands which had been reclaimed from the sea. The Municipality could have sold these lands at a very good price, and it could have built an endowment, but my successor returned the lands to the federal government. In my opinion the municipal government should not go around begging for handouts from the private sector . . . and make sure that you write in your study that what the municipalities need in Mexico is to have endowments.

In 1967 the Chambers of Commerce of the state presented a third variation, suggesting less economic centralism on the part of the state. According to the chambers, the state should authorize the municipalities to collect some of the taxes that the state had been collecting. The chambers proposed that the state should allow the municipalities to tax business firms whose capital ranges up to 50,000 pesos rather than up to only 15,000,[16] claiming that any loss to the state treasury would be compensated for by the efforts the state was then making to improve its system of tax collection.[17]

The governor and even the municipal presidents opposed the proposal of the chambers and agreed that no problems would be solved by taking money away from the state and giving it to the municipalities. The governor added that the state treasury was also depleted. A local newspaper reported his statement:

It is not possible to take away money from one purse to put it in another. And he added that the State had many more obligations than the municipalities . . . indicating that the municipalities were administrators of services while the State carried out the works of construction.[18]

A few weeks later the governor commented that the function of the municipalities was not to carry out public works but rather to provide services. The public works were to be built by the state or the federal government:

The municipalities do not even have a sufficient police force. They do not even have money to pay the electric bills, and they do not seem able to provide the basic public services which are demanded by the people. Then what is the purpose of investing their money in public works which the state can do? The municipalities cannot even obtain loans because they have no credit, the state has to be their surety. Works are distractions for the municipalities and force them to look for more resources and to neglect their services . . . It might be possible to think about a new tax to increase the revenues of the municipalities or about some other system for increasing their income . . . I have not sought new taxes because it is our goal to increase revenues by improving the system of tax collection.[19]

Nevertheless, the Chamber of Commerce, the Centro Patronal, and other groups in the private sector insisted that a thorough reorganization of the municipal fiscal system was necessary before they could overcome the problems confronting them. The upper socioeconomic groups opposed the centralized government policies, claiming that its organization was wasteful and that only a few citizens—those of the industrial and business sectors—contributed to the public treasury. The following newspaper editorial summarizes this point of view:

As could be expected, the suggestion of the Chamber of Commerce to increase the income of the municipalities has provoked many commentaries . . . The problem is that the State has taken over many of the functions which are properly the domain of the municipality . . . a typical example is the case of the urban services of water, drainage, pavement, etc., which have been carried out by the State under not very clear constitutional grounds . . . The suggestion of the Chamber of Commerce is very just. It is high time that the municipalities are restructured. Our state can be a pilot test in this direction for the nation . . . [20]

Since fiscal changes must be approved by the state legislature, which is under the control of the governor, the final disposition of the conflict between the public and private sectors of the community lies entirely with the governor.

In spite of the comments and suggestions from the private sector, the governor not only disregarded the proposal of the chambers but made some changes in opposition to those suggested. For example, instead of allowing the municipality to collect taxes from firms with capital up to 50,000 pesos as suggested by the chambers, for 1968 the governor limited the municipality to taxing firms with capital up to 5,000 pesos rather than up to 15,000 pesos as in 1967. In Ensenada, all signs pointed to increased financial control of the municipality rather than to relaxed control. By the end of 1967 the state had made plans to create a state commission to run the city water system, the largest of the utility services still under the control of the municipality. The policy-making power is held by the governor and, as in many other facets of the Mexican political system, the community groups are given a share in policy-making only through a system of formal and informal consultations.

The tax conflict should be viewed more in terms of politics than in terms of economics. Poverty is imposed on the municipalities by the governor, who through the servile state legislature controls the income laws of the municipalities.

Maintaining the present political system seems to require that the governor control the municipal economies. As will be seen shortly, such control produces higher revenues for the state.

GOVERNMENT ATTEMPTS TO IMPROVE LOCAL GOVERNMENT

The Mexican government has consistently rejected proposals that might reduce its political and economic dominance over municipalities, firmly believing that these controls are necessary to guarantee its continuance in power. Instead, it has been experimenting with methods of its own, for it is aware of the inadequacies of the present system of local government. Two recent attempts suggest that the government is searching for solutions to improve local government with these implicit conditions: (1) The municipal government must be left as it is, without decision-making power and as a patronage system for the lower socioeconomic groups and a mechanism for the political and social integration of the community. (2) The more affluent sector of the community and its money must be incorporated into positions of decision-making through new structures, under some loose but effective government surveillance. The new structures must be eminently apolitical, to reduce the conflict between the private and the public sectors and to restore trust in the political system. *De facto,* the new structures would be the municipal government.

Boards of Moral, Civic, and Material Improvements

The first major attempt to organize apolitical institutions with local decision-making power in Ensenada and throughout Mexico was the organization of the Boards of Moral, Civic, and Material Improvements. The PRI municipal committee described the nature of the boards in one of its bulletins:

It is, therefore, necessary to create an organization *strictly of a private nature* which would count with the support of the government. This organization would allow *all citizens* in the country to participate in the activities of the community . . . [21]

One of the main goals of the boards was to bring the private, affluent sector into community programs:

The harmonious union between the public and private resources will result in the extraordinary progress of the nation and will give the participants the satisfaction of contributing to the welfare of the country ... These previous considerations inspired the President of the Republic [Adolfo Ruíz Cortines] to find the means *to bring together all the dispersed forces of the community,* organizing all citizens who do not have public functions without distinction of sex, creed, or *political beliefs.*[22]

In Ensenada in the middle fifties, as in the rest of Mexico, several boards were established in the city and the rural villages. The boards promoted community services, the improvement and construction of schools, water projects, street repairs, and similar services. They obtained funds from private contributions, bazaars, raffles, small government subsidies, and selling beer without having to pay liquor license fees. A few years after their organization, the boards lost their political autonomy and, consequently, their reason for existing at all. The affluent private sector withdrew the support it had given to them. A local informant explained:

The boards accomplished something, but eventually they became political and they lost their usefulness. What we need are nonpolitical organizations because the Municipal Government is already an institution for giving representation to the different sectors of the Party.[23]

By 1967, only ten of the twenty-eight original boards were still functioning, and most of them were in the rural areas where they were limiting their activities to improving school buildings. During the summer of the same year the governor had to intervene personally to stop several abuses by board leaders.[24] The neighbors in one *ejido* complained about the behavior of the local Board of Moral, Civic, and Material Improvements, and the local press reported:

The complainants were particularly upset because the members of the Board had opened a tavern and were selling beer to obtain funds for the Board. The tavern keeper, president of the Board, had a lucrative business and without anybody knowing what was happening to the money. The worst part of the affair—it was reported by the *ejidatarios*—was the fact that the disguised bar had become the shame of the *ejido.* Drunkards hung around the bar molesting bypassing women and bringing scandal to the village.[25]

In spite of recent efforts to reorganize the boards, it is clear that their original goals were never accomplished. A similar fate has been reported for the boards in Xalapa (state of Veracruz). The study traces the downfall of the boards in Xalapa to the point at which they lost their autonomy to the state:

The development of the Junta [Board] institution in Xalapa is particularly interesting because of its onetime leadership by nonpoliticians as well as for efforts actively to involve the public in its programs ... In recent years succeeding Juntas have become increasingly inactive, and at the same time have lost all decisional autonomy in 1963 ... Thus with the disappearance of an active, politically autonomous Junta, Xalapa lost its only significant traces of participant democracy.[26]

Board of Municipal Collaboration

The organization in 1967 of the Ensenada Board of Municipal Collaboration (Junta de Colaboración Urbana del Municipio de Ensenada) was a new official attempt to give decision-making power to the private sector. This board had been in the drafting stage since 1965, and two years later, the state legislature had rubber-stamped the governor's bill, creating the board in the municipality of Ensenada to function as a pilot project for the entire state. The objectives and nature of this board were functionally the same as those of the Boards of Moral, Civic, and Material Improvements. The method used to attain goals was different, since the new board was not attempting to mobilize directly many persons. Seven distinguished citizens formed the city's single board: five representatives of the local chambers (one for each chamber), one representative of the state government, and one representative of the municipal government. The two government representatives were very well known and highly esteemed persons in the community with little involvement in politics; the apolitical nature of the board was thus guaranteed. The members were selected by the governor after each chamber proposed three candidates.

The president of the board explained its objectives:

The purpose of the Board is to give more continuity to municipal works. In three years municipal administrations do not have time to complete the works they start. Their term is too short. Often the administration leaves things half completed and the new administration begins something else instead of completing previous projects. The Board will also be an organism for consultation by the state, federal, and municipal governments before they begin works in the Municipality. For example, if during the time of the PRONAF this Board had existed, the Board would have opposed the investments of the federal government in the types of works that the PRONAF did. The water problem was much more urgent in the community. In the future, the Board will be a pressure system to have the government do the things which are more important. We do not want to oppose the works of the federal government; they have the money. But we do want the government to take into account the needs of the community.

The politically autonomous nature of the board also became apparent when the Centro Patronal protested because it had no representative on the board. In one of the sessions of the Centro Patronal the problem was discussed: "The Board is formed by representative organizations of the private sector. Therefore, if the Centro Patronal is excluded, many firms would be left without representation on the Board."[27] When the Centro Patronal began to pressure for representation, it was told that the labor federations would also have to be represented if the Centro were granted its demand. The board would then have become merely a replica of the municipal government.

Similar boards have been set up in other Mexican cities and apparently have been successful. Informants frequently referred to Guadalajara (state of Jalisco), Chihuahua (state of Chihuahua), and Hermosillo (state of Sonora) as examples of cases where boards of collaboration have produced positive results. One prominent lawyer commented:

These Boards have achieved excellent results in some cities, in Hermosillo, for example. There the private sector accepted a tax increase under the condition that they themselves would handle the funds. What they wanted was honesty. I am sure that there would be no problem in Ensenada if something like this were to be organized. The Governor has recently established in Ensenada the Board of Municipal Collaboration. The only problem with this Board is that it still has no endowment but rather a promise of 2 million pesos from the Governor . . .

It is too early to assess the results of the Board of Collaboration in Ensenada. One can conjecture that the board's success will depend on how well it is endowed by the government and how well it resists pressures to become political after it receives its endowment. Nevertheless, a general sense of optimism does pervade the business sector of the community. Possibly this very hope helps considerably to reduce the intensity of the conflict between the more affluent sector of the community and the government.

Much credit should be given to the original idea that local government can be improved by creating apolitical local institutions with decision-making power and maintaining at the same time the formal municipal government. One of the most interesting consequences of this dual system is the integrative effect that it has on the community. The lower socioeconomic groups are given a share in the municipal government, and at the same time the more affluent sector of the community is brought into the *de facto* local government.

The obvious question now is: As an alternative way in which to improve local government, would it not be possible, and perhaps easier, to change the PRI process of recruiting municipal functionaries? A more democratic way of recruiting would select better qualified, more capable officers, at the same time recruiting some of them from the lower socioeconomic groups. The answer to this question is simple. The PRI did this in some selected states of the nation, on an experimental basis, in the municipal elections of 1965. Baja California was one of the experimental areas, and the information gathered in this study is valuable in analyzing why the experiment of "internal democratization" of the PRI was a total failure (see Chapter 7). After the experiment, the Mexican government returned to its old system of dispensing offices as political patronage.

The many trial-and-error efforts to improve local government are clear indications of the government's attempts to keep its tight grip on power with the endorsement of the popular vote, and of its awareness that the recruitment process for candidates and public functionaries affects the community unfavorably. In a way, the attempts to improve local government are remedies intended to balance these effects.

PERFORMANCE OF STATE GOVERNMENT

Public Works and Services

On the basis of the previous discussion one might expect that the state is a generous benefactor of the municipality, and that it carries out the local public works needed in the city. This is hardly the case. The picture that emerges from an analysis of the state's performance in the city is that it does very little besides pay employees (see Table 14, p. 89). The state is responsible for a good share of the educational services, two hospitals, part of the security service, the judicial courts, a tourist office, an office of agriculture, and an office of public works. During the last eight years the state has limited its efforts in public works to the construction of some schools, a large water project that finally had to be completed by the federal government, and a handful of other projects. Table 21 summarizes the data.

TABLE 21
PUBLIC WORKS CARRIED OUT BY THE STATE IN THE
MUNICIPALITY OF ENSENADA, 1959–1967
(in thousands of pesos)

Public Works	Cost Subtotal	Cost Total
Building and repairing urban schools	1,648	
Building and repairing rural schools	807	
Total Schools		2,455
Water and drainage		2,665
Others		219
Construction and maintenance of state offices		127
Total		5,466

Calculated from yearly reports obtained at the Ensenada State Office of Public Works.

From 1959 to 1967 the average yearly investment of the state in public works in the municipality was 607,000 pesos. Many public works are financed only by the state and the money eventually returned to the state coffers by the individual beneficiaries. A policy change regarding state public works has deemphasized school construction and increased financing of public work projects, and since 1963 the state has built no new schools in Ensenada. This change has resulted in a considerable reduction of state investments in the city (Table 22).

TABLE 22
YEARLY STATE EXPENDITURES IN PUBLIC WORKS
IN ENSENADA, 1959–67
(in thousands of pesos)[a]

1959	1,527
1960	597
1961	480
1962	1,394
1963	176
1964	132
1965	147
1966	740
1967	273

[a] The 1962 figure includes the total expenditures for the construction of a water canal work begun in 1959. Its total cost was 1.2 million pesos.
From Ensenada State Office of Public Works.

Table 22 also shows erratic changes in expenditures over the eight years, indicating a lack of long-range planning. Probably the local office in Ensenada has difficulties in adjusting to the variations of expenditures; during some years the local staff may be overloaded, whereas during other years it may be idle.

In the fall of 1967 the state began a large project involving installation of new water pipes in one section of the city. The total estimated cost was four million pesos, to be financed by the state. The money was to be returned through yearly payments by those living in the neighborhood over a five-year to ten-year period, and then to be used to finance new public works. In this sense the state became a public financing agency, obtaining loans for the project from federal and private sources.[28] This system will be used more and more to solve the problems of public works and services in the cities of Baja California. A state bank for public services may be organized in the future along the same lines as the Federal Bank of Public Works and Services. During the summer of 1967 a bill was introduced in the state legislature that sought to find legal means for guaranteeing a high return on public loans and at the same time to outline a public program for investments. What seems clear is that the state will spend less and less of its revenue on public works and will limit itself to financing projects. In a country like Mexico, where capital is indeed very scarce, the service given by the government in financing public works should not be minimized. Perhaps this alternative is better from a political point of view than that of increasing taxation, and it may even prove economically wise in a society where tax evasion is common.

Economic Inputs and Outputs

The state government took fifteen million pesos in tax revenues from Ensenada in 1966.[29] The amount that the federal government returns to the state from the taxes it collects in Ensenada from fishing and harbor activities must be added to this. In 1966 the federal government collected more than five million pesos in fishing taxes in Ensenada, 50 percent of which was given to the state. The state in turn gave half of the amount it received to the municipality.[30] The state also obtains a considerable income from fees and franchises in the city, but these figures were not available. Although it is not possible to make an accurate economic study of inputs and outputs, the information available will give an idea of the political effects produced by the economic dominance of the state.

On the basis of the state payrolls it was estimated that the average annual salary of the state bureaucrats was approximately 24,000 pesos in 1966 and that the state spent a total of 10,872,000 pesos in the municipality for salaries during that year. The average yearly expenditure in public works was added to this amount, and an estimated expenditure for maintenance was calculated from the general expenditures in the state budget. Table 23 presents the estimated expenditures of the state in the municipality.

TABLE 23
ESTIMATED STATE EXPENDITURES IN MUNICIPALITY
OF ENSENADA, 1967
(in thousands of pesos)

Item	Cost
Wages	10,872
Public works	688
Medical general expenses	297
Educational expenses	2,336
General expenses	400
Total	14,593

Calculated from "Ley de Egresos del Estado de Baja California Para el Ejercicio Fiscal de 1967," *Periódico Oficial* (Mexicali), Vol. 74, No. 36.

Political Uses of State Income

It is clear that a large sum, perhaps as much as ten million pesos, is taken from the municipality by the state each year and is not returned. What does the state government do with it? A partial answer to the question can be found by looking into the official state budgets.

The 1967 budget for the state of Baja California totaled 222 million pesos.[31] Two important considerations are the existence of a large bureaucracy in Mexicali and the absence of effective checks on spending. At the state level political patronage is very high. The state legislature spends in salaries and general expenses more than three million pesos per year, but the public finds the state legislature of little use. The public image of a state deputy is an individual who has been "invested" in his job because of political influences. The local newspaper frequently uses cartoons to emphasize the inability of the deputies to represent the people and to legislate effectively; the punch line of one cartoon said, "It is advisable that the State Deputies do not try to reform the laws any more. They should engage themselves in their usual chores: visit bars, go out for walks, pick up their checks, go to receptions or be decorative figures at official acts. In this way, nobody will pay attention to them and they will not make such fools of themselves."[32]

A survey of appropriations in the state budget shows a number of ill-defined entries that are difficult to account for. Vaguely defined appropriations allow mishandling of funds. Thus, under the heading "Personal Expenses of the Governor" there is an appropriation of a quarter-million pesos for "social research," an amount equal to almost half what the state spends on public works in Ensenada. No one outside the small gubernatorial circle can find out whether the research is carried out, and if so, how useful it is to the state. The governor does not have to account for his activities to anybody in the state; he is the supreme ruler there. His basic yearly salary is 120,000 pesos, but the 1967 budget includes three other appropriations for him, expenses of representation, personal expenses, and extraordinary expenses, which total an additional 300,000 pesos. In all, 700,000 pesos are earmarked for the governor, not including 100,000 pesos for maintaining his residence. His secretarial staff is paid more than two and a half million pesos per year in salaries. These expenditures are clearly extravagant when the needs of the municipalities are considered.

Other vague appropriations are the subsidies for groups and associations, to which more than a million pesos is assigned. Again, one cannot tell how much of this money is given away or how the groups to receive the funds are chosen. (It seems likely that a large amount of these subsidies goes for political patronage of labor groups.)

The secrecy surrounding government spending has been pointed out by some observers. It is impossible for the political opposition to voice specific and well-documented protests, which would in any case be of little use because there are no legal mechanisms for processing such protests. The state legislature and the state supreme court are the docile servants of the governor.[33] In this light it is possible to understand why the PRI has guarded zealously the outcome of the gubernatorial and state deputy elections. Any inroads of the opposition into these offices would upset the economic and political system of spoils.

To summarize: one of the important dysfunctional effects of the regime's dominance in the state as seen from the point of view of the provincial city is that the tax money collected by the state is not returned to the city in services but is spent on offices that are sinecures. The few services with which the state provides the city are inadequate and insufficient. State hospitals are overcrowded, court calendars overloaded with cases, and justice is slow. State roads are in poor condition and the quality of education is inferior. The conflict between the more affluent persons of the private sector who pay taxes and the public sector that misappropriates the taxes becomes evident again.

PERFORMANCE OF FEDERAL GOVERNMENT

The welfare and economic development of Ensenada depend on Mexico City. Perhaps one of the most distressing realizations to the local people and local government is that they are powerless to resolve local problems. The federal government exercises total control in all major projects in the city and rural areas, including the harbor, airport, and highways. The most important public works are drawn up, approved, and financed in Mexico City. The 206-million-peso port facilities, the 400-million-peso toll road between Tijuana and Ensenada, the 60-million-peso National Border Program (PRONAF) are all recent works that were designed wholly in Mexico City. The federal government also controls directly or indirectly most aspects of water and drainage services. These projects are carried out at times by federal agencies, at other times by state agencies; in those areas under state supervision, the financing and even the blueprints for the projects come from Mexico City. Most phases of public health, all public sanitation, electrification projects, low income housing programs and school construction, and more than half of the public school teachers are also under the control of the federal government. It has direct control over many of the economic activities of the community, such as the franchising of fishing and harbor activities and the financing of fishing cooperatives, *ejidatarios,* and small farmers through the three federal banks (Fomento Cooperativo, Agrícola, and Ejidal). Also, because of proximity to the United States, import controls by the federal government have a direct impact on many local merchants and producers.

A detailed study of the economic inputs and outputs of the federal government in Ensenada would be extremely useful, since it would help one to assess with greater precision the political conflict between the public sector as represented by the federal government and the private sector. Unfortunately, these data are not available. Tax and licensing revenues collected by the local delegation of the federal Secretary of Finance were considered classified information.[34] Some knowledgeable persons in town indicated that the amount collected by the federal government from the municipality was between forty five and sixty million pesos per year. On the other hand, some of the federal expenditures could not be estimated with any degree of accuracy. For example, the value of free textbooks for grammar school children, which are sent from Mexico City, could not be determined precisely, nor could the value of the thousands of medicines sent from Mexico City to the local health center.

It is even more difficult, if not impossible, to understand the finances of the local branches of the national banks or of the social security services. These involve complex economic problems of public finance and long-range plans for public investments.[35] The economic data obtained are very limited, but within these limitations are valuable for obtaining an insight into the activities of the federal government in the municipality.

Decision-making Process for Infrastructural Works and Federal Investments

It is not known how decisions are made in Mexico in regard to the large infrastructural works, nor why a particular project in one state is given preference over a project in another state when both projects seem to be of equal importance. The following information was gathered from knowledgeable local individuals and from study of several cases.

1. The governor is the key messenger and representative of the people of his state before the federal government. The state senators and deputies in the national congress do not have representative functions before the Federal Executive. The governor makes several trips to Mexico City every year, and he meets at least once with the President of the nation and several times with the Secretary of the Interior, or with other secretaries and subsecretaries, as well as with the directors of federal agencies and commissions.

2. In order to be successful the governor must be politically a *persona grata* and economically must present a façade of responsibility and sound judgment. Personal contacts *(padrinos políticos)* are extremely useful to the governor in obtaining his requests. The decision-making mechanism in Mexico City is extraordinarily personal.

3. Each federal secretary and agency is very independent and operates

under its own assigned budget. One agency may favor a project in one region, while another may prefer to invest somewhere else. From the local level one can see no sign of coordination at the federal level, a fact that may have serious consequences in a centralized economy. Thus, while the Federal Commission of Tollways was investing 400 million pesos in the Tijuana-Ensenada toll road, the mayor of Ensenada was declaring that the city did not have adequate hotels to accommodate the expected increase in the number of tourists. The Federal Tourist Office made no study of the situation, and the PRONAF Interdepartmental Commission began to build a luxury hotel on the outskirts of the city, which was unrelated to the basic needs of the town as a tourist center. At the same time, private investors knew that the lack of water was the main difficulty in transforming Ensenada into an attractive site for the American tourist, a problem that could be solved only by the Secretary of Water Resources.

4. At times the governor is assisted in obtaining federal funds and projects by important private financiers who have economic interests in the city but reside in Mexico City. For example, General José Clark, an estate developer in Ensenada and Tijuana and the major shareholder in Ensenada's cement plant, obtained the contract for construction of the port facilities; it can be assumed that he would use his influential contacts in Mexico City to see that the construction of the port facilities was not in any way interrupted.

5. In Baja California the municipal presidents meet with the governor frequently, perhaps more than once a month, in both formal and informal gatherings. The municipal presidents brief the governor on the most urgent needs of their respective municipalities, and in some cases the governor sends them to Mexico City to transact small matters with subsecretaries. When the federal secretaries and subsecretaries visit the state—in general, some of them do so two or three times a year—the governor, local authorities, and members of the private sector take advantage of the visit to make known the needs of the state and municipalities.

6. The decisions made in Mexico City frequently take into account economic profits to be had from a contemplated investment. These decisions can be made independently by each secretariat or agency, which will operate in those areas where it can obtain the highest profit. In this sense the federal commissions and agencies are moved by the same principles that motivate the private sector. The nationalization of some industries in the Mexican economy has resulted in unfair competition for the private sector. It is naïve to believe that the federal government nationalizes industries only when the private sector is unwilling or unable to carry on in the best interests of the nation; the government takes over an industry if it sees an opportunity to make a good profit and if the nationalization is not expected to create great

opposition in the private sector. During the summer of 1967, the Bank of Fomento Cooperativo bought most of the largest fish canneries in the municipality of Ensenada and a few others in different areas of the country, all owned by the heirs of former President of Mexico General Abelardo Rodríguez. The total price paid by the bank was 500 million pesos. The fishing industry had been controlled by foreigners, mostly Spaniards, and by the industrial complex of Antonio Sacristán, a Spanish immigrant.[36] In 1960 the government had forced the Sacristán group to undersell its interests, and the Matancitas cannery in Baja California with a capital of forty million pesos was bought by Abelardo Rodríguez for eight million pesos.[37] It was sold subsequently by Rodríguez to the federal bank at a good profit. With the last acquisitions the government has virtually total control of the fishing and canning industries in Baja California, a very profitable industry (see Chapter 1, Table 3).

7. At times investment decisions are made in Mexico City for political reasons. A governor may indicate to the Federal Executive that some group is dissatisfied; according to Raymond Vernon the Federal Executive is responsive to some of these demands, since it knows that popular support during elections is generated by satisfying the wants and needs of the electorate.[38] Some economically unwise demands are satisfied nevertheless. Other demands for needed services that produce no immediate economic profit for the government, but that may produce political support by the large lower classes, may also be met.

Public Works and Services

The federal government is responsible for the largest share of educational and health services. In recent years it has built most of the new schools in the municipality through the CAPFCE agency, and teachers paid by the federal government staff more than half of the schools. Through the IMSS, the ISSSTE, and the Health Center, the national government provides most of the medical and sanitation services for the city, and is also responsible for the construction of low-income housing, although up to this point the number of units that have been built is negligible. The housing is financed by the National Bank of Public Works and Services and administered by the National Institute of Housing (INV). The bank is planning to add 125 units to the 100 units already completed, at a total cost of 10 million pesos. The price of each unit will be 80,000 pesos, to be paid in fifteen years at 9 percent interest. It is clear that these housing projects are not designed for the proletariat but rather for the upper lower and middle classes. The national government also

assumes the cost of repairing and maintaining all paved roads in the municipality.

In addition to works on the infrastructure, the federal government carries
out a considerable number of public works. The chief agency for public
works is the Federal Board of Material Improvements (Junta Federal de
Mejoras Materiales), an office that is dependent on the Secretary of the
National Patrimony. The board receives 3 percent of the duties collected at
the local custom house and a variable subsidy from Mexico City. It was
originally established to carry out works involving the preservation of the
natural resources of the nation, but at present it spends an average of
1,775,000 pesos per year in public works in Ensenada, an amount almost
three times that which the state spends on public works in the city. Table 24
presents the expenditures of the board from 1960 to 1967. The board finances public works in a manner similar to that of the state government,
advancing money for projects and receiving payment on its investment after
completion of the projects.

TABLE 24
EXPENDITURES FOR PUBLIC WORKS BY FEDERAL BOARD
OF MATERIAL IMPROVEMENTS OF ENSENADA, 1960—67
(in thousands of pesos)

Item	Expense
Water works	5,943
Street paving	5,418
Street lighting	1,066
Others	453
Total	12,880

Calculated from yearly reports obtained from the Ensenada Federal Board of Material
Improvements.

Since the board receives annually 3 percent of the taxes collected at the
local custom house, and since a large part of the money it spends on public
works is returned by those who benefit directly from the works, it might be
expected to have an ever-increasing endowment. This is not the case, although
what happens to the money is not clear. Some may disappear because of graft
and some simply never be returned by the people. This board is one of the
prime examples of misuse of money channeled through the federal government, and it serves to multiply the amount of bureaucratic activity involved
in public work projects. The municipality maintains an office of public works
with sixty-seven employees and no money. There is a state office of public
works, which also has few resources. It might be asked why the federal
government does not return its 3 percent to one of those local offices. The
answer could be that the government at the federal level needs as many

offices as possible to pay all its political debts. The political system is based on a system of patronage, and it is often necessary to increase the number of sinecures even if there is no need for the additional government officials.

A Case Study: Darkness in the Midst of Lights

The following example illustrates the conflict that the system of sinecures creates at the local level, the lack of coordination at the federal level, and the weakness of the municipal government at the local level. The respondent, clearly irate when talking about the topic under discussion, was a prosperous merchant and very critical of the way things are done in the city:

Why should I pay for the installation of the street light posts? None of the neighbors on the street were consulted about it. We were not asked to sign a contract, but the Board of Material Improvements went ahead and made the installations. And now they want us to pay the bill. I have so many feet of street frontage, therefore I have to pay so much. The most amazing thing about all this is that when we (the merchants of the main shopping street) installed the lighting on Ruíz Street through a private contractor, the cost per foot of frontage was half what we are asked to pay now. These people (referring to the government) are a bunch of thieves. Of course, everybody has refused to pay and we cannot be forced to pay, because we did not sign a contract. As a result of this nonsensical situation now we have the most modern lamp posts and the streets are darker than ever because the Board removed the old ones, and refuses to connect the new ones until they are paid for.

Several other citizens commented on the street light problem. Newspaper editorials criticized the government on this point and suggested that the increase in vandalism and robberies in the city was the result of poor street lighting. In 1967 the board continued to install more lamp posts in the city.

In June of the same year the Federal Commission of Electricity (CFE), a decentralized agency, warned the municipality that it would stop the electrical supply unless the accumulated debt of 1.7 million pesos was paid. Although the municipal president explained that his administration was responsible for only half of the debt and that the rest had been inherited from previous administrations, the CFE was not at all interested in who was responsible for the debt, and by the middle of the month it began to disconnect service. The municipality still did not make the payment. The municipal president continued to explain, saying that the bills were very high because the municipality had to pay for lighting the federal zones, such as the harbor, and for lighting all of the federal and state offices. The CFE remained unimpressed, and by the end of the month the streets of the city, with the exception of two small sections on Main Street, were blacked out. The people and the mass media began to criticize the municipal president severely, and editorials pointed to the lack of coordination between government agencies. One headline said: "Amusing. The Board of Material Improvements installs lights and the CFE shuts them off." Two months later the governor intervened, and an agreement was signed between the municipality and the CFE by which the former could pay the debt in monthly installments of 30,000 pesos over a twenty-seven-month period. The CFE required that the state be the surety for the contract.[39] As a result of the conflict between the municipality and the CFE, the town was in darkness at the peak of the tourist season, a coincidence that surely did not help the tourist industry.

A Case Study: How To Bury Millions in the Sand

Perhaps the most impressive example in the history of the city of public mishandling of capital resources was the recent work conducted under the aegis of the Federal Border Towns Program (Programa Nacional Fronterizo, or PRONAF), an interdepartmental agency created during the presidency of López Mateos (1958–64) for the purpose of helping the border towns through industrial planning in urban renewal and economic development programs. Ensenada was included by PRONAF among the border towns, and the projects for Ensenada were perhaps the most extravagant of all. The program called for investing hundreds of millions of pesos to construct a marina town, high-rise hotel complexes, and other such fantasies. The tourist trade in the city was researched only meagerly, and PRONAF economic studies of the municipality did not go beyond analysis of the data available in the national censuses.

The PRONAF works began in 1962. The first step called for renewal of an elegant but defunct casino, which PRONAF planned to use as an exhibition center for Mexican crafts, and a shopping complex in the same area. The PRONAF started to construct a large, expensive hotel on the beach as part of the marina town. Two years later the skeleton of the hotel had been completed, at a cost of 40 million pesos; it was estimated that another 40 million pesos would be needed to complete the building. In 1964 the new president, Díaz Ordaz, cut back the expensive PRONAF projects, and the Ensenada works were stopped. In 1967 the hotel project was abandoned; within a few months the shell was deteriorating and the buildings were half buried by drifting sand. Renewal of the old casino was never completed, and the surrounding grounds were worse than before.

In the summer of 1967, several private groups, among them the chambers and the Centro Patronal, wrote a letter of protest to the President of the nation in which they complained about the "destruction works" made by the PRONAF.[40] Public opinion was very critical of the misuse of public money.

The unions resented the sudden stoppage of work, which had left hundreds of construction workers jobless. The criticism was summarized by the director of one of the local high schools:

There is another type of stupid public works, and these are those whose cost is miscalculated. I imagine that this is the case of the works here in Ensenada of Punta Estero. After investing more than 40 million pesos it seems that the PRONAF will abandon the construction at the halfway mark, and together it will abandon the taxes of the people. With that money the problems of urbanization of Ensenada could have easily been solved . . . it is amazing that the very expensive works of water and drainage are left to the municipality, which, as we know, lives in misery . . . On the other hand, when federal works are planned the federation forgets the most urgent needs, the most necessary works, and it goes ahead with the most grandiose projects such as the new customs house, Punta Estero, and the coastal boulevard . . . it is more important to think about paving the streets, about water and electricity . . . Obviously, if we are thinking about attracting tourists, we are not going to bring them to walk on human refuse because the city has no drainage system . . . let us think first in a hierarchical rationalization of our needs.[41]

The lack of coordination and common sense on the part of the federal agencies and secretaries in solving local problems pervades provincial towns, and many cases could be cited to confirm this observation. The problems are acute, since the federal government is responsible for most of the public services in the city.

Building Political Support

In Ensenada, 53.3 percent of all federal employees (See Table 14) are employed in education and health services, which directly benefit the lower income groups of the community. The upper economic groups send their children to private schools, which are mostly church affiliated, and go to private doctors. Another 23.8 percent of the federal employees are engaged in public maintenance and such public works projects as school construction, pipeline installation, and street paving, efforts that are especially appreciated by the lower economic groups. The middle and upper economic groups live in neighborhoods where public services have been provided by estate developers.

This fact is politically important, for the government expects to generate support among the large lower socioeconomic segments of the community by providing services that they badly want. The quality of the services is inferior, for reasons similar to those pointed out during the discussion of the performance of state and municipal governments: the federal government too limits its functions almost entirely to salary payments. The lower economic groups, however, are not very concerned about the quality of the services; they are pleased if their children can go to school, if they receive some medical attention, if they have water piped into their homes for four or five hours at night. The federal government thus can build political support at relatively low cost to itself. For example, in 1965 the IMSS in Ensenada had 8,240 insured persons and 16,910 beneficiaries.[42] The IMSS, in effect, operates as an insurance company. The workers pay 25 percent of the premium, the industry or employer 50 percent, and the government the remaining 25 percent. Yet there is little doubt in the minds of the workers that the IMSS is a government service.

Some economists believe that economic centralization is a prerequisite for national economic planning leading to better resource allocation. Our observations, however, suggest that centralization there has resulted in economic waste produced by the very cause that centralization would be expected to remove: a tremendous proliferation of agencies, commissions, committees, institutes, and organizations operating without much coordination or central planning.[43] The federal government (and to a lesser extent the state and municipal governments) needs the political support of the large, lower economic groups of the community. To guarantee itself a high level of support in elections, the government tries to satisfy some demands at minimal cost to itself and at the expense of the smaller upper economic groups. The support it receives from the lower economic groups permits the government to promote a system of political patronage and sinecures that is harshly criticized by the economically more powerful but less numerous groups.

NOTES

1. Pablo González Casanova has commented at some length on the nature of the centralization, *La Democracia en México* (México, D.F.: Editorial Era, 1965), pp. 32 ff. Between 1900 and 1960 the municipal's percentage share of the public income decreased in Mexico from 12.9 to 2.6. See James W. Wilkie, *The Mexican Revolution: Federal Expenditures and Social Change Since 1910* (Berkeley and Los Angeles: University of California Press, 1967), p. 3. The PAN has constantly attacked the heavy centralization of the Mexican political system and it has pointed out all the evils that result from the centralist policy of the PRI regime. See Partido de Acción Nacional, *Diez Años de México* (México, D.F.: Acción Nacional, 1950), pp. 201 ff, 243 ff.

2. H. Hernández Tirado, "El Municipio," *El Mexicano* (Ensenada), July 21, 1967, p. 2.

3. The formal organization and functions of the municipalities in the state of Baja California were established in the "Ley Orgánica Municipal para el Estado de Baja California," *Periódico Oficial Organo del Gobierno del Estado de Baja California* Vol. 56, No. 3 (Mexicali: December 31, 1953).

4. During the five municipal administrations in Ensenada (1954–68) that have held office since the Territory of Baja California became a state, there has been only one lawyer on the council (1959–62). In the elections on June 2, 1968 the PRI candidate for the municipal presidency won the election. He is a lawyer.

5. Interview with José Prado, Councilman, July 19, 1967.

6. The warden is the protégé of a former municipal president who gave him a job at municipal hall, during which time he made friends with members of the administration of the incoming President; as a consequence he was given the job at the jail. At the same time he was able to obtain a permit for operating a taxicab and also was appointed chief of the Census and Electoral Registration Office.

7. The rate of growth of the population was relatively constant during this period, with a slight decline after 1965.

8. Tesorería Municipal de Ensenada, "Corte de Caja" (Ensenada: December 31, 1966).

9. The law establishes that the municipal council submits a budget proposal every year to the state legislature before November 1; "Ley Orgánica Municipal," op. cit., Art. 10, Sec. 3a.

10. Gobierno del Estado de Baja California, "Ley Orgánica Municipal," op. cit., Art. 21, VI. It is obvious on the basis of these changes that municipal expenditures for education and public lighting were practically nonexistent. These changes occurred with little public knowledge.

11. An accurate account would have to add to the basic salary figure of 288,657 the social security expenses of the unionized employees and some other gratuities.

12. This idea was expressed by former councilman Eugenio Landa, interview, October 23, 1967. The lowest fine is four dollars (almost one dollar higher than the minimum wage). An accused violator has no legal redress and must pay cash when he is fined. If he cannot pay the fine, he must turn in his driver's license, which can be redeemed at the Traffic Office only after payment of the fine. It frequently occurs that a violator has neither cash nor license. In such a case, he is jailed.

13. As will be indicated, the 15,000-peso ceiling was reduced to 5,000 pesos in 1968. These ceilings are determined by the governor every year.

14. *El Mexicano* (Ensenada), August 14, 1967, p. 2.

15. During the first five municipal administrations in Ensenada (1954–68), 29.4 percent of all the chiefs of the municipal offices were members of the labor movement and *ejidatarios*. See Chapter 7, Table 32.

16. According to the state constitution the state congress *(de facto* the governor) approves every year a tax law for each municipality. The 1967 municipal tax laws allowed the municipalities to tax only businesses with declared capital of less than 15,000 pesos. The state taxed businesses with capital of more than 15,000 pesos.

17. Cámara de Comercio de Mexicali, "Boletín de Prensa" (Mexicali: July 18, 1967).

18. *El Mexicano* (Ensenada), July 21, 1967, p. 1.

19. *Ibid.*, August 22, 1967 p. 1.

20. Rafael Martínez Retes, "Inopia Municipal," *El Mexicano* (Ensenada), July 21, 1967, p. 2.

21. Comité Municipal de Ensenada del PRI, "Juntas de Mejoramiento Moral, Cívico y Material. Boletín." (Ensenada: n.d.), p. 1. [My emphasis]

22. *Ibid.*, p. 2. [My emphasis]

23. *Field notes*, November 7, 1967. The boards were more successful in other parts of Mexico. The decision-making power of the boards in Xalapa (Veracruz) has been studied in greater detail by William S. Tuohy; "Institutionalized Revolution in a Mexican City: Political Decision-Making in Xalapa" (Stanford University: unpublished Ph.D. dissertation, 1967), pp. 181 ff.

24. *El Mexicano* (Ensenada), May 9, 1967, p. 1.

25. *Ibid.*, August 13, 1967, pp. 1–2. In some of the villages the boards were the only "store" selling beer.

26. William S. Tuohy, *op. cit.,* pp. 181 ff. Marvin Alisky studied the performance of the boards in Monterrey and Hermosillo in 1964 and, according to his observations, these boards were still successful. His article presents an interesting and brief account of the historical development of the boards in Mexico. See his "Mexico's Special Districts: Municipal Civic Betterment Boards," *Public Affairs Bulletin* (Arizona State University), Vol. 4, No. 2 (1965).

27. Centro Patronal de Ensenada, "Libro de Actas" (Ensenada: meeting minutes of March 28, 1967).

28. For this particular project the state obtained loans from the Federal Bank of Public Works and Services (Banco de Obras y Servicios Públicos). The project will increase the number of households in Ensenada with running water from 6,000 to 10,000. The beneficiaries will be the lower income groups of the community.

29. The exact amount was 15,390,325.33 pesos or 162 per capita. Information provided by the Oficina de Recaudación de Rentas del Estado en Ensenada.

30. Interview with Fernando Lugo, Chief of the Federal Office of Inspección Fiscal de Pesca y Sal, November 27, 1967. The exact amount of taxes for 1966 was 5,187,377.92 pesos.

31. It is not possible to analyze in detail the state budget at this time. It also has to be taken into account that Ensenada benefits from some of the state offices in Mexicali. For instance, the state supreme court and the central labor board see cases on appeal, and some central agencies do a certain amount of planning for Ensenada. Baja California has one of the highest taxes per capita in Mexico. According to Paul Yates Lamartine, *El Desarrollo Regional de México* (México, D.F.: Banco de México, 1962), p. 75, in 1957 the combined municipal and state tax per capita in Baja California was 269 pesos. Baja California was second to Chihuahua, with 322 pesos per capita. In that year the lowest state was Oaxaca, with 20.6 pesos per capita.

32. Bancalari, "Cartones Nuestros," *El Mexicano* (Ensenada), February 22, 1968, p. 2.

33. Members of the state supreme court are appointed by the governor, who also appoints all the judges in the state. These appointments have no tenure and the appointees can be removed at the will of the governor.

34. Interview with Ricardo Betina, subdirector of the local Federal Delegation of Finance (Delegación Federal de Hacienda de Ensenada), June 28, 1967. It is worth noting that secrecy increases with level of government. The information about state revenues in Ensenada was promptly given by the local chief.

35. Interview with Torcuato Sandoval, assistant manager of the Banco de Fomento Cooperativo, September 21, 1967. The respondent commented that during some previous administrations of the local branch there had been times when the yearly balances had shown losses. Other years they had shown profits.

36. Antonio Sacristán, a Spanish refugee banker organized the financial complex Sociedad Mexicana de Crédito Industrial, which by 1962 owned more than 80 large businesses. See Frank Brandenburg, *The Making of Modern Mexico* (Englewood Cliffs, N.J.: Prentice-Hall, 1964), pp. 267 ff.

37. Interview with Lic. José Escudero, former manager of Pesquera Matancitas, July 8, 1967.

38. Raymond Vernon, *The Dilemma of Mexico's Development.* (Cambridge, Mass.: Harvard University Press, 1965), p. 14.

39. Ensenada was not the only city in Baja California with a debt to the CFE. The city of Tecate owed 420,000 pesos and Mexicali 850,000. The governor had to mediate in these two cities, which had also been warned by the CFE. The governor talked to the

national director of the CFE, and agreements similar to the one in Ensenada were reached.

40. Consejo de la Iniciativa Privada de Ensenada, "Expediente" (Ensenada: June 1967).

41. Juan Manuel Cullingford, "Debe Cuidarse Más la Inversión Oficial," *Huella* (Tijuana), March 1967, No. 4, p. 12.

42. Gobierno del Estado de Baja California, *Baja California en Cifras, op. cit.*, p. 41.

43. For an insightful analysis of the political economy of the Mexican government, see Fernando Carmona, "La política económica," and Alfonso Aguilar M. and Fernando Carmona, *México: Riqueza y Miseria* (México, D.F.: Ed. Nuestro Tiempo, S.A., 1967), in particular Chapter 4.

6

Mechanisms of Political Control: The Nature and Roles of the PRI

LOCAL MEMBERSHIP

The nature of the PRI has puzzled many students of the Mexican political system, who generally disagree on its roles. Their disagreements are probably a consequence of the different views that each author has about the Party as a political institution.[1] As has been indicated by Vernon, one finds within the PRI the entire spectrum of ideologies that one would find in a European parliament.[2] A local PRI official affirmed:

Within the Party there are several ideologies. In principle the Party accepts everything from right to left. The question is to compensate the tendencies and as a result to get something in the center. You can have one secretary from the right and one from the left. In a city like Ensenada there are few tendencies. Here we don't have Alemanistas or Cardenistas. You may find some ideological tendencies among schoolteachers, and generally it could be said that the labor workers and the peasants tend towards the left.

Party membership does not have much meaning under these circumstances, and many members belong to the PRI merely because it helps them in their jobs, or to get better jobs. A PAN officer commented, "We know that——was a PAN officer before he came to Ensenada. He sympathizes with us but because of his present job [director of a local newspaper] he has to be a member of the PRI."

In general, the rank and file members of the PRI are what could be called passive Party members. Their names were entered in the Party lists, and they did not object. It costs nothing to be a member of the PRI, entails no obligations, and in some cases may be beneficial. One labor leader captured the spirit of this affiliation when he said, "We all are *voluntarily forced* to be PRI members."

In 1967 the number of PRI members with Party cards in the municipality was 8,500 out of an estimated population of 90,000, or somewhat below 10 percent. Table 25 shows the number of registered voters and the number of those with PRI membership. The overall PRI membership was 20.2 percent of the registered voters. In the rural areas this percentage was considerably higher (31.6 percent), while in the city it was only 15.0 percent. (A higher number of PRI affiliates in the rural areas is common in Mexico.[3])

Table 25 also shows the PRI stronger among males than among females, in both the urban and the rural areas. This is probably in part because fewer women than men are organized in the labor movement.

Affiliation Drives

Those members whose names simply appear on Party lists feel very little sense of identification with the Party. Their affiliations take place through the organized labor movement and organized peasant movement; they are mass affiliations, and most prospective members do not care whether or not they are members. The card is given to them at no cost.

The instructions sent by the PRI national executive committee to its local headquarters indicate that the Party attaches great importance to the number of people officially holding Party cards. The local headquarters in Ensenada sends monthly reports to the regional committee in Mexicali, and one of the items always reported is the number of new cards issued. The local PRI spends a considerable amount of time and money renewing affiliation cards of members. The affiliation drives (campañas de afiliación), which should more properly be called "drives to renew affiliation cards," seem to have become a ritual. The Party prefers to issue new cards to all members when a new president of the national executive committee takes office,[4] and these occasions are also used to recruit new members. The Party began an affiliation drive in Ensenada as in the rest of the country in 1966, when Lauro Ortega assumed the presidency of the national executive. The drive was officially completed within one year, and a special ceremony was conducted at headquarters in which 220 members (the VIPs) were given their cards by the regional president of the Party. The rest of the cards, more than 8,000, were personally given to the members by the local PRI president or one of his representatives. The cost of this to the local Party was in the vicinity of 20,000 pesos, as each card had to carry the individual member's photograph.

Table 26 presents the percentage of PRI members among the registered voters and the percentage of the PRI vote against the total vote in the election for federal deputies on July 2, 1967, by electoral precinct. The Party membership figures represent the total PRI membership in Ensenada as the data were gathered in October after the official closing of the affiliation drive. According to common statistical procedures, the correlation, r, between num-

TABLE 25
REGISTERED VOTERS AND PRI MEMBERSHIP, MUNICIPALITY OF ENSENADA (1967)

Voter Residence	MEN			WOMEN			TOTAL		
	Registered Voters	PRI Affiliated	Percent PRI	Registered Voters	PRI Affiliated	Percent PRI	Registered Voters	PRI Affiliated	Percent PRI
City	14,760	2,686	18.2	13,730	1,572	11.4	28,490	4,258	15.0
Rural	8,594	2,953	34.4	4,785	1,289	27.0	13,379	4,242	31.6
Total	23,354	5,639	24.4	18,515	2,861	15.4	41,869	8,500	20.2

Official figures from the local electoral committee and local PRI headquarters.

TABLE 26

PERCENTAGE OF PRI AFFILIATES AMONG REGISTERED VOTERS AND PERCENTAGE OF PRI VOTES AMONG TOTAL VOTES, ELECTION FOR FEDERAL DEPUTIES, ENSENADA (JULY 2,1967)

Urban Precincts			Rural Precincts		
Precinct Number	Percent PRI Affiliated	Percent PRI Votes	Precinct Number	Percent PRI Affiliated	Percent PRI Votes
1	12.7	72.0	37	52.2	90.0
2	12.8	66.4	38	49.6	78.1
3	13.8	66.6	39	33.7	80.5
4	11.2	80.4	40	12.9	81.9
5	8.9	65.5	41	14.1	75.6
6	10.2	76.1	42	21.2	94.7
7	12.5	71.5	43	53.5	91.4
8	9.8	64.8	44	79.0	96.8
9	18.0	73.1	45	36.9	94.5
10	7.5	70.5	46	32.4	91.9
11	9.5	66.1	47	2.9	92.1
12	29.6	75.0	48	25.1	87.5
13	29.4	68.0	49	50.6	96.2
14	15.6	70.0	50	39.3	85.8
15	26.6	70.1	51	31.5	91.1
16	13.7	68.2	52	87.0	93.8
17	11.3	67.1	53	51.0	95.0
18	9.1	72.5	54	35.7	92.9
19	11.6	60.5	55	–	94.1
20	14.3	71.8	56	–	97.4
21	11.1	70.6	57	1.9	91.6
22	7.9	64.0	58	58.1	81.0
23	21.2	70.3			
24	14.0	62.2			
25	11.4	71.0			
26	15.2	68.2			
27	10.5	54.7			
28	16.0	72.4			
29	13.2	64.5			
30	18.6	68.5			
31	12.5	63.5			
32	9.0	71.1			
33	23.2	74.4			
34	11.6	62.2			
35	16.3	67.5			
36	14.9	65.8			

Official figures from the local electoral committee and local Party.

bers of card holders and electoral returns in the urban precincts was computed to be $r = 0.69$. This value is significant at the 0.05 level. In the rural precincts, $r = 0.24$, which is not significant at the same level. In the city, then, the PRI seems to be rewarded at the electoral tables as a result of its mass affiliation drives. In the rural areas, while poor communication and long distances preclude the Party's carrying out effective mass affiliation drives, at election time the peasants vote overwhelmingly for the PRI, regardless of whether they are officially members of the Party. This fact suggests that the political behavior of rural and urban dwellers is different in the municipality of Ensenada.

Party Finances

Weak party identification is also manifested in the almost total absence of financial contributions to the Party by its members. A study of Party financial reports shows that only the Union of State and Municipal Bureaucrats has made monthly contributions to the Party (five pesos per member), and these contributions are not given voluntarily but are automatically deducted from the pay checks and sent directly to the Party by the state and municipal cashier, per agreement between the Party and the union. The members of the municipal council and a few other municipal officers give voluntary monthly contributions to the Party ranging from twenty-five to seventy-five pesos (two to six dollars). In spite of recent attempts by the national executive committee to collect dues from members, there is not one party member, except for those already mentioned, who gives regular contributions to the Party in Ensenada, including the members of the PRI executive committee.

When money is needed for an extraordinary event, such as when the PRI built its local headquarters in Ensenada or when a presidential candidate or the President of the nation visits the city, an *ad hoc* financial committee is organized. In 1964 when Gustavo Díaz Ordaz visited the city as a presidential candidate, the committee for his reception spent 109,275 pesos for decorating the city, campaign signs, and the reception banquet. The money was donated mostly by businessmen and merchants, many of whom were not party members and some of whom were PAN affiliates or sympathizers.

It is no secret that the local Party depends on the government for its operating expenses. The salaries of the small secretarial staff are paid by the municipality, which also pays for phone service and utilities, a monthly contribution of 4,000 pesos.[5] The day-to-day expenditures of the Party are very small; it owns its headquarters, and its political activities are minimal, except for the elections. Political propaganda for national elections is sent from Mexico City. State and local elections are financed by the candidates themselves. Expenses for other extraordinary political activities are paid by the state, and affiliation drives and party conventions are also state financed.

An insight into the poverty of the local party is given in a CNOP report to the national CNOP executive committee:

It was agreed that we would contact the Municipal President to see whether he could help us with some financial assistance. We are in dire need of the most elementary things: a typewriter, stationery, and have no money to pay the secretaries. This Assembly also agreed to ask you to mediate before the National CNOP Executive Committee to see whether it is possible to send us a small subsidy.[6]

There is no need to elaborate on the fact that the local PRI in Ensenada has no financial resources and that the members do not maintain their party.

LOCAL ORGANIZATION AND ACTIVITIES

Sectional Committees and Party Sectors

The PRI tries to generate grass-roots support through the sectional committees, which are the lower organizational units in the pyramidal structure of the Party. In the municipality in 1965 there were twenty-nine sectional committees in the city and eighteen in the rural areas—one committee for each electoral precinct, with the electoral precincts generally coinciding geographically with neighborhoods. Originally, the sectional committees were intended to carry out the following activities: (1) mediate between neighbors and the municipal authorities for the improvement of public services; (2) indicate to Party authorities the social work projects that are needed in the *colonia*; (3) organize cultural and educational activities; (4) affiliate new members to the Party (for which purpose the committees were subdivided according to street blocks, with a chief, *jefe de manzana*, responsible for affiliation campaigns in each block—in theory, affiliation is a matter of proselytizing, convincing the people of the progressive nature of the Party); (5) represent the Party at the electoral tables.[7]

In 1965 the Ensenada municipal committee sent a memorandum to the regional committee in Mexicali claiming that the sectional committees of the municipality were completely disorganized and inactive and that most of the persons chosen to head them, hurriedly selected in 1965 for the primary elections, were not competent to carry out the political and social goals of the Party.[8]

With very few exceptions, the sectional committees were never well organized or very active. Their single activity was to represent the Party at the electoral tables; the other activities were either not carried out or were performed by the sectors of the Party. Thus, as was indicated, affiliation was accomplished through the sectors, and demand articulation for social and public services was the responsibility of the CNOP in the city and the CNC in the rural areas.

Our observations suggest that the failure of the sectional committees is related in part to competition among the leaders of the Party sectors.[9] Leaders wish to increase the importance of their own sectors by increasing their membership and capitalizing on the welfare services that they provide for their members. This competition is fostered partly by the fact that the leaders have to recruit members from the same lower socioeconomic sector of the community and, partly by the fact that political patronage is distributed through the sectors of the Party. The original structure of the Party—with the sectors—was at first corporate in nature but has now lost most of its original purpose.

Informants reported that the Party sectors are very independent of one another. The three sectors never meet jointly except during unscheduled Party conventions, and each generally resolves its business alone. They consult directly with their regional or national offices rather than with the municipal or regional executive committees. The PRI has a dual organizational power structure (Figure 14); the evidence in Ensenada indicates that this is a source of internal cleavages. The sectors have also weakened the effectiveness of the sectional committees, and as a result the work of proselytizing has been substituted for mass affiliation and this has weakened the sense of identification that the members feel toward the Party.

A Case Study: The Conflict between the Ejido Sánchez Taboada and the CNOP[10]

The town of Maneadero (population 1,375 in 1960) lies a few miles south of the city and is inhabited mostly by members of the very wealthy and progressive *ejido* Rodolfo Sánchez Taboada, which was organized during the presidency of Lázaro Cárdenas. Several hundred farm laborers are hired during the tomato and pepper seasons and, according to some labor leaders, much of the wealth of the *ejidatarios* results from exploitation of these hired hands. (The labor federations would like to unionize those workers but are opposed by the CNC, a fact that points up the conflicting interests of the two sectors of the Party.) According to city officials, the lands of the *ejido* contain the only large underground water source in the vicinity of the city. The water is pumped up and used to irrigate the *ejido* lands. In 1960 an expensive project (estimated cost, six million pesos) was begun to construct a system for exchanging the water disposed of by the city for the *ejido* water. The waste water was to be treated chemically in a plant built for that purpose and then sent to the *ejido* through a canal also built specifically for the purpose.

The works were completed by mid-summer 1967, with the exception of a well in the *ejido*.

The *ejidatarios* had objected to the water exchange; they feared that the city would take too much. They alleged that geological studies showed that the transfer would accelerate seepage of nearby seawater and ruin the *ejido* lands forever. City officials rebutted by saying that the waste water would compensate for the water being pumped out, that the treated water might even be beneficial for agricultural purposes. But the *ejidatarios* made it clear that they would defend their water by every legal and political means. They

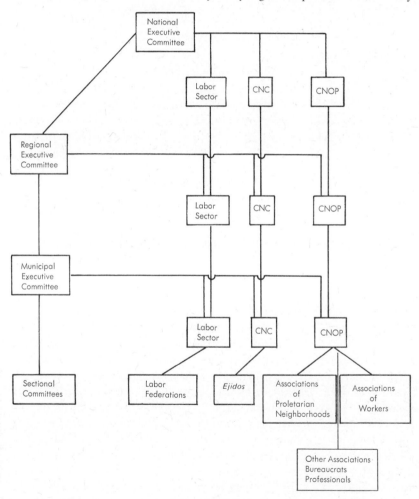

FIGURE 14.
DUAL ORGANIZATIONAL STRUCTURE OF THE PRI

hired a geologist to explore other sources of water for the city and, after a geological survey of several nearby valleys, hired a private company to test drill at the most promising site known as El Gallo.[11] In 1967 they went several times to seek the governor's help, and the governor went twice to inspect progress at the drilling site.

The municipal president (a CNOP member) and the president of the Federal Board of Material Improvements decided to begin drilling a well at the *ejido* without waiting for the results at El Gallo, citing as authority a document that they said had been issued by President Gustavo Díaz Ordaz in 1964 granting permission for the drilling. To circumvent the *ejidatarios* the Board of Material Improvements chose a drilling site along the federal highway, on federal property from which the *ejidatarios* could not evict a federal agency.

This action outraged the *ejidatarios*. They immediately sent wires to the President of the nation, the national CNC, the governor, and several other authorities. Their plea was simple: Why could the municipal authorities not wait for the results of the drills that the *ejido* was financing at El Gallo? At the same time they sponsored full-page ads in the local newspaper, attacking the municipal president and the president of the Board of Material Improvement as ignorant, irresponsible officials, enemies of the poor classes, incapable of understanding the problems of the working people because the two had been born into wealth. The municipal president, afraid that the *ejidatarios* would resort to violence, sent most of the municipal police to the *ejido*. This made the *ejidatarios* even more angry and they continued to attack the municipal president in the newspaper.

In the meantime, the PAN had sent some members to the *ejido* to distribute pamphlets showing sympathy for the case of the *ejidatarios* and capitalizing on the "antirevolutionary" spirit of the municipal president and some of the federal authorities.[12]

The local CNOP leaders sent telegrams supporting the municipal president to the President, the CNOP national executive committee, the governor, and several secretaries. At the same time the CNC staged a massive rally supporting the people of Maneadero, attended by *ejidatarios* from several other *ejidos* as well. The labor sector remained uncommitted during the conflict, but many workers sympathized with the *ejidatarios*.

The following field note reflects the internal conflict in Ensenada's PRI municipal committee:

Juan, one of the leaders from Maneadero, arrived at the PRI headquarters with a document that had been prepared by the *ejidatarios*, a manifestation of support for the cause of the *ejido*. Juan asked the manager of the PRI (*oficial mayor*) to have the document endorsed by the PRI municipal committee and published in the newspaper. The manager read the document and said that it could not be published because it would create many problems.

Juan understood and asked to have the document delivered to the President of the PRI municipal committee. He said that it had been very difficult to keep the people in the *ejido* calm and that the leaders were making an effort to avoid violence because they did not want to give cause for a misunderstanding about the real issue of the *ejido*. The manager commented that the Party could not take a stand because the municipal president was also a member of the PRI and continued to explain that these situations when the two groups fighting were members of the Party was quite common . . . Juan said that he was not very sure of what would happen if the Party did not take a stand because the people were very disappointed; the PAN had begun to support the *ejidatarios*, and the people had begun to comment that the PAN was supporting them more than the PRI. Juan added that it was possible that the PRI would lose the next elections in the *ejido*.

In December a compromise solution came from Mexico City. The federal government ruled to stop the works of the Federal Board of Material Improvements until the drilling at El Gallo showed results. Then if the results at El Gallo were negative, the *ejidatarios* would have to exchange their water; if some water was found at El Gallo, the *ejido* would supply the rest; if the well at El Gallo would produce enough water, the *ejido* water would not be sent to the city. The *ejidatarios* were given six months to complete their exploratory drilling.

In this case the local CNOP and CNC were competing for Party support. The municipal committee's inability to support the *ejidatarios* alienated them and weakened their sense of party identification.

DEMAND ARTICULATION FOR LOWER CLASSES

Students of the PRI have pointed to the dominant position of the CNOP sector of the Party over the CNC and the labor sector. Table 27 shows that the CNOP is numerically the largest sector of the PRI in Ensenada, having 46.6 percent of the total Party affiliation, followed by the CNC with 29.8 percent and labor with 23.5 percent. However, the sectors do not cleave along the occupational structure. There are 513 peasants who are members of the CNOP. They are small farmers who own their own land, and are becoming more and more numerous in Baja California as the irrigation system expands, for the government policy in Baja in recent years has been to distribute and sell land to individuals rather than to organize *ejidos*. Of course, there are also peasants who are members of the CNC; most of these are *ejidatarios*, but a few farm peons are second-class members. There are peasants in the labor sector; members of unions in the agricultural farms. (In fact, the largest union in Ensenada is the Unión de Trabajadores de Olivares Mexicanos, which has five hundred workers laboring on the largest olive plantation in Mexico.) The same analysis can be applied to fishermen. In Chapter 2 it was explained that the CNOP association of workers and the other associations of workers should all be considered as part of the labor movement. Consequently, the three sectors of the Party no longer respectively represent in Ensenada the peasantry, the urban working class, and the white collar and business groups.

Confusion about the sectors is further increased by deviations from procedures in the affiliation of members. For example, wives who are members of the PRI are supposed to affiliate in the same sector as their husbands, but in practice most wives of city labor workers affiliate with the CNOP because they are members of one of the CNOP neighborhood associations (see Table 27). The CNOP has more women than men, whereas the labor sector has 1,731 men and only 270 women, most of whom are themselves laborers in the fishing canneries. The same applies to the youth membership.

TABLE 27
NUMBER OF PRI MEMBERS WITH PARTY CARDS, BY SECTOR[a]
MUNICIPALITY OF ENSENADA (OCTOBER 1966–OCTOBER 1967)

Unit	Men	Women	Total	Percent of Total Membership
City of Ensenada (urban)				
CNOP	1,484	1,393	2,877	33.8
CNC	17	–	17	0.2
Labor	1,185	179	1,364	16.0
Subtotal	2,686	1,572	4,258	50.0
Rest of Municipality (rural)				
CNOP	495	592	1,087	12.8
CNC	1,912	606	2,518	29.6
Labor	546	91	637	7.6
Subtotal	2,953	1,289	4,242	50.0
Total Municipality (urban + rural)				
CNOP	1,979	1,985	3,964	46.6
CNC	1,929	606	2,535	29.8
Labor	1,731	270	2,001	23.5
Total	5,639	2,861	8,500	99.9

[a]Does not include youth members under 21 years of age, under 18 if married. The only sector of the Party with a youth organization was the CNOP with 393 youth members of which 250 were in the city.
Calculated from Party files.

CNOP Sector as Representative of Urban Lower Classes

Contrary to the observations made by some students of the PRI,[13] data gathered in Ensenada show that the CNOP sector there does not represent the middle classes but rather the lower socioeconomic groups of the community. Furthermore, the three sectors of the Party represent only the lower socioeconomic groups and articulate only a few of their demands, demands for public works and welfare services. Table 28 shows the membership composition of the CNOP.

TABLE 28
CNOP MEMBERS IN MUNICIPALITY OF ENSENADA (1967)

Group	Number of Members	Percent of Total Membership
Urban		
Federation of Proletarian Neighborhoods	2,100	52.9
Bureaucrats	481	12.1
Labor associations	258	6.7
Professionals	38	1.0
Rural		
Peasants	513	12.9
Fishermen	574	14.4
Total	3,964	

From official CNOP figures.

The Federation of Proletarian Neighborhoods. The federation is formed by the associations of neighbors in the poor *colonias* of the city and is by far the largest CNOP group. Most association members are women, and the federation articulates their demands for public services, particularly water, electricity, school buildings, transportation, and the legalization of estate property titles.[14] The federation is one way in which the Party exchanges votes for services. During the 1967 general assembly of the federation, the CNOP secretary general said, "The Federation of Proletarian Neighborhoods will continue to be a social organization and will at the same time be a political organization, organized according to the rules of the popular sector." A CNOP report included the following:

We have distributed 1,254 lots size 20 by 30 meters to humble people at the price of 1,200 pesos, 900 pesos and 600 pesos per lot according to location. The *compañeros* have been given six months to pay for their lots. In regard to water, we have been mediating before the authorities to have water installed in several of the proletarian *colonias*. We are confident that our mediation will bring positive results. In regard to electricity we are also mediating to see if some of the *colonias* can be given light. In regard to titles to the land we hope that our work before the state and federal government will be fruit-ful . . . [15]

Some public works, such as water, electricity, and street paving, are financed only by the state or federal government, and the neighbors have to repay the government for the work. In some cases the government or federal agency may demand a down payment from the neighbors before beginning construc-tion. On several occasions the Federation of Proletarian Neighborhoods has been in charge of collecting funds from the people, and there have been frequent accusations of fraud. Legalization of titles and distribution of lots also allow for a great deal of profiteering, which has produced innumerable factions within the Federation and the CNOP, fights among leaders, and the secession of associations of neighbors from the Federation. It has weakened the trust of the neighbors in the Federation. In spite of these problems, the Federation of Proletarian Neighborhoods continues to be a relatively efficient demand articulator for public services, the only one available to the lower classes. The governor and the municipal council seem to be aware of the voting power of the slum dwellers; they promise improvements, and some-times keep their promises.

The bureaucrats. The relationship of the bureaucracy to the PRI was ex-plained in Chapter 4. The unions of bureaucrats refuse to deal with the CNOP regarding their problems. They make their demands through their state or national federations, and the presence of the bureaucrats in the CNOP is nominal. The CNOP leaders have no control over them.

The labor associations. These associations have formed a federation called Agrupaciones Proletarias Liberales de Ensenada (APLE), consisting of self-employed workers, street vendors, street musicians, and other lower income laborers. The APLE uses the Party to articulate the specific demands of its associations, such as franchises and licenses from the government for street vendors; taxi drivers, distilled water distributors, and truck drivers.[16] Their demands generally conflict with those of the labor federations, which have similar associations. The CNOP and the labor federations also clash over membership, since the CNOP wants all self-employed workers to be associ-ated with it rather than with the labor sector. One of the proposals of the CNOP leaders at the Ensenada General Assembly of the PRI was "that the taxi drivers, the street vendors, and in general all the association members of the labor federations should be organized within the CNOP sector of the Party to which they belong as self-employed workers."[17]

Not unfrequently there are conflicts between the CNOP associations and the labor federations. On one occasion, for example, the CNOP organized an association of street musicians composed of several musicians who had been expelled from the CTM. The CTM union wrote a letter of protest to the PRI Municipal Committee complaining about the CNOP action. The letter said:

"You would understand that this would increase the divisions among the street musicians. We members of the union have been fighting for many years to defend the interests of our workers. All these efforts would be destroyed by other enemy groups working under the protection of the brother sector CNOP .... "[18] Clearly the CNOP labor associations are formed by persons who belong to the lower socioeconomic groups and who also could be organized under any of the labor federations.[19]

The professionals. The small CNOP professional group is composed of a few chief bureaucrats, who are affiliated with the Party in hopes of promotion; other professionals, mostly lawyers and engineers, who can profit in their private professions by being affiliated with the Party (the engineers, for example, look for public work construction contracts); some wealthy merchants and managers who hold no professional degrees but who are considered professionals because of their wealth. Some members of this group aspire to municipal office, particularly the municipal presidency. The professionals do not hold meetings, elect officers, or articulate demands. Their demands are articulated through professional associations such as the Lawyers Association, the Association of Architects and Engineers, and the Association of Writers, civil associations that are organized outside the Party.

The CNOP farmers and fishermen. By and large, members of these groups belong to the low socioeconomic sector of the municipality. The farmers do not use the CNOP to articulate their demands. This function is performed for them by nation-wide groups very much like the chambers, for example, the Union of Vegetable Producers in Ensenada, which is federated to other unions throughout the country and uses its national headquarters in Mexico City to present demands to the Federal Executive. The fishermen affiliated with the CNOP are members of the cooperatives, which are also federated nationally. The headquarters of the Federation of Fishing Cooperatives of the Northern West Coast is in Ensenada. This is a powerful group whose demands are articulated through its national headquarters in Mexico City.[20] The secretary general of the CNOP commented that the CNOP had had serious difficulty in affiliating the members of the fishing cooperatives with the CNOP, a problem created by deep personal animosity between the secretary general of the CNOP and the secretary general of the Federation of Fishing Cooperatives.

On the official list of CNOP associations were twenty-two other associations. Some of these groups existed for only a few weeks and then disbanded. The rest were ghost organizations; some permanent, others organized merely on paper by unscrupulous politicians before political campaigns.

The popular sector of the PRI has failed to attract the middle and upper classes. In 1967 the PRI municipal committee held an official gathering to distribute the new affiliation cards to the Party's VIP members. Private white

collar employees, businessmen, merchants, and technicians were conspicuously absent. Of the two hundred selected to be PRI VIP members there
were only sixteen merchants and businessmen, eleven technicians, and seven
private white collar employees. The manager of the Centro Patronal confirmed these observations: "Members of the Centro belong to whatever political party they wish. We as an organization have nothing to do with the PRI,
we simply ignore it. The CNOP sector would be our sector but here in
Ensenada it does not have leadership."[21]

The PRI as a Welfare Agency

In Ensenada the PRI gives considerable importance to welfare work, particularly medical and educational assistance, and home economics classes are
given for the benefit of the lower classes. A reading of the PRI monthly
reports and the minutes of the general assemblies shows the concern of the
PRI for improving the living conditions of the poor people. This is one of its
most important activities. A medical clinic was organized in 1959 and for
several years was very successful. Local doctors gave their services free and
sample medicines were donated by the drug industry. A few months after the
organization of the clinic the PRI reported, "A few months ago we saw the
need to organize a medical clinic for the many indigent persons who have no
means of paying doctors and of buying medicines . . . Until today our doctors
have attended over 11,000 persons and distributed medicines of an approximate value of 100,000 pesos . . ."[22]

In 1967 the PRI organized a free legal office with six lawyers donating an
evening's time apiece each week, but a few months later the service was
discontinued for lack of clients.

These services are sporadic and their success and continuity depend to a
considerable extent on the personal drive of the members of the PRI municipal committee. However, these activities are probably viewed as good-will
gestures, and in turn generate support for the Party.

The local PRI, then, articulates the demands for public and welfare services
of the lower socioeconomic groups of the community. The PRI as a national
political institution also symbolizes the revolutionary forces and legitimizes
(but does not articulate) the demands of the labor movement, the rank and
file bureaucrats, and the peasantry before the federal government.[23]

In assuming these roles through the PRI, the Mexican government frequently finds itself arbitrating conflicting demands from the opposite ends of
the socioeconomic continuum. For example, demands from the labor movement for franchises conflict with demands from the managerial groups to
liberalize commerce and exploit natural resources. The fishing industries op-

pose the franchises given by the government to the fishing cooperatives for the exploitation of some marine species. The Chamber of Commerce constantly protests against the franchises granted by the local government to street vendors of the labor movement. Demands for wage increases, price controls, profit sharing, and social security from the labor movement conflict with demands from the managerial groups organized outside the Party in the Centro Patronal and the chambers.

NOTES

1. Robert E. Scott, *Mexican Government in Transition* (Urbana: University of Illinois Press, 1964), pp. 145 ff, views the PRI as a dominant pragmatic party with the traditional functions of other Western parties, namely, with aggregative functions, with decision-making power, and responsible for the integration of the political system. Frank Brandenburg, *The Making of Modern Mexico* (Englewood Cliffs, N.J.: Prentice-Hall, Inc., 1964), pp. 3 ff. and 142 ff, considers the PRI an instrument of the Federal Executive whose function if any would be electoral. L. Vincent Padgett, *The Mexican Political System* (Boston: Houghton Mifflin Co., 1966), pp. 48 ff, sees the Party as an important political mechanism which facilitates the aggregation of demands. Pablo Gónzalez Casanova, *La Democracia en México* (México, D.F.: Editorial Era, 1965), pp. 115 ff, considers the PRI and the other Mexican parties political instruments manipulated by the real holders of power. He warns students of the Mexican political system that the Mexican political parties should not be studied by the standard data of party membership and electoral results. For him, the Mexican party system is a deviant case as the total Mexican system is very special and unusual in the Western world.

2. Raymond Vernon, *The Dilemma of Mexico's Development* (Cambridge, Mass.: Harvard University Press, 1965), p. 14.

3. Raymond Vernon, *op. cit.,* p. 16, explains this peculiarity as a response of the *ejidatarios* to the "paternalistic and solicitous" attitude of the government toward the *ejidos.*

4. At least this has been the case with the last three presidents of the PRI national executive committee. When Lauro Ortega began an affiliation drive in 1966, the Carlos Madrazo affiliation drive had not even been completed. Soon after Ortega's drive was completed in October 1967 he was removed from office.

5. Comité Municipal del PRI, "Datos del Municipio de Ensenada" (Ensenada: October 27, 1960). The same amount was given by the municipality in 1967.

6. Liga Municipal de Organizaciones Populares, CNOP de Ensenada, "Carta al Secretario General del Comité Ejecutivo Nacional de la CNOP" (Ensenada: June 23, 1963). Financially the sectors of the Party are independent. The municipal subsidy to the PRI in Ensenada is given to the municipal committee.

7. Comité Ejecutivo Regional del PRI, "Circular No. 1" (Mexicali: June 29, 1953).

8. Comité Municipal del PRI de Ensenada, "Memorandum" (Ensenada: October 15, 1965).

9. Observers at the national level have also indicated the existence of deep rivalries and cleavages among leaders of the Party sectors. Philip B. Taylor, Jr. believed it would even be possible that the sectors of the Party would break away and become independent parties. Philip B. Taylor, Jr., "The Mexican Elections of 1958: Affirmation or Authoritarianism?" *Western Political Quarterly,* Vol. 13, September 1960, pp. 722-44.

In an interesting study of political factionalism in a municipality of Puebla, Henry E. Torres-Trueba found that political conflict was in part the result of contrasting value orientations among PRI members. See his "Factionalism in a Mexican Municipio," *Sociologus,* Vol. 19, No. 2, 1969, pp. 134-52. Observations in Ensenada also suggest that factionalism in the PRI is not so much caused by ideological differences as by sociocultural factors. This is an important and little studied aspect of the Mexican political system.

10. The information to illustrate this case was gathered from several interviews and from the local newspaper *El Mexicano.*

11. The site was the property of a wealthy Ensenada family who evicted the construction company. The family filed a writ of *amparo* and the case was brought before the federal circuit court. This court denied the *amparo* on the grounds that the drilling had taken place in a dry river bed that according to the Mexican Constitution was the property of the nation. This action cost the *ejidatarios* time and money.

12. Comité Municipal del PAN de Ensenada, "Manifesto a los Campesinos del Valle de Maneadero" (Ensenada: November 8, 1967).

13. L. Vincent Padgett reports: "Mexican politicians speak of it as the 'organized middle class,' or 'the organized middle class on the march.' Formation of the CNOP marked the beginning of ascending political fortunes and more effective representation in the political system for many interests that had before remained on the periphery of the Revolutionary Coalition. Unlike the peasant and labor organizations, the organized middle sector of the Revolutionary Coalition is not rooted in the traditional issues of 'revolutionary' conflict . . . " *op. cit.,* p. 123. And Robert E. Scott, *op. cit.,* p. 31, indicates that: "One indication that this process leading toward the last step in the transition to a full Western-type political system may already be occurring lies in the composition of, and the role played in the political process by, the so-called Popular sector of the official party. This sector is not composed of functionally, specialized groups, as are the Farm and Labor sectors, but of a central core of government bureaucrats and a large number of heterogeneous associational-type groups such as civic betterment groups, professional groups (medical men, lawyers, engineers, architects) even student and women groups."

14. Interview with Gustavo Fernández, president of the Federation of Proletarian Neighborhoods, May 19, 1967.

15. Liga Municipal de Organizaciones Populares, CNOP de Ensenada, "Informe" (Ensenada: June 27, 1963).

16. The APLE frequently writes letters to the PRI regional committee in Mexicali asking the committee to pressure the municipal president into giving all the permits for street vendors to the APLE. See, for example, Asociaciones Proletarias Liberales de Ensenada, "Oficio" (Ensenada: January 3, 1967).

17. CNOP, Ensenada, "Ponencia a la Asamblea General del PRI" (Ensenada: June 14, 1963).

18. Sindicato de Filarmónicos y Trovadores de Ensenada, Sec. 44, CTM "Oficio 50/00.63" (Ensenada: July 14, 1963). The CNOP also complains about the competition of the labor federations against the CNOP workers: "We would like to indicate that we have had a considerable amount of problems with the CTM labor federation. The CTM has not allowed our *compañeros* street vendors to work peacefully. In this report we would like to make a formal complaint against them." Liga Municipal de Organizaciones Populares, CNOP de Ensenada, "Informe" (Ensenada: July 14, 1963).

19. When the CNOP Association of Small Merchants approached the CROC Federation with the possibility of joining their ranks the CROC leaders consulted the central

executive committee of the confederation in Mexico City. The small merchants had thought that a labor federation would be a better articulator of their demands than the CNOP before the local and state governments. The central executive committee answered with a report. This document emphasized that it was important for the labor movement to approach groups like these. It went on to say that it was of particular importance to cooperate in keeping the prices of basic commodities low. The document added: "The members of the Association of Small Merchants fall within the category of workers and can be affiliated to the CROC. This has been studied in our 15th National Council where it was agreed to fight in order that self-employed workers who live in modest economic conditions be considered subjects of the labor law. Consequently, we do not see any problems in the affiliation of the Association." Comité Ejecutivo Nacional CROC, "Expediente 4-2(3), Oficio 2358./58" (México, D.F.: April 30, 1965). The labor federations are very anxious to expand their membership since, as has been indicated, there is a relation between their size and the rewards they receive from the government. It is indicative that the small merchants approached the largest labor federation in Ensenada.

20. In 1959, for example, the Ensenada fishing cooperatives demanded a seat on the municipal council. The representatives of the cooperatives went directly to Mexico City to present the demand to Lic. Alfonso Corona del Rosal, at that time president of the PRI national executive committee, instead of going to the local CNOP. Their demand was satisfied. Information obtained from Comité Municipal del PRI de Ensenada, "Expediente" (Ensenada: April 7, 1959).

21. Interview with Lic. Gustavo Acevedo, manager of the Centro Patronal, May 30, 1967. The tone of the remarks reminded me of Rossi's comment about the relations of businessmen and politicians in his study of Mediana: "The politician is viewed by the businessman as a pariah." But in Mediana he added " . . . community leaders can have access to those who control the economic institutions of the community." Peter H. Rossi, "The Organizational Structure of an American Community," in Amitai Etzioni, ed., *Complex Organizations: A Sociological Reader* (New York: Holt, Rinehart and Winston, 1966), p. 307. In Ensenada one of the problems was that the government officials did not have effective access to the economic leaders.

22. Comité Municipal del PRI, "Informe de Labores" (Ensenada: January 29, 1960).

23. In the last few years students of Mexican politics have begun to question the meaning of the Mexican Revolution to contemporary Mexican society. According to some writers the Revolution has ceased to exist, for others it has been betrayed, for still others it continues to exercise its influence. For a collection of interesting articles presenting contrasting points of view and arguments, see Stanley R. Ross, ed., *Is the Mexican Revolution Dead?* (New York: Alfred A. Knopf, 1966). Our observations suggest that in Ensenada the symbolic meaning of the Revolution is still very much a reality among slum dwellers, union workers, and bureaucrats. As a symbol it has important effects on the political system.

7
The Political Contest

PERFORMANCE OF THE PRI

Electoral Performance

Study of how successful the PRI has been in gaining the legitimation of its candidates at the polls in Ensenada can be of particular interest, for Baja California is one of the few states in Mexico in which the PRI has encountered considerable opposition from the PAN.

The PAN presented candidates for the first time in Ensenada in the 1958 national elections. This study is limited because the results of the 1958 and 1962 municipal elections could be found neither in Ensenada nor in Mexicali.[1] The analysis of the electoral results is also restricted by the absence of public opinion polls that could help to identify the voters of the two parties by age, sex, religiosity, and socioeconomic and occupational characteristics. The high rates of migration make it difficult to know with any precision the number of eligible voters, and therefore the rate of absenteeism is also unknown. Consequently, the following analysis should be taken as extremely tentative. It may, however, demonstrate the potential usefulness of the study of state electoral results in the Mexican political system.

Table 29 presents electoral results from selected elections in the municipality. The following points emerge.

1. The PRI is much stronger in the rural areas of the municipality than in the city. In the rural areas it has never received less than 73.8 percent of the total vote and it has received as much as 91.3 percent. Conversely, the PAN is much stronger in the city than in the rural areas, and won the gubernatorial and state deputy elections in the city in 1959.[2]

2. With the exception of the elections for senators and federal deputies in

152

1964, a higher percentage of registered voters vote in the rural areas than in the city.[3]

3. There seems to be an increasing tendency among registered voters to abstain from voting, observable equally among the rural and urban voters. Elections for the President of the Republic attract the highest percentage of registered voters to the polls. Increasing absenteeism is observable in the election for federal deputy: In 1961, 70.4 percent of the registered voters voted, in 1964, 67.5 percent, and in 1967, 53.7 percent. However, with the available information one cannot tell whether the number of *eligible* voters abstaining from the polls is also increasing. According to the 1960 census, the number of eligible voters (persons over twenty-one years of age, plus married persons over eighteen) was approximately 28,800.[4] This figure, adjusted to the 1959 and 1961 population, indicates that there were approximately 26,000 eligible voters in 1959 and 32,000 in 1961, suggesting only 43 percent of the eligible voters voted at the turn of the decade. It is possible but not probable that an ever-increasing number of eligible voters have been registering during the decade, in which case absenteeism would not be as serious as has been indicated above. The 1970 census will reveal the percentage of eligible voters who voted in the 1968, 1970, and 1971 elections.

4. The range of voting percentages for the parties in the selected elections is 27.1, with extremes for the PRI of 80.2 (presidential election of 1964) and 53.1 (state deputy elections of 1959). These figures suggest the existence of a considerable number of voters who vote for the person rather than according to the party line. The 1959 gubernatorial election shows an unusually high return for the PAN, 35.7 percent. It is probable that many persons who ordinarily would have voted for the PRI voted for the PAN because of dissatisfaction created by outgoing PRI Governor Braulio Maldonado and because of the imposing personality of the PAN candidate, Lic. Salvador Rosas Magallón, a prominent and highly respected lawyer from Tijuana. On the other hand, Ensenada's PRI candidate for the municipal presidency in the same year was a well-known surgeon while the PAN candidate was a little-known merchant. The PRI candidate obtained 65.1 percent of the vote and the PAN only 22.3. In 1959 some of the same people voted for the PAN gubernatorial candidate and the PRI municipal candidate.[5]

Who were the nearly 5,000 persons who opposed the official Party in the city in the 1967 election? Only a public opinion poll could answer this question with any precision, but in the absence of polls some insight can be gained by the following observation: The percentage of PAN votes in the urban precincts was checked against the socioeconomic rankings of the neighborhoods. The PAN votes were evenly distributed throughout the city and were cast in the slum *colonias* in fairly similar percentages to those cast in the

TABLE 29

ELECTORAL RESULTS IN MUNICIPALITY OF ENSENADA (SELECTED ELECTIONS)

Election	Registered Voters (A)	Total Votes Cast (B)	Percent Voting (B/A)	Percent PRI Votes	Percent PAN Votes	Percent PPS & PARM Votes	Percent Void Votes[a]
1959 Governor							
City	—	9,346	—	42.7	42.9	0.0	14.4
Rural	—	4,543	—	77.2	21.0	0.0	1.7
Total	—	13,889	—	54.0	35.7	0.0	10.3
State Deputy							
City	—	9,312	—	41.5	44.0	0.0	14.5
Rural	—	4,238	—	78.6	19.5	0.0	1.9
Total	—	13,550	—	53.1	36.3	0.0	10.5
Municipal Council							
City	—	7,144	—	54.2	26.9	0.0	18.9
Rural	—	4,220	—	83.5	14.6	0.0	1.9
Total	—	11,364	—	65.1	22.3	0.0	12.6
1961 Federal Deputy							
City	12,833	8,447	65.8	46.4	38.7	1.2	13.7
Rural	6,550	5,202	79.4	73.8	14.1	1.7	10.5
Total	19,383	13,649	70.4	56.8	29.3	1.4	12.5
1964 National President[b]							
City	19,107	15,065	78.8	75.3	25.7	—	—
Rural	8,390	6,650	79.3	91.3	8.7	—	—
Total	27,497	21,715	79.0	80.2	19.8	—	—
Senator I							
City	19,107	12,512	65.5	67.5	32.5	0.0	—
Rural	8,390	5,390	64.2	89.0	11.0	0.0	—
Total	27,497	17,902	65.1	74.0	26.0	0.0	—

Senator II						
City	19,107	13,014	68.1	71.4	28.6	0.0
Rural	8,390	5,709	68.0	91.0	9.0	0.0
Total	27,497	18,723	68.1	77.4	22.6	0.0
Federal Deputy						
City	19,107	13,036	68.2	67.9	30.2	1.8
Rural	8,390	5,533	65.9	88.9	10.0	1.1
Total	27,497	18,569	67.5	74.2	24.2	1.4
1965 Governor						
City	22,100	11,201	50.7	67.2	32.8	0.0
Rural	10,104	5,457	50.4	89.6	10.4	0.0
Total	32,204	16,658	51.8	74.6	25.4	0.0
State Deputy						
City	22,100	10,368	46.9	65.1	34.9	0.0
Rural	10,104	5,034	49.8	89.4	10.6	0.0
Total	32,204	15,402	47.8	73.0	27.0	0.0
Municipal Council						
City	22,100	10,585	47.9	64.6	35.4	0.0
Rural	10,104	5,074	50.2	90.3	9.7	0.0
Total	32,204	15,659	48.6	72.9	27.1	0.0
1967 Federal Deputy						
City	28,490	15,035	52.9	69.5	29.2	2.9
Rural	13,379	7,300	54.6	89.5	8.3	2.1
Total	41,869	22,335	53.7	75.7	22.2	1.9

aAfter 1961 in the "official" electoral returns found in the archives of the PRI in Ensenada the column Void Votes does not appear again.
bIn the presidential election of 1964 the PPS (Partido Popular Socialista) and the PARM (Partido Auténtico de la Revolución Mexicana) endorsed the PRI presidential candidate.
Official figures found at the Ensenada headquarters of the PRI.

upper-class and middle-class neighborhoods. Little else can be drawn from the available information.

The PRI continues to have a comfortable lead at the polls in Ensenada. However, the challenge of the PAN to the official party should be understood in light of the following considerations.

Campaigns

The PRI candidates spend much more money on their campaigns than do the PAN candidates. In 1965 the PRI candidate for the municipal presidency spent about 150,000 pesos, the PAN candidate less than one-tenth of that amount.[6] This is logical; the PAN candidate's chances of being elected are slim, and no candidate wants to make a big investment in a campaign where the odds are so much against him. The position of the PRI candidates is altogether different: In office they will have the opportunity to recoup their campaign investments, with good interest.

The PRI campaigns are more carefully planned than those of the PAN because of the PRI's extensive resources. The municipal campaigns generally begin three months before the election, and during this time the candidates are occupied full-time with the campaign. Gubernatorial and presidential campaigns begin four to six months before the election. Greater resources allow the PRI candidates to travel to every inhabited corner of the municipality.[7]

An examination of the PRI campaign schedules and the diaries of several campaigns indicates that campaigning is intended to increase mass support for the candidates and to provide the populace with a channel for communicating some of its demands. Table 30 shows the number of public appearances of the PRI candidate for municipal presidency in 1962.

But why does the PRI carry out such heavy campaigns, when it has almost certain victory at the polls and also has, when necessary, the means to rig the election outcome through control of the Electoral Commission? First, PRI national candidates have always toured the country extensively, visiting even far-off villages and towns, a policy institutionalized in the Mexican political system since Cárdenas. The regime wants to give the Mexican political system democratic appearances, and democratic electoral contests require candidates who go to the people to gain support and votes. The national policy is followed by local candidates. Second, the PRI uses the campaigns to distribute propaganda about the regime and to indoctrinate the masses with the idea that the regime is the legitimate heir of the Mexican Revolution. The Mexican political calendar has elections almost every year.[8] The campaigns offer a channel for frequent propaganda, legitimized by the democratic appearances of the elections, thus avoiding a "Big Brother" image for the government. The

TABLE 30
NUMBER OF PUBLIC APPEARANCES OF THE PRI CANDIDATE
FOR MUNICIPAL PRESIDENCY OF ENSENADA
(MAY 12–AUGUST 5, 1962)

Urban visits to:	Number
Labor unions	57
Neighborhoods	17
Social clubs and chambers	9
Other groups and organizations	14
Mass rallies	4
Civic acts	3
Rural visits to:	
Ejidos	17
Rural villages	16
New agricultural centers	14
(Nuevos Centros de Población Agrícola, NCPA*)*	
Rural colonias	3
Rural associations	2
Indian communities	2

Calculated from Partido Revolucionario Institucional "Diario de Campaña. Discursos y Actas" (Ensenada: 1962), manuscript.

elections give the PRI a legitimate opportunity to go almost every year to labor union meetings, *ejidos,* and other groups, an inexpensive system of propaganda for the Party since the candidates pay their own expenses. Third, elections are seriously contested by the PAN in Ensenada and the rest of Baja California. If the PRI did not carry out a well-organized, heavy campaign, its lead at the polls would be reduced dangerously. Finally, elaborate campaigns afford many people the opportunity to participate in the political process and to gain political experience, a goal that under certain limits and controls the PRI seems to be honestly interested in carrying out.

The PAN campaigns stand in stark contrast to the magnitude of the PRI activities. The PAN candidates, for example, spent only four days visiting the rural areas in the 1965 municipal campaign;[9] it is no surprise that the PAN has so little support in the rural areas. The PAN campaigns are poorly organized not only because of insufficient funds but also because of the shortage of candidates. One PAN official commented on the difficulty of finding candidates, "This is a very grave problem for the party," and added, "Many times the party has not been able to find the candidates until a couple of days before the closing time for the inscription of candidates with the electoral commission."

Many PAN officials and independent citizens said that affluent members of the community who were also PAN sympathizers and who could afford to pay the expenses of their own campaigns were not willing to be publicly identified with the PAN, fearing reprisals that might damage their businesses. A reliable informant said, "You know——, he is a PAN member and was very active in the Party. Now he is the manager of factory x, and has to stay out of politics. His job is of great responsibility, it is a big business and his active political stand for the PAN could create serious problems for the firm." Obviously the PRI businessmen do not have these problems.

When PAN leaders were asked why the many important citizens of the community who were PAN sympathizers could not form a common front to avoid reprisals, they answered that it was impossible, that nobody was that interested in politics.

The PRI also has the complete backing and support of the local press and mass media. The government controls the press through paper quotas and radio and television through the issuing of operating permits. In fact, the four radio stations are owned by PRI politicians. Consequently, the PRI candidates make front-page headlines almost every day during the campaigns; the PAN candidates may be given side references every other week.

The PRI has control of the state and local electoral commissions. The presidents of the commissions and the presidents of all the electoral precincts are trusted PRI members. The PAN consistently complains about this situation, to no avail,[10] and PRI members enjoy relating the many tricks used to cheat at the polls. There is little doubt that the PAN is the underdog party in Ensenada.

ROLE OF THE PAN

How, under these unfavorable circumstances, does the PAN frequently obtain between 30 and 35 percent of the returns in the urban precincts? The answer to this question is not simple.

Perhaps, as several PAN members advanced, the proximity of Baja California to the United States exposes the inhabitants to the United States two-party system and influences the political behavior of the people of Baja, who in increasing numbers find it difficult to reconcile democracy with the existence of one dominant party.

High PAN returns can also be explained by the following hypothesis. The urban population of Baja and Ensenada occupies a privileged position in the Mexican socioeconomic structure. The urban dwellers are more enlightened political subjects because of their relative wealth, and they can become dissatisfied more easily with the recruitment system of the official party and with the spoils system. Their resentment toward the government is further increased by corruption and inefficiency in the public sector. At the same time, an increasing number of voters needs less and less the welfare services that the Party can offer to win their votes.[11] They either abstain from voting or vote for the PAN in order to show their dissatisfaction with the government and its official party. For example, PAN leaders in Ensenada were aware that those who voted for the PAN in 1967 were in reality voting against the PRI. During a weekly session at PAN headquarters, one of the main speakers commented on the recent victory of the PAN in the municipal elections in the city of Hermosillo (state of Sonora), "It is clear that the PAN did not win in Sonora—the PRI lost there."

Several things suggest that the PAN's role is that of recipient of the votes of the dissatisfied. The PAN platform in Ensenada consists of negative criticisms of the PRI and of promises similar to those of the PRI.[12] Criticism is directed particularly at the alleged corruption in government, the absence of democratic forms in the PRI, and the fraudulent behavior of the electoral commission under the control of the government. The PAN also advocates more municipal autonomy; as has been indicated, there is already general agreement in the community that something has to be done to improve local government.[13]

There are no other noticeable ideological differences between the PRI and the PAN, at least not as the two parties represent themselves to the Ensenada voter.[14] The local PAN conspicuously avoids any reference to religious issues, and even PAN propaganda from Mexico City omits reference to religion.[15] The PAN criticism of Article 3 of the constitution has little significance. *De facto*, there is educational freedom in the city, with four large religious schools, where, incidentally, children of the upper classes—children of PRI and PAN members, Sinarquistas, Masons, and Knights of Columbus—are educated.

The PAN leaders insist that the Party has no relation with the small group of Sinarquistas in Ensenada, and some of the more church-oriented members of the PAN favor the separation of Church and State. Many PRI leaders themselves agree that the religious issue has been overcome in Mexican politics. Consequently it is unlikely that the PAN draws partisans for religious considerations. Ensenada is a very secular community and it is difficult to believe that many voters there would vote for the PAN for religious reasons, as they might in more religious regions of Mexico such as Guadalajara, Puebla, or Monterrey.

There are other similarities between the two parties. PAN members, like PRI members, will not support their party with regular fees. (The PAN does receive contributions from wealthy sympathizers during campaigns.) The ideological range of the PAN is broad, as is that of the PRI, with both right-wing and left-leaning members. Incumbent PAN officers in Ensenada

were moderate and did not lean toward the right. Referring to a former
leader, the incumbent PAN president commented, "We don't want to see
— —too much around here—he is too extremist [right]." The PAN uses the
political tactics of the PRI. During several of their weekly sessions, PAN
members discussed ways to organize welfare services and thereby generate
political support from the lower classes: a medical clinic, literacy courses for
adults, a small reading room, and so forth. The local president of the PAN
municipal committee commented, "Our problem is that we don't have
money. We are planning now to begin a medical clinic. For the PRI it is very
easy, they get the money from the government. If we could have the money
that the PRI has, we would do the same, probably more and better."

The PAN also appeals to the lower socioeconomic classes of the community, and approximately one-third of the members of the PAN municipal
committee are blue collar workers. Table 31 shows that the occupational
composition of the PRI and PAN municipal committees is not very different.

TABLE 31
OCCUPATIONAL COMPOSITION OF OCCUPANTS OF THE FOUR MOST
IMPORTANT OFFICES, PRI AND PAN MUNICIPAL COMMITTEES[a]

Officeholders	PRI (1953—68)	PAN (1958—68)[b]
Professionals	4	0
Semiprofessionals	4	1
Businessmen and merchants	12	11
White collar	3	2
Military	1	0
Workers	12	6
Total	36	20

[a]The PRI offices selected were: President, Secretary General, CNOP Secretary
General, and Treasurer. The PAN offices were: President, Secretary of Organization,
Secretary of Propaganda, and Treasurer.
[b]The first PAN municipal committee in Ensenada was organized in 1958.

The most noticeable difference is the presence of professionals and semipro-
fessionals (generally schoolteachers) in the PRI and a larger percentage of
merchants and small business owners in the PAN. These differences are understandable. Many professionals work in the bureaucracy and expect to use the
party for promotion and other benefits. On the other hand, the small private
business owners and merchants are generally those members of the community who pay the most taxes in relation to the benefits they obtain from
the government, and, consequently, they oppose it.

The PRI naturally regards the opposition party in Ensenada and Baja
California with increasing concern as the municipality becomes more urban.

The popularity of the PAN signals that the PRI's role of exchanging welfare services for votes and of legitimizing the demands of organized labor is not producing the expected returns in the affluent urban centers of Baja California. The PRI has reacted to the pressures of the opposition by searching for new avenues to attract voters. One such attempt was an experiment to liberalize the recruitment process of its candidates for public office. But it was beyond the power of the PRI to reduce bureaucratic corruption and patronage; only the Federal Executive could attempt to do so.

PRI MUNICIPAL PRIMARY, 1965

Baja California was selected as one of several states for a PRI pilot project to democratize the system of electing party candidates. Under the leadership of Lic. Carlos Madrazo, newly appointed president of the national executive committee of the PRI, the experiment allowed selection of PRI candidates for municipal council by direct popular vote.

The primary election was a novelty in Mexico. Procedures for it were explained by circulars sent from Mexico City to the regional committee in Mexicali and from there to the local party. The electoral tables were to be supervised by a representative of the national executive committee, a representative of the local PRI municipal committee, and three other representatives, one from each sector of the Party. Only Party members could vote in the primary, and members were to be identified by Party credentials. The instructions stated that eligible voters had to be Party members and register before voting but that registration could be done at the electoral tables immediately before voting.[16] This part of the instructions was confusing, and the regional CNOP committee sent its own instructions to the local CNOP committees, clarifying the instructions by saying that persons could also join the Party at the electoral tables.[17] Obviously, the CNOP was the sector that could profit most from this direction; the CNOP had the largest number of possible joiners, while the labor sector had been affiliated to the Party through mass affiliations and the CNC was numerically smaller.

Each sector of the Party was allowed to register a slate of three candidates only for the six offices of municipal councilmen. The candidates for the municipal presidency entered the primary contest without *official* endorsement from the sectors. Each voter was given two ballots, one with the names of the candidates for municipal president, one with the nine names proposed by the three sectors for councilmen, identified on the ballots by sector "to help the voter in making his choice."

Three candidates entered the contest for the municipal presidency. They were very wealthy members of the upper class (this time they might have to pay the costs of two campaigns). Two were lawyers and public notaries,[18] the third a high school teacher and superintendent of the federal school system in Ensenada who also owned one of the radio stations in the city. The candidates were well known in the community and were members of the exclusive Rotary and Lions clubs. Two were also members of the Masonic lodges and were Shriners. One had been president of the PRI municipal committee for two years, another was the incumbent president, had built the local Party headquarters during his tenure, and had been secretary general of the CNOP for several years. The third candidate had not held any important offices in the local party, but had powerful *padrinos* in Mexico City.

In Ensenada there was general confusion concerning the primary. The leaders of the labor groups and political organizations did not know how to go about selecting a candidate for the municipal presidency. They had been accustomed to endorsing the PRI candidate officially on behalf of their groups, and had never had a problem in doing this because there was only one Party candidate. Now these organizations, accustomed to backing the candidate corporately, did not consider allowing their members to make their own choices. The voting procedures seemed also to foster divisions along the lines of the Party sectors. It was necessary for the organizations to select one candidate and see what kind of rewards he could provide in exchange for their support, but it was equally important to choose the candidate with the best chance of winning. The problem was how to choose among the three candidates.

The increasing confusion in the state prompted Lic. Carlos Madrazo to visit Baja California and meet with groups and organizations to explain the nature of the primary. The state CROC Confederation reported to its national executive committee after Madrazo visited Baja California's federations:

The visit of Lic. Carlos Madrazo had been very useful because the novelty of the election had confused many CROC members. Prior to the visit it had become clear that some *compañeros* had acquired political ties with some persons who pretended to be pre-candidates. The CROC was trying to unify its people behind one candidate. During the visit of Lic. Carlos Madrazo it was clearly explained that the PRI National Executive Committee did not wish to impose its will in the selection of the candidates in the primary, and that *this function was left to the local organizations. They should select the best candidates for the offices of popular elections.*[19]

One week after the visit the CNOP regional committee sent instructions to the local CNOP committees asking members and their relatives to vote for the municipal council *(regidores)* candidates proposed by the CNOP. The instructions read, "As members of the CNOP sector and true *cenopistas* we have the ineludible duty to make sure that our *compañeros,* in the CNOP obtain an overwhelming victory at the primary and also at the constitutional elections."[20] At the same time the Ensenada CNOP officially endorsed one of the three candidates for the municipal presidency. The CNOP controls only the Federation of Proletarian Neighborhoods, which is numerically a large organization (2,100 members in 1967). Some leaders in the slum *colonias* were promised employment in the City Hall. The leaders began to work zealously in the *colonias* to win supporters for their candidate. (Incidentally, this candidate won the election and kept the promises.)

The CROC Federation, representing 2,600 workers, convened a special session to discuss which candidate it should endorse. All but two of the federation unions agreed to support the candidate proposed by the federation leaders, and in a final vote the dissenting unions decided for the sake of unity to join the others, so that the CROC unanimously endorsed one of the candidates. The minutes of this session reflect the importance that the federation attached to collective support of the candidate: "The Secretary General said that we should be united, and that now that the Federation has taken the decision to back one of the candidates the important thing is to win and to defend the candidates of the Federation *whoever they are as far as they are our candidates.* "[21]

The candidate chosen by the CROC was not the same one selected by the CNOP, and the two numerically powerful groups were confronting each other. The primary was splitting the local party and creating deep animosity among candidates and followers. The candidates were promising rewards to their followers and at the same time creating fear among the other candidates' followers that if they should lose they would be excluded from jobs in the municipal administration. The three candidates spent considerable amounts of money and time campaigning. One of the losing candidates commented, "I spent 50,000 pesos on the campaign and I was told that I had not spent enough. One of the other candidates spent much more than I, but he also lost."

April 11 was the day of the primary election. By the end of the day two candidates had claimed victory, but *officially* the CNOP candidate had won.[22] The third candidate and his followers complained that one of the other candidates had deceived the voters by broadcasting on the radio during the day that the third candidate had withdrawn from the election. The Party secretary reported that he had been an eyewitness to electoral fraud, that even children had been allowed to vote in the slum *colonias,* and that there was little doubt that some ballot boxes from the rural areas had been opened before arriving in Ensenada and that the votes had been changed. Many people in the city believed that the elections had been fixed in Mexico City. The candidate endorsed by the CROC claimed that he had won the election and the CROC leaders, with many other people in town, declared that the election had been irregular. The CROC wrote a letter to the PRI national executive via the CROC national executive, expressing their grievances and saying that their members, along with many other people, were expressing with great alarm their disapproval of the way the elections had been conducted:

According to our people, the local PRI bureaucrats have forced the elections favoring candiate X. The CROC members affirm that in all truth candidate Y received more votes, and that his opponents in an incredible manner voided precinct 42 which corresponds to the region of El Rosario. This was done without any reason or explanation.[23]

The CROC national executive forwarded this letter to Madrazo, adding:

The CROC National Executive Committee considers it very important to act cleanly in this first time when a democratic procedure was used for the selection of pre-candidates to municipal offices. Besides it is a matter of justice. It is imperative to begin creating a climate of confidence and a political conscience in order that this very important first step be successful. We beg you to pay attention to the mentioned facts. And if they are true we beg you to revoke the agreement to select candidate X and to decide in favor of Y.[24]

Indeed, the issue at stake was very important for the CROC. Its leaders were seriously concerned that the winner would make reprisals and deprive the federation of the municipal delegations and other offices in the municipal administration that they had traditionally held. In 1959, when some of the CROM leaders had supported a PRI leader running as an independent candidate for the municipal presidency against the Party directives, the CROM had been punished and deprived of its council seat.[25]

The supporters of the claimant organized to present an official denunciation of the election and dispatched a commission to Mexico City. The commission tried unsuccessfully to change the *official* results of the election, presenting evidence of electoral fraud. Madrazo explained to them that one of the unsavory results of the primary system was that only one candidate could be chosen. The CROC leaders went to see Madrazo for the second time, to explain that the CROC Federation "had acted with civic and political maturity" during the election and to ask for guarantees that no reprisals would be made against the federation. The meeting gives one an idea of the problems that the primary created in Ensenada, illustrated by the following CROC document:

The purpose of our visit with Lic. Carlos Madrazo was to let the winner of the primary election amply express guarantees of a fair treatment for our *compañeros* during the forthcoming political campaign and when the candidate reaches the Municipal Presidency. Secondly, it must remain absolutely clear that all resentment and reprisals between the two groups [the winners and the losers] will be erased, and that our *compañeros* will be accepted not as political enemies but as valuable contingents of the Party during the forthcoming campaign. Thirdly, that the people of our organization will be given the opportunity to participate and to have leadership in the campaign. The right to this opportunity is derived from the large number of people our organization represents.[26]

Madrazo had the winner of the Ensenada primary attend the meeting with the CROC leaders, and in their presence Madrazo made him recognize "the full rights of the CROC to participate in the campaign and later on in the municipal administration."[27] After the winner of the primary won the constitutional election and took office, he gave the CROC a token participation in the municipal administration, cut the subsidy that the municipality had traditionally given to the federation, and failed to appoint two CROC members as municipal delegates in the rural towns where the CROC had traditionally held those offices.

After the primary election the unity of the Party in Ensenada was badly damaged. Leaders of various groups resented each other, their differences became more profound and more intense, and the rivalry lasted an unusually long time.[28] The objective of the primary—so the people of Ensenada had been told—had been to create trust and confidence in the PRI by liberalizing the system of electing candidates for public office. It did not accomplish this goal, and it probably produced the opposite result. The 1965 primary had similar effects in Ciudad Juárez,[29] a remarkable coincidence that suggests that the Ensenada event was not unique and that any "democratization" of the Party may require first some important structural modifications.

After this pilot project primaries were not held again in Mexico, and Madrazo was deposed from the presidency of the PRI national executive committee. What Madrazo's intentions had been was questioned by some PRI leaders in Ensenada. As one explained:

The PRI and the government are one and the same thing but the Party is the political machine. The idea of the primaries was good in itself. The problem was that with the system of the primaries the PRI Central Executive Committee reserved for itself the power to give the final acceptance to candidates. By the traditional system of selecting candidates this power has been held by the government. The government realized that the power was being transferred to the machine, and in the final analysis to Madrazo. And the government also realized that in a few years there would be a couple of thousand municipal presidents who would owe their position personally to Madrazo. The government could not accept the shift of power and deposed Madrazo. He was a very skillful politician and he was preparing himself for the National Presidency by achieving political control of the primaries.

The insistence of the Party on using sectors and labor organizations may have been detrimental to the primary. In a relatively affluent setting like Ensenada, the sectors of the Party as they are presently organized could begin to be dysfunctional.

The 1965 primary election could be a useful guide in future attempts to democratize the Party. It also indicates how complex the problem is. Indeed, many changes will have to take place within the Party and many years elapse before the selection of gubernatorial candidates and deputies can be liberalized.

INTEGRATION OF THE COMMUNITY

Thus far, the PAN's challenge to the official party does not seem to have produced deep cleavages in the community. The conflicts between labor and management, the dissatisfaction of the affluent sector of the community with the bureaucratic performance, and the disregard of the businessmen for the politicians have not polarized the community.

Our findings contrast markedly with the report by D'Antonio and Form on Ciudad Juárez (state of Chihuahua), where the authors found "deep-seated cleavages" that prevented cooperation among various sectors of the community. The authors noted that the business community was unable to cooperate with politicians as a group on any single occasion during the seven years covered by their study. Moreover, D'Antonio and Form added that "a large proportion of the business influentials found it impossible to work with the PRI for purely ideological reasons. Out of this split within business a fairly strong PAN organization emerged."[30] It has already been pointed out that in Ensenada the two parties were not found to fight one another merely for reasons of ideology, that both are very pragmatic. In addition, it has been demonstrated that the emergence of the PAN in Ensenada and Baja California is accounted for by the increasing dissatisfaction of the people with their government's performance, and that PAN support comes from all socioeconomic classes.

The polarization found in Ciudad Juárez was explained as being the result of conflicting attempts by business leaders and career politicians to control decision-making. It is difficult to accept this interpretation, because observations in Ensenada and in other cities of Baja California, as well as the findings of other observers of the Mexican political system, suggest that there is little decision-making power at the local level, and the local PRI is clearly not the locus of power at this level. The local PRI is the articulator of only a few demands of the lower socioeconomic groups. Nothing suggests that local businessmen want to control the local PRI, unless for personal reasons: The PRI is one way (but not the only way) by which one may enter the upper ranks of the bureaucracy, and through which one may receive political patronage and offices in the municipal administration.

The six municipal presidents that the municipality has had since 1953 have been prominent businessmen and professional persons. Five were members of the exclusive service clubs, four were high-ranking members of the Masonic lodges and Shriners, and one was a prominent Catholic leader. All were members of other professional, business, and civic associations. On the other hand, only three of them had occupied offices in the local PRI, a clear indication that business leaders have access to positions of local decision-making without having to control the local political machine.

Finally, and contrary to the conclusions made by the students of Ciudad Juárez, the data gathered in this study show that one of the latent functions of the official Party is to facilitate the integration of the community through a system of political brokerage. Before elaborating on this function of the Party, it may be useful to present a case in which conflicting groups were able to overcome their differences and to cooperate in an attempt to obtain benefits for the total community.

A Case Study: Community Fight To Lower Fare on Tijuana-Ensenada Toll Road[3] [1]

A federal decentralized agency, Caminos y Puentes Federales de Ingresos y Servicios Conexos (CPFISC), has a government franchise to build and operate all toll roads, toll bridges, and ferry services in Mexico. When in April of 1967 the CPFISC officially inaugurated the 105.5-kilometer toll road from Tijuana to Ensenada, the agency was already operating 581 kilometers of toll road in Mexico, seventeen bridges, and four ferries. The round-trip fare from Tijuana to Ensenada on the scenic, controlled-access toll road was fixed by the CPFISC at 60 pesos ($4.80 U.S.), a price officially approved by the Secretary of Communication and Transport. The people were dismayed.

Immediately after the highway opened, the Chamber of Tourism convened a general meeting and invited representatives from the other four chambers, the five labor federations, and the Centro Patronal, the secretary generals of the most important unions, the Federation of Fishing Cooperatives, the Association of Commercial Sport Fishing, and various other groups. They agreed to form an *ad hoc* committee to fight the high fare. The labor groups agreed to ask for the support of their organizations across the state, and volunteered to picket the toll gates. On May 4 representatives of the managerial sector went to see the governor in Mexicali, who agreed with their protest and promised to take up the matter with the federal government during his next visit to Mexico City. He did so but was not successful. The members of the *ad hoc* committee continued to search for other channels to exercise influence with the Federal Executive.

On May 11 the Chamber of Tourism organized a public campaign to mobilize local support for the *ad hoc* committee. The Lions Club and the Rotary

Club joined the other groups. The Governor dispatched a state economist to Mexico City, asking him to represent the *ad hoc* committee in the capital and to see what could be done about the toll.

On May 22 several miles of the new road collapsed into the sea due to a geological fault, and the road was closed for several weeks. The repairs were to last several months and were to cost three million pesos. This incident and the several car accidents that had occurred on the road triggered many new criticisms against the CPFISC. The secrecy with which the agency kept the details of the disaster and the fact that the local agency chief refused to disclose the official figures on the number of vehicles using the road exacerbated the Ensenada committee and many other members in the community. During all the public antagonism toward the CPFISC, the agency merely emphasized the fact that the fare had been calculated after taking a consumers' survey and after an estimate of expenditures for maintenance and the amortization of the debt. The toll had been estimated exclusively on an economic basis; the toll was high because construction costs had been high.

In mid June members of the committee representing twenty local groups—most of the important groups of the community, including labor, management, and the municipal, state, and local federal bureaucracy—sent by wire a memorandum to the President of the Republic expressing the profound dissatisfaction in the community with the new road and pointing out that the road was not producing the desired result, bringing more tourists into Ensenada from the United States. This document added that the fare was out of proportion to the minimum wages in the area and that consequently *de facto* discrimination was affecting the labor class, for whom the 60-peso fare was prohibitive.

One month later one of Baja California's senators came from Mexico City to the state and declared that he would use all his contacts in Mexico City to remedy the situation. The Ensenada committee organized a meeting with the senator, the municipal presidents of Ensenada and Tijuana, the secretary generals of several unions, and several business leaders. They agreed to make a survey of toll road use, since the CPFISC still refused to make its figures public. The municipal presidents offered the service of their police forces to carry out the survey at the toll gates in the two cities. A commission was then to be dispatched to Mexico City, where the senator was to make sure that the commission was properly received at the federal offices. The senator offered to pay the commission's expenses.

On July 28, just a few days after the visit of the senator, the Director of Prices of the Secretary of Communication and Transport made a brief stop at the Tijuana airport on his way to Los Angeles and in a press interview made it clear that under no circumstances would the Secretary reduce the toll road fare. He said that the CPFISC was not forcing anybody to use the new road;

that they had received no complaints from tourists; that the old road would always be there for those who did not want to pay the toll, and that the new road had diverted some traffic, thereby making the old road safer than before. (During the 1950–60 decade the old Tijuana-Ensenada road had registered the highest number of fatal accidents in the republic.) The president of the Ensenada Chamber of Tourism retorted that the summer of 1967 had been the first summer in years in which the city's tourist centers had not been filled, and blamed the high toll for this situation. However, when the municipal police surveyed the number of cars using the new road, they discovered to the surprise of everybody except the CPFISC that the number of users was much higher than the local critics had anticipated.

The results of the survey and the uncompromising tone of the director's remarks caused the commission to cancel its planned trip to Mexico City. Although the *ad hoc* committee continued to meet throughout the summer, with the sporadic encouragement of some politicians and organizations, by the end of the summer it was obvious that the community had lost the case. In October the CPFISC released official figures for the first time: During September, 133,534 motor vehicles had used the toll road. The agency itself had anticipated only 118,000. After the agency released these figures the case of the toll road became a dead issue.

Several points emerge. Of particular relevance is the ability shown by the leaders of the community to organize for common action. It is remarkable that the Chamber of Tourism brought together representatives of the managerial and labor sectors with such ease. Labor leaders, business leaders, and municipal and state authorities worked together harmoniously through the *ad hoc* committee during several months, overlooking mutual antagonisms on other fronts. Members of conflicting social classes, members of the frequently opposing private and public sectors, members of the PRI and PAN (although not acting as such), Masons and Catholics were able to meet many times under the same roof, work out common tactics, and plan together for a common cause during a five-month period that included a political election (federal deputies, June 1967).

This is not an isolated occurrence in Ensenada. As has been indicated in previous chapters, labor leaders, business leaders, and representatives of the public sector frequently interact through the mixed commissions, the labor boards of conciliation, informal state consultations, and formal conventions. The interaction between leaders of conflicting social classes takes place also at the PRI headquarters.

The case also confirms observations made in the analysis of previous cases; that is, the federal and state deputies and the municipal councilmen were notorious for their lack of involvement. During the conflict the state legislature was in session, yet the issue was never discussed by the legislators. Only one of the state senators offered to help, and he did not suggest that the case be brought to the national congress for study or investigation but rather offered to use his personal contacts in the federal bureaucracy. The personalistic nature of the Mexican centralized bureaucracy becomes obvious once again. It is not surprising, therefore, that the political parties were never used by the local leaders. The parties' capacity for articulating this type of demand or mediating in these conflicts is minimal. Most members of the local PRI municipal committee were involved at one time or another in the case, not as PRI officials but rather as representatives of the local groups, labor unions, and chambers.

Latent Functions of PRI

In his book *La Democracia en México,* Mexican sociologist González Casanova points out the contradictions that exist in the Mexican political system: that, on the one hand, the framers of the 1917 Mexican constitution incorporated into the political system of the nation political institutions borrowed from the Western tradition, i.e., a bicameral congress, a federal system, political parties, and the three branches of government; that, on the other hand, these institutions have never performed in the Mexican system the functions they perform in the other Western societies that developed them. In other words, Mexico never assimilated these institutions. The country developed a political style of its own, unrelated to the imported forms. Thus the three branches of government have never served as a means of checks and balances; the executive branch has had total dominance over the legislative branch and has exercised a tight surveillance over the judicial branch. The sovereignty of the individual states has been merely symbolic, and the political parties have neither aggregated the demands of the masses nor recruited the political candidates. According to González Casanova, the parties are fronts behind which the real power holders operate.

One need not agree fully with these views to admit that they do present meaningful insights into the realities of the Mexican political system. The question that should be asked is: To what purpose does the regime keep alive the semblance of these dead political institutions?

In part, it does so because it regards the "traditional" institutions as constitutive elements of a democratic society, and keeps them as symbols that in Mexico do not generate democratic behavior but are worth preserving because they allow manipulation of the masses. The symbolic nature of these institutions is apparent in the frequent appeals to the spirit of the Revolution, a myth that continues to be invaluable.

The Ensenada data provide some other insights into the question. It is extremely doubtful that the regime considers the present political system in a transitional stage moving toward the full functioning of the traditional political institutions, as some observers have indicated, or perhaps desired. Our hypothesis regarding why the institutions are retained is as follows. The regime has adapted these institutions to the performance of new functions crucial for the political stability and economic development of the nation. The transformation of the institutions is so profound that attempts to restore them to their original functions would probably be unsuccessful and might even imperil the regime. The failure of the 1965 primary elections suggests how difficult it would be for the Mexican political system to establish a competitive multiparty system. The following comments of a PAN leader are striking and suggest that even the opposition does not seriously expect the "democratization" of the Mexican party system. The respondent said:

At times I think that it is much better if we don't win the elections. As our national leader has told me on several occasions, if we would win we would get into all kinds of trouble. It has to be recognized that the PRI has not done everything wrong. In fact, they have done many things right. We have unity in the country, and this has to be credited to the PRI. Mexico needs strong governments and at times I think that it is better if things continue as they are.

These startling declarations came from the number-one PAN stalwart in the city, a well-known person who had been under house arrest several times for political reasons and the editor of a weekly paper in which he had strongly attacked the PRI and the regime. His paper had been closed down several times in the preceding ten years and was then publishing without an official permit. This attitude supports our previous analysis: The PAN does not perform the functions of a competitive party in a free electoral system, but carries out other important functions—to check on the performance of the official party, and to warn the regime about the degree of popular dissatisfaction, measured by the number of votes the PAN receives. Some writers on the Mexican political system have wrongly interpreted this role of the opposition as indicating that the opposition parties are controlled by the regime.

The PRI performs other latent functions that have contributed to the stability of the political system because they help integrate the society: (1) The cooptation into the PRI of community leaders with different socio-economic backgrounds; (2) interaction among these leaders; (3) the brokerage function that this interaction produces. As a result, the cooperation among opposing social classes is greatly enhanced, and class cleavages are considerably reduced.

Cooptation of labor leaders into Party. In Chapter 2 the recruitment and socialization of labor leaders were described. One fascinating aspect of the Mexican political system is that the PRI has accepted the labor leaders and has ascribed to them a second leadership role, a political role. Significantly, PRI acceptance of the leaders is subsequent to their emergence in the labor federations. The political roles follow the labor roles; consequently, the legitimacy that has been acquired in the first role can easily be transferred to the second one. Following Philip Selznik, this process can be described as *cooptation.*[32]

The mobility that the labor movement provides and the cooptation of upward-mobile workers into the PRI reduces considerably the potential alienation of the most able and articulate workers. Politically, it decreases the potential opposition of those workers who could be most hostile to and effective against the regime. The process of cooptation, of course, also generates some political stability.[33] It can be suggested that the relatively small success of proletarian parties in Mexico is due in part to cooptation.

Table 31 showed that one-third of the most important offices in the PRI municipal committee were given to workers. These coopted labor leaders generally pass from the PRI municipal committee to offices in the municipal administration. Table 32 shows that 28.8 percent of the chiefs of municipal offices were workers. As has been mentioned previously, labor leaders who occupy municipal offices are liaisons between the labor federations and the

TABLE 32
OCCUPATIONAL COMPOSITION OF MUNICIPAL OFFICIALS
AND ADMINISTRATORS, ENSENADA, 1954—68
(percentage)

Occupation	All Offices[a] (N=118)	10 Most Important Offices[b] (N=56)	5 Most Important Offices[c] (N=27)
Professionals	6.8	12.5	14.9
Businessmen and merchants	22.0	32.1	33.3
Schoolteachers	16.1	19.6	18.5
White collar	17.7	23.2	29.6
Military	1.7	3.6	0.0
Workers	28.8	1.8	3.7
Housewives	0.9	0.0	0.0
Vacant offices	5.9	7.1	0.0

[a]There were 23 offices. The office of *oficial mayor* was excluded because it was vacant in four of the five municipal administrations.

[b]The ten most important offices according to knowledgeable informants were: municipal president, *síndico*, secretary, treasurer, tax collector, chief of police, chief of traffic department, chief of water department, chief of public works, and civil registrar.

[c]The five most important offices were: municipal president, secretary, treasurer, chief of traffic department, and chief of public works.

municipal administration, and through its leaders the labor movement articulates some of its demands to City Hall. However, Table 32 also shows that
the percentage of labor leaders occupying high municipal office in the municipality drops from 28.8 to 3.7 when only the five most important offices are
considered, which seems to suggest that the most important offices are reserved for political leaders coopted from the professional and business sectors
of the community, and that the decisional power of the labor leaders in the
municipal administration is symbolic.

Cooptation of business and professional leaders. While most labor leaders
are coopted into the PRI, many leaders of the professional and business
community are politically indifferent and others overtly or covertly support
the PAN. But so far the PRI has been able to coopt some professional and a
few business leaders of the community.

Among the professionals, lawyers, medical doctors, engineers, and schoolteachers are frequently coopted. Most of them are interested in politics for
professional reasons. Very few businessmen are coopted by the PRI. Some are
contractors who are rewarded with building contracts; others, such as public
notaries or custom brokers, have been franchised or expect to be franchised
through contacts in Mexico City with very profitable permits or patents. A
few merchants and industrialists of the upper class also are coopted into the
PRI. They try to make contacts with the bureaucracy through the Party that
would be useful in cutting red tape, marketing their products, or receiving
import permits. Generally, they handle very large businesses. Other merchants
in the Party are former bureaucrats who made their money in the bureaucracy, then returned to private life and became successful, wealthy businessmen.

To obtain an approximate idea of the number of members of the upper
socioeconomic groups who have been coopted into the PRI in Ensenada,
membership lists of the Lions and Rotary clubs were checked against membership lists of the PRI municipal committees, municipal officials, and
members of the state legislature from 1953 to 1968. The Rotary and Lions
clubs, the most exclusive social organizations in the city, do not include all
business and professional leaders since some leaders are not interested in
membership. However, checking the membership lists of the service clubs
against the executive committees of other organizations such as the Centro
Patronal, the chambers, the Harbor Association, the Association of Commercial Sport Fishing, and the Bar Association showed that a large number of
persons who had served on their executive committees were also members of
the service clubs. Approximately 18 percent of the members of the two
service clubs had been coopted into the PRI. Table 33 presents these findings.

We call the labor leaders and the professional and business leaders who are
coopted into the PRI *political brokers.*

TABLE 33

MEMBERS OF ROTARY AND LIONS CLUBS WHO WERE
POLITICAL BROKERS, ENSENADA (1967)

Members who, during 1953–67:	Number
Have occupied office in the PRI municipal committee and/or in the municipal administration	7
Have not occupied office, but are active PRI members	3
Have received special franchises, patents, or contracts	4
Have been state deputies	2
Have been chiefs of federal or state offices	8
Total Political Brokers	24
Total Membership of Service Clubs	134

Calculated from official membership lists.

Interaction among political brokers. One of the latent functions of the PRI is to provide the ground on which labor leaders and upper-class leaders coopted into the PRI can interact. The interaction takes place on many occasions during each year. Every year the Party schedules activities during which the political brokers meet. For example, after the President's state of the nation message, the local Party leaders hold a conference at which studies of the President's speech *(glosas)* are presented. Delivery of party membership cards is another ceremony that brings the political brokers together. During patriotic celebrations such as Benito Juárez's birthday, Independence Day, and the commemoration of the Revolution, the political leaders meet at Party headquarters to give speeches. On these occasions some rank and file members are also present, but by and large they belong to the lower socio-economic groups of the community. When high chiefs of the PRI central executive committee or the federal government visit the city, the PRI organizes elaborate receptions. Many commissions are formed, each responsible for a different aspect of the reception. Political brokers from the lower and upper socioeconomic groups mingle in these commissions. The PRI also carries out several welfare activities in Ensenada, and occasionally these activities call for the presence of political brokers; for example, for inaugurating a new activity, giving diplomas to those who have attended courses offered in home economics or language, or distributing prizes to winners of athletic competitions or art exhibits. The sporadic party conventions also bring together the political brokers. Perhaps the most intense interaction is provided by the frequent political campaigns, during which political brokers work together during months of planning and carrying out the campaign.

As has been indicated, numerous political leaders go from the PRI municipal committee to municipal administration. Here, during the term of each administration, is intense interaction between the labor leaders who occupy some offices and the members of the upper classes who occupy others. Frequently, lasting friendships develop among the members of the different social classes. It is not necessary to delineate all the occasions on which political brokers from different social classes interact. Interaction does take place and often develops into friendships that in turn lead to new, informal social interaction. For example, some members of the upper class go home from their downtown offices and change into casual clothing before going to a Party meeting in the evening—and laborers, on the other hand, will also change, and they will show up at Party headquarters dressed impeccably in suits and ties.

The role of the political broker is time consuming. He must take time to assist meetings, time to attend the business of the commissions, and also—particularly the upper class brokers—time to participate in welfare services. Some doctors give free medical care to Party members in the slum areas; some lawyers give free legal advice to Party sympathizers who are poor; some businessmen write letters of recommendation or find jobs for others who have need. These good-will gestures show the interest of the "haves" for the welfare of the "have nots."

The Function of political brokerage. Political brokerage is the process of bringing together sectors of the community that have conflicting interests. It is important to the integration of the community.[34] Labor leaders have easy access to upper-class leaders and, through them, to other business leaders in the community. In a society that is highly personalistic, brokerage is effective. It facilitates meetings at City Hall when the municipal president wants to consult with or to inform various sectors of the community about a problem. It may facilitate the bargaining process between labor and management, and it may help the government to perform its mediatory role between labor and management through consultation and through the labor boards of conciliation and arbitration. It facilitates the work of the mixed commissions, where labor, management, and representatives of the government try to find solutions to common problems.

Political brokers are important in easing the tensions between the public and private sectors. Formal and informal consultations between state and federal executives and business groups are made easier by the presence of the political brokers, who are the middlemen. Through this latent function the PRI has substantially contributed to community integration.

NOTES

1. Two trips were made to Mexicali to locate that data. At the regional headquarters of the National Electoral Commission I was told that all information on elections was sent to Mexico City. At the PAN and PRI regional headquarters the data could not be found. Similar difficulties have been indicated by other students of Mexican communities. Lawrence S. Graham commented, "regardless of many attempts to obtain electoral statistics from the state capital and many polite assurances as to their availability, the researcher was unable to gain access to such data." *Politics in a Mexican Community* (Gainsville, Fla: University of Florida Press, 1968), p. 46. The unavailability of political and economic data is the effect of a policy of secrecy by the government, and it gives an indication of the limited freedom tolerated by the Mexican political system.

2. The municipality of Ensenada constitutes the ninth electoral district in the state of Baja California, and it elects one deputy to the state congress. Generally, the PRI candidates for deputies in the ninth district had been CNC leaders. The municipality of Ensenada and the Valley of Mexicali (all-rural population) constitute the third federal district in the state and it elects one federal deputy. The number of registered voters in the Valley had generally been about three times larger than in Ensenada. Consequently, the results of the election are controlled in the Valley. Generally, the PRI candidates for the third district had been CNC leaders from the Valley, and the alternates had been labor leaders from Ensenada.

3. These findings cast some doubt on González Casanova's hypothesis of rural marginalism: "Rural dwellers are marginal to the parties, passive instruments of their leaders; . . . the rural population . . . correlates with low voting behavior, in its general tendencies the rural population is marginal to voting . . . ," *La Democracia en México* (México, D.F.: Editorial Era, 1965), p. 118.

4. The exact figure could not be calculated because the census breakdown of population by age makes it impossible to know the correct number of married persons between 18 and 21 years. However, the number of married people between those ages is very small and our error negligible.

5. Lawrence S. Graham also noted in his study of a Mexican city in the central plateau that voters cast split ballots: "Apparently many people identified with the PRI and voting the PRI ticket in local and state elections were casting their ballots for the PAN candidate during national elections." *Op. cit.,* p. 46.

6. This information was elicited in an interview with Antonio Luján, secretary general of the CNOP, September 14, 1967. The informant had been one of the campaign managers of the candidate. I had heard the same information from several other sources. The PAN information was elicited by Professor Manuel Estévez, PAN candidate for the municipal presidency in 1965, interview on November 9, 1967. Professor Estévez estimated that he had personally spent about 15,000 pesos. According to some PRI officials the gubernatorial campaign cost the candidate over one million pesos in 1965.

7. It should be remembered that the municipality of Ensenada is the largest in Mexico, with an extension of 53,352 square kilometers.

8. The electoral dates of the state of Baja California since it was given statehood in 1952 have been:

      1953 Constitutional Assembly
      1953 Governor, State Deputies
      1954 Municipal Council, Federal Deputies
      1956 Municipal Council, State Deputies
      1958 President of the Republic, Senators, Federal Deputies

1959 Governor, State Deputies, Municipal Council
1961 Federal Deputies
1962 Municipal Council, State Deputies
1964 President of the Republic, Senators, Federal Deputies
1965 Governor, State Deputies, Municipal Council
1967 Federal Deputies
1968 Municipal Council, State Deputies

9. Partido de Acción Nacional de Ensenada, "Programa de Jira a El Rosario" (Ensenada: June 13, 1965).

10. The control of the PRI over the electoral commission was made explicit by the PRI party secretary. She commented that the commission always asks the Party before elections to send the names of trusted members for the appointments to the presidency of the electoral precincts.

11. Barry Ames in a quantitative analysis of six national elections (1952-67) found that low levels of urbanization were associated with higher percentages of votes for the PRI. Ames also found that low percentages for the PRI in the border states could not be associated with their proximity to the United States, thus invalidating the hypothesis that the United States two-party system may have a demonstration effect in the neighboring Mexican states. However, he admits that the demonstration effect "may carry over into the *cities* (rather than border *states*)" but without affecting the total vote of the state. Barry Ames, "Bases of Support for Mexico's Dominant Party," *American Political Science Review,* Vol. 64 (March 1970), pp. 153-67.

12. See, for example, Partido de Acción Nacional, "Plataforma Política de Gobierno para el Municipio de Ensenada" (Ensenada: April 18, 1965) and Partido de Acción Nacional, "Plataforma Política de Gobierno para el Estado de Baja California, 1959," in Carlos Ortega G., *Democracia Dirigida con Ametralladoras. Baja California 1958-1960.* (El Paso, Texas: Talleres la Prensa, n.d.), pp.159-60.

13. See Partido de Acción Nacional, *Diez Años de México* (México, D.F.: Acción Nacional, 1950), pp. 201 ff and 243 ff. Similar observations about the PAN's political platform have been made by several other students of the Mexican electoral process. Robert E. Scott's observations of the campaigns and of the performance of the PAN are particularly insightful, *Mexican Government in Transition* (Urbana: University of Illinois Press, 1964), pp. 223-43.

14. Kenneth F. Johnson has characterized the ideology of the PAN as restorationist. However, the author also suggests that the PAN is being coopted into the PRI. Kenneth F. Johnson, "Ideological Correlates of Right Wing Political Alienation in Mexico," *American Political Science Review,* Vol. 59 (September 1965), pp. 656-64. Lawrence S. Graham, *op. cit.,* p. 47, found that in the city he studied the PAN was playing the role of a loyal opposition. Local PAN leaders defined the role of the Party as one of forcing "the local PRI to function more in accord with the democratic norms built into its party statutes." This observation seems to confirm the view that the functions of the party system in Mexico are different from those of other Western systems.

15. Partido de Acción Nacional, *Principios de Doctrina, Su Proyección en 1965* (México, D.F.: XVIII Convención Nacional del PAN, May 16, 1965). See also Partido de Acción Nacional, *Plataforma Política y Social* (México, D. F.: February 12, 1967).

16. Partido Revolucionario Institucional. Comité Directivo Estatal, "Mecanismo de Elecciones Internas. Indicaciones Generales" (Mexicali: n.d.). [Mimeo.]

17. Federación Estatal de la CNOP, "Instructivo" (Mexicali: March 25, 1965).

18. In Mexico only career lawyers can be public notaries. The licenses for the public notaries are issued by the state government and they are valid for life. The licenses are

very restricted—in Ensenada there were only three public notaries—and they are given away to friends of the governors as political patronage. Public notary is a very lucrative occupation, fees are high, and it does not take much time as the paper work is done by the secretarial staff.

19. Confederación Estatal CROC, "Informe Gira del Lic. Carlos Alberto Madrazo" (Mexicali: March 20, 1965). [My emphasis]

20. Federación Estatal de la CNOP, "Instructivo" (Mexicali: March 25, 1965), p.1.

21. Federación CROC, "Libro de Actas" (Ensenada: meeting minutes of April 5, 1965). [My emphasis]

22. It was not possible to locate in Ensenada the official results of the primary election.

23. In Confederación Nacional CROC, "Expediente O.I.A., Oficio 2197/65" (México, D.F.: April 19, 1965).

24. *Ibid.*

25. Interview with Ignacio Silva, secretary general of the CROM Federation, July 24, 1967. The respondent indicated that almost ten years had elapsed since the incident and that the CROM had been unable to regain the council seat. He was confident that in the next elections in 1968 the Party would return the seat to the federation.

26. Confederación Nacional CROC, "Expediente O.I.A., Oficio 2202/65" (México, D.F.: April 23, 1965).

27. *Ibid.*

28. Two years later, in 1967, the scars left by the primary were still very evident. Some PRI leaders fell short of declaring themselves public enemies of other PRI leaders. In an effort to reconcile the factions the PRI national executive committee selected as the Party candidate for the 1968 municipal elections the unsatisfied loser of 1965.

29. William W. D'Antonio and Richard Suter, "Elecciones preliminares en un municipio mexicano: Nuevas tendencies en la lucha de México hacia la democracia," *Revista Mexicana de Sociología,* Vol. 29 (January 1967), pp. 93-108.

30. William D'Antonio and William Form, *Influentials in Two Border Cities* (Notre Dame: University of Notre Dame Press, 1965), p. 190.

31. The materials to illustrate this case were obtained from documents made available by the Centro Patronal, the Chamber of Commerce, from information obtained from the local daily, *El Mexicano,* from May to November 1967, and from information obtained from personal interviews.

32. Philip Selznik, *TVA and the Grassroots* (Berkeley: University of California Press, 1949).

33. Cooptation, political stability, and economic growth are nicely tied together in the model presented by Bo Anderson and James D. Cockcroft, "Control and Cooptation in Mexican Politics," *International Journal of Comparative Sociology,* Vol. 7, (March 1966), pp. 11-27. The authors emphasize particularly the cooptation of dissident leaders. Philip Selznik's concept of cooptation is broader as it refers to the absorption of "new elements into the leadership . . . as a means to avert threats . . ." Philip Selznik, *op. cit.,* p. 259. Cooptation in Ensenada was not limited to dissident leaders but to most labor leaders and to some upper-class leaders and, of course, to some members of the middle classes.

34. The system of cooptation and its effects on the local community have also been studied by Lawrence S. Graham, *op. cit.,* pp. 48 ff. His findings are remarkably similar to my own. Graham suggests that there was no cleavage between the PRI and the business community because of the political skills of businessmen and the use of cooptation by the PRI. However, Graham did not find a high degree of social integration.

8
Conclusions

Baja California is one of the economically most highly developed and urbanized states in Mexico. Unless some unforeseeable, major changes occur in national or international politics, it can be suggested that as other Mexican states modernize they will follow political and organizational patterns similar to those observed in this study. The data gathered in Ensenada could in that case be useful in projecting some aspects of the future development of the Mexican political system. This author is aware of the dangers of generalizing from one case study. The few political studies of Mexican communities make generalizing especially difficult and risky. Then, too, in many ways Ensenada is not a "typical" Mexican city.

The validity of these generalizations is not based on typicality, but on the observation during this study of grass-roots processes of political institutions that exist throughout Mexico. It seems certain that as students of Mexican politics observe more and more grass-roots operations, generalization and prediction will become more precise.

Countervailing Powers and Pluralism

The performance of the Mexican political system as it was observed at the local level can be summarized as follows. The Mexican political system has been relatively successful in peacefully solving the labor-management conflict, and, consequently, the class conflict. Labor and management are well organized and presently their power vis-à-vis each other is fairly evenly distributed. The process of solving the labor-management conflict has been routinized; violence is never considered a viable method of solution. When direct bargaining fails, the government frequently mediates between labor and management through a process that could be described as indirect bargaining.

179

The government is careful to maintain the balance of power, for it needs both the votes of the numerically large labor groups and the cooperation of the business sector to spur industrial development and obtain needed revenues.

The routinization of labor-management relations has been achieved by a plurality of mechanisms: (a) The peculiar organization of the labor movement, which includes self-employed as well as unionized workers; (b) the openness of the labor movement, which allows for selection of the most capable members as leaders by the rank and file; (c) the existence of the labor law, a progressive piece of legislation that is frequently reinterpreted and amended and that provides a legal frame within which the conflict must be solved; (d) the labor boards of conciliation and arbitration, which provide relatively quick and inexpensive redress for the workers; (e) the mixed commissions, valuable mechanisms of interaction between labor and management. Salary increases are regularly provided by the government every two years, after consultation with labor and management through these commissions, an action that also helps to control inflation; (f) the frequent formal and informal consultations by federal and state government with labor and management to study common problems and find acceptable solutions; (g) the responsiveness of the government to some of the demands of labor and management—the government is aware that it must use its power with discretion if the system that gives it power is to continue.

It can be suggested that the existence of countervailing powers provides the basis for a pluralistic society in Mexico.[1] The PRI has performed an important function in developing these powers. The official Party, as a symbol of the Mexican Revolution, has legitimized the demands and aspirations of the labor movement and has given the political system the brokers who have facilitated interaction and communication between the leaders of different socioeconomic groups. This political brokerage has reduced social tensions and enhanced the integration of the society.

Several authors have argued that the development of a stable political system in Mexico would require internal democratization of the PRI and development of a multiparty system. Our study suggests that a multiparty system would have only fragmented the Mexican society and probably would not have allowed for a peaceful routinization of the labor-management conflict. The basis for a pluralistic society would not have developed under a multiparty system in Mexico.

The political institutions borrowed from other Western societies have been adapted and transformed to Mexican conditions and to the realities of its political culture. These transformations have been thorough. The primary election of 1965 suggests that at present the internal democratization of the Party cannot be accomplished without destroying the present political arrangement, affecting the balance of power, and producing some disintegrative

effects on the precarious societal cohesion that the one-party system has
achieved.

Centralization and Development

The regime has heavily centralized the political and economic systems of
the nation to ensure its own perpetuation in power. Political centralization
means that the key political offices, such as high PRI offices, governorships,
and the presidencies of all important municipalities, are appointed by or with
the approval of the Federal Executive. Generally, state legislators and federal
congressmen are also implicitly or explicitly selected by the Federal Executive. Economic centralization is not imposed particularly for reasons of
economic planning and development. At the local level it has been observed
that centralization is not accompanied by central planning. On the contrary,
the innumerable federal commissions and agencies are poorly integrated and
uncoordinated and operate on a personalistic basis. The evidence of several
case studies indicates that centralization is a heavy burden on the economy
and leads to waste of already scarce resources.

Economic centralization seems to be imposed for two main reasons: (a) to
reinforce political control over the governors through control of state finances (similarly, the governors control the municipal presidents through
control of municipal finances); (b) because the regime relies on a system of
spoils to secure trusted followers and consequently needs to create as many
federal agencies and commissions as possible to reward its political protégés,
pay political debts, and patronize future political followers. The instability of
the bureaucratic chiefs is also in part a consequence of the need to reward as
many political trustees as possible. These actions are responsible to a great
extent for the poor performance of the bureaucracy and for graft by bureaucratic chiefs.

Similar practices are followed by the state executives. Local resources are
used to enrich the governor and his protégés and to maintain a state legislature whose seats are given to political brokers extracted from the labor and
business sectors. The state legislature does not legislate, nor does it check the
performance of the other two branches of the state government.

Party leadership in the city is generated by attracting persons who want to
occupy municipal office, or expect to be given office in the upper ranks of
the bureaucracy, to receive franchises, or to make important business and
professional contacts. The municipal bureaucracy is overloaded with people
who are on the municipal payroll as a reward for their help in political
campaigns.

The low performance of the three bureaucracies produces dissatisfaction among the business sector of the community, the main contributor to the public treasury. The Ensenada study also suggests that as their increasing demands are not met by the regime, the emerging working class is beginning to show signs of dissatisfaction.

Raymond Vernon has characterized the Mexican dilemma as the government's struggle between the increasing demands of the citizens and the inability of the economic system to produce the resources necessary to satisfy the demands.[2] Our study suggests that the Mexican economic system has the resources to meet these demands, and the hypothesis is as follows: The Mexican economy can generate resources to satisfy the most pressing new demands. However, the scarcity of public resources is produced by diversion of public funds into the private purses of the bureaucratic chiefs and protégés and by the wastefulness of an inept and uncoordinated bureaucratic apparatus. Under these circumstances it may be difficult for the regime to meet the growing demands, and then, unless some reforms are made in the bureaucratic machine and unless the regime can rely on other ways to recruit its followers, the more highly developed urban centers will manifest increasing dissatisfaction with the regime.

Viability of One-party System

The PRI is the instrument of the regime in charge of legitimizing the perpetuation of the government via the electoral process. The Party carries out political campaigns and attempts to build popular support for the candidates chosen by the Federal Executive. In order to generate popular support, it is allowed to articulate through the CNOP and CNC a few demands for public and welfare services for the lower socioeconomic groups. As a symbol of the Revolution, the Party also legitimates the demands of the labor movement and rank and file bureaucrats, but it does not articulate those demands.

In this process of exchanging votes for public services and the legitimation of labor demands, the government finds itself arbitrating the conflicting demands of the lower socioeconomic groups and the more affluent sectors of the nation that want a larger share of the economic output and fewer government restrictions. In order to facilitate the work of the PRI, the government has been particularly careful to find compromises for these conflicts. However, electoral results for Baja California and Ensenada indicate that the PRI is failing to legitimize the candidates of the regime at the polls. The large number of votes that the opposition is obtaining under very unfavorable conditions manifests public dissatisfaction with the regime and suggests that as dissatisfaction increases in other parts of Mexico, it will become increasingly more difficult for the PRI to win the support of the masses at the polls.

The day the PRI loses its political supremacy at the polls in Ensenada—and this day may be very near—the regime will have two courses of action, or a combination of the two. The first alternative will be to allow the Party to defraud the votes. The second will be to use the necessary physical coercion to stay in power. The former probably will be the first choice and will be used as far as possible without making an obvious mockery of the electoral system. The efforts of the regime to reduce tensions and create consensus in the community suggest that physical coercion will be used only as a last resort. (In the past, some illegal physical coercion has been used in Ensenada, and during the 1959 elections the army was on the alert.)

It is also possible that an opposition victory at the polls will be reluctantly accepted by the regime. The regime might turn such an event into a warning to its Party and demand better future performance and some internal changes. The question to be asked is whether it is possible for the Party to carry out meaningful and successful internal reforms within the blueprints and under the conditions dictated by the regime. In the final analysis, the viability of the present Mexican political system and its increasing democratization seem to be contingent on the possibility of the regime's reducing the system of political patronage without destroying itself.

NOTES

1. William D'Antonio and William Form, *Influentials in Two Border Cities* (Notre Dame: University of Notre Dame Press, 1965), p. 231, have suggested that in the United States pluralism also emerges in the community " . . . when the business-professional groups are successfully challenged by the working class and ethnic groups."

2. Raymond Vernon, *The Dilemma of Mexico's Development* (Cambridge, Mass.: Harvard University Press, 1965), pp.188 ff. It should be taken into account that Vernon studied Mexico during the early sixties at the time the country was experiencing a mild economic recession.

Bibliography

Books and Articles

Alba, Victor. *Politics and the Labor Movement in Latin America.* Stanford, California: Stanford University Press, 1968.

Alisky, Marvin. "Mexico's Special Districts: Municipal Betterment Boards," *Public Affairs Bulletin,* Vol. 4, No. 2 (1965).

Almond, Gabriel A. and Bingham G. Powell. *Comparative Politics. A Developmental Approach.* Boston: Little Brown and Co., 1966.

Ames, Barry. "Bases of Support for Mexico's Dominant Party." *American Political Science Review,* Vol. 64 (March, 1970), pp. 153–67.

Anderson, Bo and James D. Cockcroft. "Control and Cooptation in Mexican Politics," *International Journal of Comparative Sociology,* Vol. 7 (March, 1966), pp. 11–27.

Anderson, Graydon K. *The Port of Ensenada. A Report on Economic Development.* San Diego, California: Economic Research Center. Department of Economics, San Diego State College, 1964.

Baja California, Territorio Norte. *Memoria Administrativa del Gobierno del Territorio Norte de la Baja California, 1924-1927.* n.p. and n.d.

Barret, Ellen C. *Baja California 1535-1964: a Bibliography of Historial, Geographical, and Scientific Literature Relating to the Peninsula of Baja California and to the Adjacent Islands in the Gulf of California and the Pacific Ocean.* Los Angeles: Westernlore Press, 1957–67. 2 vols. Vol. 1 published by Bennet and Marshall.

Blaisdell, Cowell L. *The Desert Revolution. Baja California, 1911.* Madison, Wisconsin: University of Wisconsin Press, 1962.

Brandenburg, Frank. *The Making of Modern Mexico.* Englewood Cliffs, N.J.: Prentice-Hall, Inc., 1964.

Burke, Henry T. "Olive Industry in Lower California, Mexico," Washington, D.C.: U.S. Government Printing Office ii, U.S. Foreign Agricultural Services, Foreign Agricultural Report No. 85, 1955.

Cámara Nacional de Comercio de Ensenada, Baja California. *Estatutos.* Ensenada, Baja California: 1967.

Carmona, Fernando. "La política económica," *México: Riqueza y Miseria,* Alonso Aguilar and Fernando Carmona, eds., México, D.F.: Ed. Nuestro Tiempo, 1967.

184

Castellanos de la Torre, Luis. "La Función Jurisdiccional de los Tribunales Laborales de Arbitraje." Unpublished thesis, Universidad Autónoma de Guadalajara, Jalisco, 1966.

Clelland, Donald A. and William Form. "Economic Dominants and Community Power: a Comparative Analysis," *American Journal of Sociology*, Vol. 69 (1964), pp. 511–21.

Cooper, Kenneth. "Leadership Role Expectations in Mexican Rural and Urban Environment." Unpublished Ph.D. dissertation, Stanford University, 1959.

Coser, Lewis. *The Functions of Social Conflict.* Glencoe: The Free Press, 1956.

Cueva, Mario de la. *Derecho Mexicano de Trabajo.* México, D.F.: Ed. Porrúa, 1959.

Cullingford, Juan Manuel. "Debe Cuidarse más la Inversión Oficial," *Huella.* Tijuana, Baja California: No. 4 (March, 1967), p. 12.

Dahl, Robert A. *Who Governs? Democracy and Power in an American City.* New Haven: Yale University Press, 1961.

D'Antonio, William W. and William Form. *Influentials in Two Border Cities.* Notre Dame: University of Notre Dame Press, 1965.

D'Antonio, William W. and Richard Suter. "Elecciones preliminares en un municipio mexicano: nuevas tendencias en la lucha de México hacia la democracia," *Revista Mexicana de Sociología,* Vol. 29 (January–March, 1967), pp. 93–108.

Diaz, May N. *Tonalá: Conservatism, Responsibility, and Authority in a Mexican Town.* Berkeley and Los Angeles: University of California Press, 1966.

Dubin, Robert. *Working Union-Management Relations: The Sociology of Industrial Relations.* Englewood Cliffs, N.J.: Prentice-Hall, Inc., 1958.

Estados Unidos Mexicanos. Secretaría General de Industria y Comercio. Dirección General de Estadística. *VII Censo General de Población.* México, D.F.: 1950.

——. *VIII Censo General de Población.* México, D. F.: 1960.

——. *VIII Censo General de Población. Estado de Baja California.* México, D. F.: 1963.

Etzioni, Amitai. *A Comparative Analysis of Complex Organizations.* New York: The Free Press, 1961.

Freeman, Linton C., Thomas J. Fararo, Warner Bloomburg, Jr., and Morris H. Sunshine. "Locating Leaders in Local Communities: A Comparison of Some Alternative Approaches," *American Sociological Review,* Vol. 28 (1963), pp. 791–98.

Fuentes Díaz, Vicente. "Desarrollo y Evolución del Movimiento Obrero a Partir de 1929," *Ciencias Políticas y Sociales* (Mexico City), Vol. 5 (July–September, 1959), pp. 326–48.

Garza, David T. "Factionalism in the Mexican Left: The Frustration of the MLN," *Western Political Quarterly,* Vol. 17 (September, 1964), pp. 447–60.

Gobierno del Estado de Baja California, *Baja California en Cifras*. Mexicali, Baja California: Talleres Tipográficos del Gobierno del Estado de Baja California, 1967.

———. *Constitución Política del Estado Libre y Soberano de Baja California*. Mexicali, Baja California: Ed. Congreso, 1953.

———."Ley de Egresos del Estado de Baja California, Ejercicio Fiscal de 1966," *Periódico Oficial (Organo del Gobierno del Estado de Baja California*, Mexicali), Vol. 62, No. 36 (December 31, 1965), Sec. 8.

———. "Ley de Egresos del Municipio de Ensenada," *Periódico Oficial (Organo del Gobierno del Estado de Baja California*, Mexicali), Vol. 62, No. 36 (December 31, 1965), Sec. 8.

———. "Ley Orgánica Municipal para el Estado de Baja California," *Periódico Oficial (Organo del Gobierno del Estado de Baja California*, Mexicali), Vol. 56, No. 3 (December 31, 1953).

———. *Ley del Servicio Civil de los Trabajadores al Servicio de los Poderes del Estado y Municipios*. Mexicali, Baja California: Talleres Tipográficos del Estado, 1959.

González Casanova, Pablo. *La Democracia en México*. México, D.F.: Editorial Era, 1965.

Graham, Lawrence S. *Politics in a Mexican Community*. Gainesville, Fla.: University of Florida Press, 1968.

Hernández Tirado, H. "El Municipio," *El Mexicano* (Ensenada, Baja California), July 21, 1967.

Homans, George C. *The Human Group*. New York: Harcourt, Brace, and World, Inc., 1950.

Huerta Maldonado, Miguel. "El Nivel de Vida en México," *Revista Mexicana de Sociología* (Mexico City), Vol. 22, No. 2 (May-September, 1960), pp. 463–527.

Hunter, Floyd. *Community Power Structure: A Study of Decision Makers*. Chapel Hill: University of North Carolina Press, 1953.

Irigoyen, Ulises. *Carretera Transpeninsular de la Baja California*. 2 vols. México, D.F.: Ed. América, 1962.

———. *El Problema Económico de las Fronteras Mexicanas. Tres Monografías: Zona Libre, Puertos Libres, y Perímetros Libres*. México, D.F.: 1935.

Johnson, Kenneth F. "Ideological Correlates of Right Wing Political Alienation in Mexico," *American Political Science Review*, Vol. 59 (September, 1965), pp. 656–64.

Klapp, Orrin E. and L. Vincent Padgett. "Power Structure and Decision-Making in a Mexican Border Town," *American Journal of Sociology*, Vol. 65 (January, 1960), pp. 400–06.

Kornhauser, Arthur, Robert Dubin, and Arthur M. Moss, eds. *Industrial Conflict*. New York: McGraw-Hill Book Co., 1954.

Lamartine, Paul Yates, *El Desarrollo Regional de México*. México, D.F.: Banco de México, Departamento de Investigaciones Industriales, 1962.

Landsberger, Henry A. "The Labor Elite: Is It Revolutionary?" *Elites in Latin America,* Seymour M. Lipset, ed., New York: Oxford University Press, 1965, pp. 256–300.

López Aparicio, Alfonso. *El Movimiento Obrero en México.* México, D.F.: Ed. Jus, 1958.

Lynd, Robert S. and Helen M. Lynd. *Middletown in Transition: A Study in Culture Conflicts.* New York: Harcourt, Brace, and World, Inc., 1937.

Maldonado, Braulio. *Baja California.* México, D.F.: Ed. Costa Amic, 1960.

Mantilla Molina, Roberto L. *Derecho Mercantil.* México, D.F.: Ed. Porrúa, 1956.

Martínez, Pablo. *Historia de Baja California.* México, D.F.: Ed. Libros Mexicanos, 1965.

Martínez Retes, Rafael. "Inopia Municipal," *El Mexicano* (Ensenada, Baja California), July 21, 1967.

"México: Historia de Dos Ciudades," *The Economist para América Latina* (London) Vol. 2, No. 14 (July 10, 1968), pp. 12–13.

México, Presidente. 1934– . *El Problema de los Territorios Federales. Mensaje Dirigido a la Nación el 28 de Septiembre de 1936.* México, D.F.: Talleres Gráficos de la Nación, 1936.

Michel, Jerry B. "The Measurement of Social Power on the Community Level: an Exploratory Study," *The American Journal of Economics and Sociology,* Vol. 23 (April, 1964), pp. 189–93.

Mills, C. Wright. *The Power Elite.* New York: Oxford University Press, 1951.

Nelson, Cynthia. "The Waiting Village: Social Change in a Mexican Peasant Community." Unpublished Ph.D. dissertation, The University of California, Berkeley, 1963.

Nunez, Theron A. "Cultural Discontinuity and Conflict in a Mexican Village." Unpublished Ph.D. dissertation, The University of California, Berkeley, 1963.

Ortega G., Carlos. *Democracia Dirigida con Ametralladores. Baja California 1958-1960.* El Paso, Texas: Talleres la Prensa, n.d.

Padgett, L. Vincent. *The Mexican Political System.* Boston: Houghton Mifflin Co., 1966.

Partido de Acción Nacional. *Diez Años de México.* México, D.F.: Acción Nacional, 1950.

——. *Más Sobre el Caso de Baja California.* México, D.F.: Ed. Jus, 1959.

——. *Plataforma Política y Social 1967–1970.* México, D.F.: Acción Nacional, February 12, 1967.

——. *Principios de Doctrina. Su Proyección de 1965.* México, D.F.: XVIII Convención Nacional del PAN, May 16, 1965.

Payne, James L. *Labor and Politics in Peru. The System of Political Bargaining.* New Haven: Yale University Press, 1965.

Polsby, Nelson W. "Community Power: Some Reflections on the Recent Literature," *American Sociological Review,* Vol. 27 (1962), pp. 838–41.

Programa Nacional Fronterizo. *Ensenada, B.C.* México, D.F.: n.d., Part 1, Report No. 7.

Ramos, Rutilio et. al. *La Iglesia en México. Estructuras Eclesiásticas.* Friburg: Oficina Internacional de Investigaciones Sociales de FERES, 1963.

Ross, Stanley R., ed. *Is the Mexican Revolution Dead?* New York: Alfred A. Knopf, 1966.

Rossi, Peter H. "The Organizational Structure of an American Community, *Complex Organizations: A Sociological Reader,* Amitai Etzioni, ed., New York: Holt, Rinehart, and Winston, 1966, pp. 301–12.

Salazar Rovirosa, Alfonso. *Cronología de Baja California: del Territorio y del Estado, 1500 a 1956.* México, D.F.: 1957.

Scott, Robert E. *Mexican Government in Transition.* Urbana: University of Illinois Press, 1964.

____. "The Established Revolution," *Political Culture and Political Development,* Lucien W. Pye and Sidney Verba, eds., Princeton, N.J.: Princeton University Press, 1965. pp. 330–95.

Selznik, Philip. *TVA and the Grassroots.* Berkeley: University of California Press, 1949.

Simmel, George. *Conflict and the Web of Group Affiliations.* Glencoe: The Free Press, 1955.

Taylor, Philip B., Jr. "The Mexican Elections of 1958: Affirmation of Authoritarianism?" *Western Political Quarterly,* Vol. 13 (September, 1960), pp. 722–44.

Torres-Trueba, Henry E. "Factionalism in a Mexican Municipio," *Sociologus,* Vol. 19, No. 2 (1969), pp. 134–52.

Treviño Arredondo, René. "La Industrialización y el Desarrollo Económico del Estado de Baja California," unpublished "licenciatura" thesis, Universidad Nacional Autónoma. Escuela Nacional de Economía, México, D.F., 1962.

Trueba Barrera, Jorge. *El Juicio de Amparo en Materia de Trabajo.* México, D.F.: Ed. Porrúa, 1963.

Trueba Urbina, Alberto. *El Nuevo Artículo 123.* México, D.F.: Ed. Porrúa, 1962.

Trueba Urbina, Alberto and Jorge Trueba Barrera. *Ley Federal del Trabajo Reformada y Adicionada.* México, D.F.: Ed. Porrúa, 1967.

Tuohy, William S. "Institutionalized Revolution in a Mexican City: Political Decision Making in Xalapa," unpublished Ph.D. dissertation, Stanford University, 1967.

Valenzuela, Arturo. *Derecho Procesal del Trabajo.* México, D.F.: Ed. Porrúa, 1959.

Vernon, Raymond. *The Dilemma of Mexico's Development.* Cambridge, Mass.: Harvard University Press, 1965.

Wilkie, James W., *The Mexican Revolution: Federal Expenditures and Social Change Since 1910.* Berkeley and Los Angeles: University of California Press, 1967.

Other Sources

Cámara Nacional de Comercio de Ensenada. "Directorio." Ensenada: August, 1966. (Mimeographed).
Centro Patronal de Ensenada. *Boletín Empresarial (Organo de Difusión del Centro Patronal de Ensenada)*, January, 1965–June, 1968.
_____. "Archivos: Oficios y Expedientes." Ensenada, 1966–67.
_____. "Libro de Actas." Ensenada: manuscript.
Díaz, Angel. "Informe del Secretario General al Décimo Congreso General de la CTM de Ensenada," speech delivered to the CTM of Ensenada on April 1, 1967. (Mimeographed).
Dirección General de Turismo del Estado de Baja California. *Boletín*. Ensenada: 1967.
Federación CROC. "Acta del Tercer Consejo Confederal Estatal CROC del Estado de Baja California. Circular 70." Mexicali: manuscript, 1967.
_____. "Libro de Actas." Ensenada: manuscript.
_____. "Reporte Anual." Ensenada: manuscript, January 7, 1965.
_____. "Archivos: Oficios y Expedientes." Ensenada, 1958–67.
Federación CRT. "Archivos: Oficios y Expedientes." Ensenada, 1963–67.
_____. "Libro de Actas." Ensenada: manuscript.
Federación CTM. "Archivos: Oficios y Expedientes." Ensenada, 1963–67.
_____. "Libro de Actas." Ensenada: manuscript.
Hirales Corrales, Román. "Estudio Demográfico de Baja California." Tijuana: Instituto de Investigaciones Sociales y Económicas. Universidad de Baja California, 1964 (manuscript).
Huella (Tijuana), monthly, May, 1967–June, 1968.
Junta Municipal de Conciliación de Ensenada. "Informe de Labores." Ensenada: manuscript, August 1, 1962–July 31, 1963.
_____. *Expediente de Huelgas*. Ensenada: manuscript, October, 1966–September, 1967.
El Mexicano (Ensenada), daily, January, 1960–July, 1968.
La Nación (Mexico City), weekly, January, 1959–December, 1959.
Partido de Acción Nacional. "Plataforma Política de Gobierno para el Municipio de Ensenada." Ensenada: manuscript, April 18, 1965.
Partido Revolucionario Institucional. "Archivos: Oficios y Expedientes." Ensenada: 1953–67.
Tesorería Municipal. "Corte de Caja por las Operaciones registradas duránte el Ejercicio Comprendido del Primero de Enero al 31 de Diciembre de 1966." Ensenada: manuscript, 1966.
El Universal (Mexico City), daily, July 11, 1967.

Index

DATE DUE
